The Many Faces
of Modern Architecture

The Many Faces of Modern Architecture

Building in Germany between the World Wars

Edited by John Zukowsky

With contributions by Kennie Ann Laney-Lupton,
Wojciech Lesnikowski, and John Zukowsky

Prestel
Munich · New York

Front cover (from top to bottom):
Dominikus Böhm, St. Engelbert's Church, Cologne, 1930;
Gottfried Schramm, Summer house, Reinbek, 1927-28;
Josef Gesing, August Bebel School, Frankfurt an der Oder, 1926;
Emil Fahrenkamp, Shellhaus, Berlin, 1930-31

Back cover (from top to bottom):
Erwin Gutkind, Sonnenhof apartment building, Berlin, 1926-27;
Friedrich Wilhelm Virck, Holstentorhalle, Lübeck, 1925;
Wilhelm Riphahn, Die Bastei restaurant, Cologne, 1924;
Robert Vorhoelzer and Hans Schnetzer,
Post office and apartment building, Munich, 1930-33

Frontispiece:
Gustav August Münzer, Marine-Ehrenmal, Laboe, 1927-36

Prestel-Verlag

16 West 22nd Street, New York, NY 10010
Tel. 212-627 8199; Fax 212-627 9866

Mandlstrasse 26, D-80802 Munich, Germany
Tel. 089-38 17090; Fax 089-38 170935

Distributed in Continental Europe by Prestel-Verlag
Verlegerdienst München GmbH & Co. KG
Gutenbergstrasse 1, D-82205 Gilching, Germany
Tel. 8105-388 117, Fax 8105-388 100

Distributed in the USA and Canada on behalf of Prestel by te Neues Publishing Company,
16 West 22nd Street, New York, NY 10010, USA
Tel. 212-627 9090; Fax 212-627 9511

Distributed in Japan on behalf of Prestel by YOHAN Western Publications
Distribution Agency, 14-9 Okubo 3-chomo, Shinjuku-ku, J-Tokyo 169
Tel. 3-32 08 01 81; Fax 3-32 09 02 88

Distributed in the United Kingdom, Ireland and all remaining countries on behalf of Prestel by
Thames & Hudson Ltd., 30-34 Bloomsbury Street, London, WC1B3QP, England
Tel. 071-636 5488; Fax 071-636 1659

Designed by Dietmar Rautner, Munich
Map by Tausendblauwerk, Absmeier & Berwanger, Munich
Cover design by F. Lüdtke, A. Graschberger, and A. Ehmke, Munich
Typeset by OK Satz GmbH, Unterschleissheim
Offset lithography by Gewa-Repro GmbH Gerlinger & Wagner, Munich
Printed and bound by Passavia Druckerei GmbH, Passau
Printed in Germany

ISBN 3-7913-1339-8   (German edition)
ISBN 3-7913-1366-5   (English edition)

Contents

Acknowledgments

When we initially discussed this project in 1988, we naively envisioned a publication that would encompass Modern Movement architecture in all of Central and Eastern Europe. After realizing that this was a task impossible to accomplish in one book, we elected to concentrate on works in eastern and western Germany, at that time a divided nation. Focusing on buildings erected in that country, one of the fabled birthplaces of the Modern Movement, would, we felt, provide us with sufficient material. In fact, further research revealed that the number of buildings far exceeded the scope of a single volume. It was then that we decided to place the emphasis on buildings constructed and published in the twenties and thirties that had not received much coverage since — on structures that constitute the mainstream of modernist architecture in Germany.

A generous grant from the Graham Foundation for Advanced Studies in the Fine Arts in 1989 funded the bulk of our initial site investigations. We are especially grateful to the Foundation's president, Carter H. Manny, Jr., for his enthusiastic support of our endeavor. Other agencies assisted us by providing funds for continued research. John Zukowsky's further research, undertaken while on sabbatical from The Art Institute of Chicago in 1991, was supported by an individual grant from the National Endowment for the Arts, both the research leave and the grant being enthusiastically endorsed by his director, James N. Wood. Wojciech Lesnikowski received a grant from the German Academic Exchange Service (DAAD) that enabled him to work on the project into 1992.

Various people here and abroad provided research assistance and access to historical documentation in Germany. They receive our warmest thanks. For archival help and information relating to Berlin, we are especially indebted to Almut Eckell, Bernd Evers, Ursula Frohne, Annemarie Jaeggi, Thomas Ludwig, Carl John Sterner, and Christian Wolsdorff. Iris Cramer, Rainer Meyer, and Luminita Sabau assisted with sites and collections in Frankfurt am Main. Many people in Hamburg and other north German cities openly shared their ideas and documentation with us, but we should particularly like to thank Norbert Baues, Hartmut Frank, Hermann Hipp, Roland Jaeger, Martina von Limont, Johann Schmidt, Wolfgang Voigt, and Anna Katharina F. Zülch. Among the numerous cooperative people in Bavaria and Baden-Württemberg who assisted us in locating buildings and providing historical data are Marion Bembé, Werner Buch, Ines Dresel, Michael Foster, Rolf and Rita Hahn, Karin Kirsch, Axel and Helga Menges, Anton Noll, Dr. Osteneck, Dietmar Rautner, Hans Schieber, Franz Stauda, Sabine Thiel-Siling, Ernst Wasmuth, and Franziska Windt. Mr. Foster and Ms. Thiel-Siling also provided invaluable advice on editorial matters pertaining to all chapters of the book. Individuals who helped with research into the Rhine and Ruhr areas include Eugene and Chucky Asse, Susan Edwards, Dr. Mary Laney, Dr. George Lupton, Wolfgang Pehnt, Lesley Raynor, and Christoph Vogtherr. For advice on buildings in Wrocław, we extend our thanks to Olgierd Czerner of the Museum of Architecture in that city. We are particularly grateful to Wolfgang Pehnt for reviewing some sections of the manuscript. The staff at Prestel-Verlag made this book a reality, and they are to be thanked for their faith in the project, even before it took on tangible shape. Michael Green's proofreading expertise and editorial advice were much appreciated, and thanks are especially due to Dietmar Rautner, who has provided us with an elegantly designed publication.

Finally, we were fortunate to have the help of people in our daily environments. Milli Zukowsky typed portions of the manuscript, and Stewart Lupton assisted with computer skills. Most of all, we are grateful to our families and friends for their patience as we prepared this study for publication.

John Zukowsky
Wojciech Lesnikowski
Kennie Ann Laney-Lupton

Introduction

John Zukowsky

The Germany of the 1920s and early 1930s, the period of the Weimar Republic, has long been considered one of the birthplaces of the Modern Movement in architecture and design. The leaders of that movement are well known to historians and architectural enthusiasts alike. Walter Gropius, Ludwig Hilberseimer, Ernst May, Erich Mendelsohn, Hannes Meyer, Ludwig Mies van der Rohe, and Bruno Taut are among those whose varying and various contributions to avant-garde design have been extensively published and discussed. Yet there also exists an entire body of work that, though not necessarily as radical or as well known as that of these designers, was nevertheless integral to the mainstream of modern architecture at the time. Such work, executed by now forgotten architects, could be found throughout Germany during the twenties and thirties. Indeed, much of it is still there, despite the extensive destruction wrought by Allied air raids and urban battles during World War II. Even more important, a number of the buildings illustrated in contemporary German architectural journals and monographs have not been published since, not even in recent local guides.

This book publishes these often neglected contributions to the architecture of the interwar years in relation to better known German landmarks. We place major sites within the broad context of architecture in the twenties and thirties, providing a generous survey of buildings in Germany from this era, particularly those with a modernist bent. This compilation serves as a documentation of buildings from the decades between the world wars. It also documents sites in what was, after World War II, a nation divided into two states: the Bundesrepublik Deutschland, or Federal Republic of Germany (West Germany), and the Deutsche Demokratische Republik, or German Democratic Republic (East Germany). Before embarking on an extensive visual tour of this architecture, it will be helpful to discuss the sites within a historical framework. We should begin by examining assumptions about German architecture of the twenties and early thirties in relation to sociocultural tendencies in that country.

Germany is divided into several regions that find their political expression in *Länder* (federal states). With the reunification of Germany within a year of the 1989 fall of the Berlin Wall, there are now sixteen *Länder*. The number of political subdivisions has, however, varied throughout German history,

and some, including a large part of what are now Hamburg and Schleswig-Holstein, were provinces of other countries — in this case, Denmark. Moreover, Berlin and the region of Brandenburg were culturally influenced by nearby Poland, whereas North Rhine-Westphalia, the Rhineland-Palatinate, and Saarland were impacted, economically, culturally, and historically, by their neighbors, France and the Benelux countries. Religious influences played a part in this interchange, as can be seen in the onion-domed Catholic churches of Bavaria, so similar to those in neighboring Austria. Specifically regional architectural expressions in Bavaria incorporate stucco, carved stone, and elaborate plasterwork. This is best illustrated by the ornate eighteenth-century churches by the Asam brothers, and these are related to Italian prototypes. Regional associations are also evident in the ubiquitous brick buildings of northern Germany. All are allied with comparable brick structures, commercial, religious, and agricultural, in the adjacent countries of Denmark and the Netherlands. These regional influences and approaches to architectural design extend into the 1920s, the most notable examples being the modernist masonry buildings of the Stuttgart School, the brick expressionist modernism of Hamburg's architects, and the classicistic stucco buildings of Munich (see, for example, pp. 116-18, 187-89, 204-6).

Although German architecture has strong regional traits, at times unifying tendencies have asserted themselves both in the country's society and in its arts. The first of these was probably Charlemagne's creation of the Holy Roman Empire in the year 800. The most famous relic of his revival of Roman architecture as an imperial style is the Palace Chapel of Aachen (796-805), but, for our purposes, an even more interesting site is the Gatehouse to the Abbey of Lorsch (c. 800), with its hybridization of classical forms and vernacular decoration based on the memory of half timber construction. Subsequent periods of German history also had classical aspirations, usually related to attempts at asserting political authority. Expressions of this range from the great Ottonian churches, such as St. Michael's at Hildesheim (1001-33), to the firm Prussian classicism of Karl Friedrich Schinkel and his Berlin contemporaries in the early 1800s. They went on to include more elaborate monuments, such as the Berlin *Siegesäule* (Victory Column) of 1865-73, which commemorates Otto von Bismarck's victories in the course of welding the German provinces into a nation state, and the more obviously grandiose buildings constructed or planned under Kaiser Wilhelm II and Adolf Hitler as part of an effort to make Berlin a rival to such classical, imperial cities as Paris and Rome.

Fig. 1 Herbert Rimpl. Entrance staircase, administration building, Heinkel factory, Oranienburg, 1935 (dismantled after World War II). From Hermann Mäckler, *Architekt Herbert Rimpl: Ein deutsches Flugzeugwerk* (Berlin, 1938).

9

Fig. 2   Ludwig Mies van der Rohe. Tugendhat House, Brno, Czechoslovakia (now Czech Republic), 1930 (renovated). Photograph 1986.

Within the two opposing tendencies of regionalism and centralization there existed a wide range of expressions and hybridizations throughout all periods of German architecture, including the post-World War I era. At that time, these multifarious expressions — the many faces of modern architecture — were, more often than not, relatively conservative or eclectic, rather than markedly avant-garde or purist. This contrasts somewhat to the stereotypical view that the radically modern buildings of the Weimar Republic were the true sociocultural manifestation of that fledgling democracy when compared with the imperial, almost Baroque, classicism of the Wilhelmine period that preceded it. True, Germany's defeat in World War I under Wilhelm II was followed, in late 1918 and 1919, by socialist revolutions in such cities as Berlin, Dresden, Kiel, Leipzig, Magdeburg, and Munich, and the coalition government of the Weimar Republic of 1920 and the various democratic permutations of that government through the twenties did bring at least a strained sense of order to the country. Yet the Republic's uncertain pluralism ultimately enabled the National Socialists, or Nazis, to gain power and to usurp democratic authority in 1933. Correspondingly, the architecture of the twenties and early thirties evinced a wide variety of modern expressions, as one would expect in a democratic, pluralistic society.

Conventional wisdom has it that "modern" in the Weimar years meant, in architecture and design, the *Neue Sachlich-*keit (New Sobriety) practiced by teachers and students at the Bauhaus. That famous school was founded in 1919 in Weimar, and then moved to Dessau when a new building was constructed for it in 1925 by Walter Gropius (Fig. 1, p. 214). Perfect examples of *Neue Sachlichkeit* include that functionalist building, Ludwig Mies van der Rohe's elegantly sparse German Pavilion at the World Exhibition of 1929 in Barcelona, and the same architect's Tugendhat House of 1930 (Fig. 2). Yet a number of alternative solutions to the problem of an architecture thought to be appropriate to the new, democratic society existed alongside what many feel are the radical, avant-garde buildings of Gropius, Mies, and others from the Bauhaus. The curvilinear expressive forms of Erich Mendelsohn (see Fig. 10, p. 24; Fig. 19, p. 27; p. 29), the highly coloristic housing projects of Bruno Taut (see Figs. 4 and 5, p. 23; Fig. 17, p. 26), the modernist masonry Stuttgart School works of Paul Bonatz (see pp. 166, 180-81, 187-89), and the brick expressionism of Fritz Höger and the Gerson brothers in Hamburg (see pp. 112-13, 116-17, 125) all provide ample evidence of the multifaceted methods of design and detailing for modern life in the twenties and early thirties. In fact, these and comparable hybridized approaches to modern architecture far outnumbered the more radical designs propagated by the Bauhaus. And even within the Bauhaus, and among other leading modernists of the twenties avant-garde, there existed a subtle diversity, as the recent book by Richard Pommer and

Fig. 3   Herbert Rimpl. Main assembly hall, Heinkel factory, Oranienburg, 1935 (dismantled after World War II).
The Heinkel He111 aircraft is in the foreground. From Mäckler, *Architekt Herbert Rimpl.*

Christian F. Otto, *Weissenhof 1927 and the Modern Movement in Architecture* (1991) and such exhibitions as "Bauhaus Utopien: Arbeiten auf Papier" (1988) and "Experiment Bauhaus" (1988) have indicated. This is hardly surprising when one compares the work of the three Bauhaus directors: Gropius (1919-28), Hannes Meyer (1929-30), and Mies (1930-33). Differences range from the more functional approaches of Gropius and Meyer to the more aesthetically inclined works of Mies.

It is also commonly held that, when the Nazis came to power in 1933, modern architecture disappeared from the German cityscape. This assumption was founded on the fact that a large number of talented architects, including Gropius, Hilberseimer, Mendelsohn, and Mies, fled the repressions of the new regime. Further verification of modernism's retreat has been sought in the shift, especially in the later thirties and early forties, toward classicism for governmental buildings (see Figs. 15 and 16, p. 25) and toward an almost mythic medievalism or medievalist contextualism for some other building types (see p. 170). Yet the situation of modern architecture in the Third Reich was far more complicated.

Books by Barbara Miller Lane (1968) and Robert R. Taylor (1974) on German architecture in the Third Reich have hinted that the Nazis were ambivalent about modern architecture, dismissing it for public buildings and housing, yet embracing it for industrial and technical facilities. More recent books and

articles by such scholars as Gerhard Fehl, Elaine Hochman, Hartmut Frank, Winfried Nerdinger, Wolfgang Voigt, Sabine Weissler, and Uwe Westphal have shown that matters were more complex than that. Part of this complexity involved rivalries among Nazi officials and differences of opinion among party administrators in the more liberal Berlin and the more conservative Munich. Another part included the acceptance of modernist architectural forms for structures that represented the new, Nazi society and the wish for increased public access to technological innovations of varying scale, from the autobahn to the home radio. Structures for transportation, in particular, witnessed an outpouring of modernist designs, from bus and railroad terminals to service stations and factories for automobiles and airplanes. The most famous of the latter is the Heinkel factory of the mid- to late thirties erected at Oranienburg near Berlin (Figs. 1, 3) to designs by Herbert Rimpl, a follower of Theodor Fischer in Munich and assistant to Dominikus Böhm in his office at Hindenburg (now Zabrze, Poland; see p. 233).

Other types of structure acceptable for modernist design in the Third Reich were devoted to the body, to sport and health. This makes sense, considering the emphasis that Nazi society placed on organized recreation in shaping the future citizens of Germany. Modern design as seen in industrial products and buildings permeated the ordered approach to recreation of the "Kraft durch Freude" (KdF; Strength through Joy) orga-

Fig. 4   Herbert Rimpl. Employees' health club facility,
Heinkel factory, Oranienburg, 1935 (dismantled after World War II).
From Mäckler, *Architekt Herbert Rimpl.*

nization, architectonically expressed in, among other things, new cruise ships commissioned for group tours and the development of the 1935 Volkswagen as the streamlined KdF car for family touring on Germany's new autobahns. With the hosting of the Olympics by Berlin in 1936, sports facilities were developed throughout the country, the most impressive being the masonry and glass stadium designed by Paul Bonatz in Schweinfurt in 1936 (see p. 181). In addition, general health care structures of modernist design were built, published, and promoted, from the Opel Baths of 1934 in Wiesbaden (see p. 97) to the Naval Hospital of 1938 in Stralsund (see p. 156). This emphasis on making the body healthy for a new Germany extended to the factory as well, with Ernst Heinkel constructing extensive sports and health facilities for apprentices and workers at his high-tech airplane factories (see Fig. 4). In many ways, the aesthetics of these structures for creating healthy bodies are directly descended from modernist, and pre-modernist, ideas on health care facilities (see pp. 43, 95-98, 182-83, 211, 242-43) and from architectural philosophy of the twenties, best exemplified in the writings of Le Corbusier, who strove to make buildings machines for living. Thus, modernist health care and sports facilities were accepted by the Third Reich because of the underlying technical nature of the buildings. In a sense, they were factories for making healthy, strong bodies to serve the regime.

There are other aspects of modernism in the Third Reich that have been somewhat overlooked. One such involves, surprisingly enough, housing. Recent literature on Third Reich housing shows that the Nazis often extended and adapted the modernist policies of the Weimar Republic. For instance, the Nazi-controlled building society GEHAG (Gemeinnützige Heimstätten Spar- und Bau-Aktien Gesellschaft) in the mid-thirties reused Bruno Taut's late twenties formula when erecting apartments in the Zehlendorf district of Berlin (see Fig. 17, p. 26), but built them with the pitched roofs deemed appropriate to the image of a "home" (Fig. 5). It was efficient to employ this planning formula, since everyone was familiar with its construction, and besides, the new government had not yet fully established definite guidelines for new housing construction and design. This recycling of a Taut design was apparently no secret: the June 1939 issue of *Monatshefte für Baukunst und Städtebau*, for example, reported on it in an article devoted to GEHAG's recent work in Berlin and elsewhere. It should be remembered, however, that this combination of modernist plan and elevation with a more conservative roofline was practiced in other countries at the time, even in social housing in Switzerland, which had a strong Modern Movement in the twenties and thirties.

Browsing through this book will reveal other conscious and unconscious survivals, combinations, and adaptations of traditional and modern forms and plans by architects of the twenties and thirties. Although the case just mentioned, together with the other uses of modern architectural forms in the Third Reich, may seem to contravene Nazi ideology, this is in keeping with other contradictions of the idealized norm within Nazi culture. According to Detlev Peukert, in his *Inside Nazi Germany* (1987), this society endorsed and accepted both conservative and modern or radical values in a personalized, almost irrational way. The book cites numerous examples of individual and group protest against the Nazi norm, the most famous being the "Swing Youth" of Hamburg and Berlin, who openly played and danced to British and American jazz all through the war. The variety and intensity of some of these protests demonstrate that in Nazi Germany, as in all totalitarian states, it is impossible for the government to control every aspect of life. This may well have found expression in several features of the German architectural community that require discussion.

The first of these is architectural publishing. A number of magazines appeared throughout the era dealt with here, but the most astonishing one was the Stuttgart-based *Moderne Bauformen*. This was the monthly journal of editors Julius and Herbert Hoffmann, whose publishing house was one of Germany's most prolific as regards architectural books. Although their magazine published all types of design, it concentrated on the eclectic modernist mainstream. Cases in point are the 1932, 1937, and 1939 issues, which presented the streamlined, yet rather eclectic work of American designer Gilbert Rohde. In keeping with Nazi Germany's policy of equipping every household with a radio — a program to propagandize the family — the October 1935 issue of *Moderne Bauformen* included an article on modern streamlined design for home radios. The magazine continued to publish both conservative and more modern architecture during the war, not ceasing to appear until 1944. Editorial policy was internationally oriented, with articles on new foreign buildings appearing alongside their German counterparts. Issues from the mid-thirties through 1942 even carried English and French translations of the articles. At this time, the magazine also printed a series of invaluable pieces titled "Ein Architekt besucht" (An Architect Visits), which are still excellent guides to buildings in such cities as Berlin, Dresden, Hamburg, Leipzig, Munich, and Stuttgart.

It is hard to say exactly why *Moderne Bauformen* continued to include modernist buildings. It is possible that the journal fits Peukert's thesis of a totalitarian regime being unable to bring everything under its control, yet it is difficult to believe that the magazine would not have been subject to censorship for its persistent publication of eclectic modernist architecture. A more plausible explanation is that the censorship authorities did not consider modernist buildings constructed outside Germany to be a matter of much importance. Albert Speer's *Inside the Third Reich* (1970, p.184) recounts how Hitler did not

care about modern art being practiced and even exhibited in France, stating: "Are we to be concerned with the intellectual soundness of the French people? Let them degenerate if they want to! All the better for us." Elsewhere (p.122) Speer describes how Hitler felt that it would be a mistake to export Nazi ideology because it would only strengthen other nations, thus weakening Germany's political and economic position. It may well be that this attitude enabled *Moderne Bauformen* to publish articles on Modern Movement buildings, especially those in other countries. A case in point is the January 1943 issue which, as in the previous year, included mainstream modernist work from German-occupied Holland and Denmark, as well as from the Axis ally Finland and neutral Sweden and Switzerland. In an editorial printed in German, French, and Italian, Herbert Hoffmann acknowledges that the war has interrupted the long-term reconstruction program instituted a decade previously by the Nazis. He notes that these reconstructive efforts incorporated a plurality of design approaches, as opposed to what he decries as the "misguided" radical international modernism that had disfigured Germany's cities in the twenties with buildings devoid of national or regional character. Further, he states that his magazine, always

Fig. 5   Design Office of GEHAG. Apartment building, Hartmannsweilerweg 18-24, Berlin-Zehlendorf, c. 1935.

interested in international developments, publishes the finest examples of varied and original approaches to modern and even rational design in all European countries, appreciating that differences in design exist both between and within individual nations. Once one looks beyond the obligatory propaganda, Hoffmann is, then, drawing attention to the fact that his magazine's policy — particularly its recognition of the diversity of design, both national and regional, within modernism — had remained consistent, before and after 1933. His observations also tie in with Hitler's comment, quoted by Speer, that hardcore National Socialism, and perhaps, by extension, its approaches to official design, should not be strictly enforced in other countries, whose traditions are different from those of Germany. Whatever the ideological background, the articles published in *Moderne Bauformen* permitted German architects to stay in touch with the national and regional variants of modernism being practiced at home and abroad in the thirties and even the forties.

More than simply being informed of international architectural developments, German architects who did not emigrate after the rise of National Socialism had some opportunities to put their own modern design training into practice. Several of them were adept at designing in any style they chose, whatever the commission. Two such are Fritz August Breuhaus de Groot and Cäsar Pinnau.

The Düsseldorf architect Fritz August Breuhaus de Groot was a follower of Peter Behrens. After service on the eastern front in World War I, he returned to the Rhineland to design a

number of large villas and housing estates. In a 1929 monograph on him, Herbert Eulenberg wrote of the architect's eclectic approach to modernism, stating that Breuhaus was an "enemy of a uniform style" who created spaces "according to life-style, always conforming to the wishes and whims of his clients without being disloyal to his artistic convictions." In the late twenties Breuhaus designed the interiors of the steamship *Bremen* as well as a spectacular *moderne* estate in Stuttgart, which he labeled the house of "Kultivierte Sachlichkeit," or refined sobriety (see p. 176). Later, he designed the interior of the airship LZ128 (which was never constructed) and a glass summer house on Berlin's Wannsee (Fig. 6) that rivaled anything done by Mies or his colleagues. Breuhaus's modernism could also be considerably tempered, if not abandoned, in other jobs, such as a little known classical office building (Fig. 7) and the conservative, wing-chaired interiors of Hermann Goering's own Junkers Ju52 airplane. Monographs on Breuhaus's work published before and after the war, however, testify to the high esteem in which his buildings were held over a span of four decades.

Hamburg-born Cäsar Pinnau was an assistant in Breuhaus's office from 1930 to 1937. Pinnau may well have been at least partly responsible for the design of that elegantly modern Wannsee summer home, as is suggested by the presence of the photograph reproduced here, and others, in the Pinnau archives. Pinnau had studied at the Kunstgewerbeschule (arts and crafts school) in Munich in the late twenties before working in Breuhaus's atelier, where he executed the interior of a

Fig. 6 Fritz August Breuhaus de Groot, possibly assisted by Cäsar Pinnau. Summer house on the Wannsee, Berlin, 1930.

Fig. 7 Fritz August Breuhaus de Groot. Berufsgenossenschaft der Chemischen Industrie (now GAGFAH) building, Rüdesheimer Strasse 50 near Breitenbachplatz, Berlin-Wilmersdorf, c. 1938. Photograph 1989.

Fig. 8 Fritz August Breuhaus de Groot, assisted by Cäsar Pinnau. Airship LZ 129 *Hindenburg*, 1935.

Heinkel He70 "Blitzflugzeug" (fast commuter airliner) for Lufthansa in 1934 and of the famed airship LZ129 *Hindenburg* in 1935 (Fig. 8). Like other architects in the Great Depression of the early thirties, Pinnau sought work designing furniture and furnishings. In 1937 he left Breuhaus to set up his own practice in Berlin, working with Speer's office and other firms on the design of various classicistic or historicist interiors, such as the lobby of the Japanese Embassy in Berlin and spaces in the Reichskanzlei (Reich Chancellery). After World War II, Pinnau continued to design large country houses, and, drawing on his mentor's expertise in ship and aircraft interiors, received a number of commissions for oceangoing vessels. Pinnau was also responsible for the design of freighters in the fifties, such as the Cap San class for the Hamburg-Sud shipping line, in use from 1955 to 1969. Moreover, he proved equally adept at designing a variety of historicist and modernist buildings.

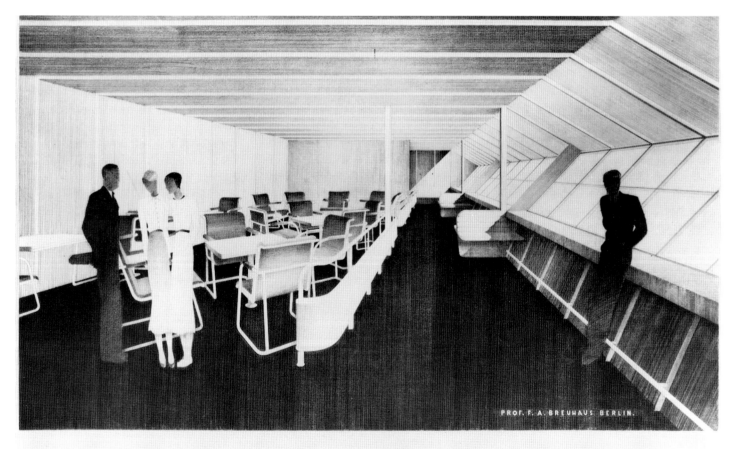

L. Z. 129 A·DECK HALLE UND STEUERBORDPROMENADE

One of his most famous skyscrapers is Olympic Tower of 1971 on New York's Park Avenue, executed with Skidmore, Owings and Merrill as associate architects.

The intertwined careers of Breuhaus and Pinnau are not exceptional, but they serve to illustrate the continuity of more than simply competent design under a variety of client conditions before, during, and after the war. In contrast to Breuhaus and Pinnau and their espousal of diverse stylistic approaches, there were architects whom many have thought to be more consistently modernist. Like Breuhaus and Pinnau, these aficionados of modernism made their mark on German design from before the Third Reich through to the postwar era. Those whose life and work are fairly well documented include Egon Eiermann (see p. 35), Hans Scharoun (see Fig. 11, p. 24), and Emil Fahrenkamp. Werner Durth's book *Deutsche Architekten* (1986) discusses the lives of these and other modernist architects, such as Paul Bonatz (see Fig. 11, p. 75, and pp. 180-81), Konstanty Gutschow (see pp. 114-15), Ernst Neufert (see p. 233), Friedrich Tamms (see p. 140), and Lois Welzenbacher, who practiced before, during, and after World War II. All often utilized the principles they had learned and practiced at the beginning of their careers. Some were in positions of sufficient prominence under Speer to be aware of the abuses of human rights in the Third Reich, particularly as pertains to forced labor from concentration camps or impressed foreigners. Those and other horrors perpetrated by the Nazi regime must be acknowledged in any history of the period. Yet, on another level, many of those modernist architects who remained in Germany were no different from their Allied counterparts who designed buildings in support of the war effort.

The stories of the better known architects who did not emigrate have already been published. Those of two other architects, however, deserve telling here in relation to this tumultuous time. The first is Carl August Bembé. Born in 1900 in Mainz, he was the son of a painter who lived with his family in Paris and Florence before World War I. After service in that "war to end all wars," Bembé studied at the Technische Hochschule (polytechnic) in Munich and eventually became an assistant to Paul Bonatz. In the twenties and early thirties Bembé designed motor yachts for the Maybach company, the streamlined sailboat *Tiger* for the Curry family, and automobiles for Opel and Adler. At the same time, he specialized in designing vernacular-modernist wood frame garden houses and summer homes (see Fig. 9 and p. 193). The late twenties and early thirties witnessed his first trip to the United States and contact with Gropius and other Bauhaus personalities. Bembé worked as an architect in Munich until 1939, one of his most famous commissions being a streamlined gas station for the new autobahn (Fig. 10). From then until the end of the war he served in the army, while his family moved to their summer home in Herrsching to escape the bombing of Munich. At war's end, he renewed contact with such architects as Bonatz, Welzenbacher, and Gropius. It was the latter who sponsored Bembé for a teaching position at Rensselaer Polytechnic Institute in Troy, New York, where he taught from 1948 until his death from a heart condition in 1955. In the postwar period he continued to design small modernist homes and wrote on architecture, including the book *Von der Linie zum Raum* (From Line to Space), published in Munich in 1953.

Fig. 9   Carl August Bembé. Thieme-
Hutchinson House, Munich-Harlaching,
c. 1929 (demolished).

Fig. 10   Carl August Bembé. Autobahn
gas station near Frankfurt am Main
(with prototype Volkswagen sedan?),
c. 1937 (demolished).

Another comparable and, in some ways, even more re-markable career was that of Werner Buch. Born in 1917, he was a student at the Technische Hochschule in Berlin in 1936. While studying under the rather conservative Heinrich Tesse-now, Karl Caesar, and Emil Rüster, Buch became interested in the radical modernist works of Mies that were published in journals of the late twenties and early thirties, which he read in the school's library. Upon hearing of Mies's move to the United States in 1938, Buch applied for, and received, an exchange scholarship to study in Lincoln, Nebraska. He visit-ed Mies in Chicago and, after an interview with him in 1939, was accepted into the School of Architecture of the Armour In-stitute of Technology (now the Illinois Institute of Technology). He studied under Mies and Hilberseimer for two years, and his reminiscences are an invaluable record of what it was like to train under them in those early years in Chicago. With the threat of induction into the American army in March 1941, he reluctantly returned to Germany. After a trip across the Pacific Ocean, via Tokyo and Moscow, Buch arrived in Berlin shortly before Germany's June 1941 invasion of the Soviet Union, which prevented him from receiving the trunk containing all the drawings he had done in America. In Berlin he met former colleagues of Mies, such as Lilly Reich, Hugo Häring (see p. 50), and Tessenow, all of whom asked eagerly after Mies's activities in Chicago. That same year, Buch was hired by Welzenbacher to work on the Siebel aircraft factory in Halle. Welzenbacher had noticed Buch's photographs of Mies's Bar-celona Pavilion and Tugendhat House pinned near his draft-ing station in an industrial architecture workshop and em-ployed him immediately upon hearing of his admiration for

those buildings. From then until he was drafted for military service in 1943, Buch worked with Welzenbacher. At the end of hostilities, while Buch was a prisoner of war, he was recruit-ed, because of his fluency in English and lack of political affiliations with National Socialism, to help create a news network for German radio in the American sector. From 1947 to 1952 he returned to architecture studies, at the Technische Hochschule in Darmstadt under Neufert and Jan-Hubert Pinand. Upon graduating, he worked for Theo Pabst, a student of German Bestelmeyer (see p. 197). In addition to working on his doctorate, completed in 1961, Buch designed modernist homes and other buildings until his retirement in 1974. He currently resides in Herrsching, near Munich.

The stories of Bembé and Buch are but two instances of countless careers that demonstrate the persistence of varied modernist design values throughout this troubled time in Ger-many. Although they did not occupy the limelight like the "star" architects of the era, their commitment to modernist design principles remained unshaken, as was most certainly the case with others like them who worked anonymously be-hind the classicistic and historicist facade of architecture in Nazi Germany. It is people such as they and their older coun-terparts who rebuilt Germany after the ravages of the war, and they all held one form or another of modernism in high regard. As authors such as Durth, Weisler, and Wolfgang Schäche have suggested, it was these modernists of the twen-ties and early thirties, further hybridized by their experiences during the later thirties and forties, who led the way to shap-ing an eclectic, yet distinctive, modernist architecture in post-World War II Germany.

The many faces of modern architecture that reemerged after the hiatus in construction during the war ranged from the industrially oriented, radically modern to the numerous strands of expressionism and contextually oriented modernist masonry building. The last two categories run the gamut from the works of Scharoun in Berlin to Ernst Balser in Frankfurt. Their contribution to the rebuilt urban fabric of Germany after the war was greater than the few high-profile commissions given to such émigré architects as Gropius and Mies. In fact, the efforts of those architects who had stayed in Germany toward fashioning a modern architecture for their country were possibly even more strongly influenced by the multifaceted postwar American modernism of a firm such as Skidmore, Owings and Merrill than by the likes of Gropius and Mies. Even in the Soviet-controlled, eastern part of Germany, native architects continued to practice and develop a postwar architecture parallel to that in West Germany.

Because many modernist buildings from the interwar years were built on the periphery of cities, they often survived the aerial bombardment that obliterated German city centers and industrial complexes. Nevertheless, many of the buildings that remained standing in West Germany were either replaced by fifties structures or so extensively repaired and renovated as to be more the work of the fifties and sixties than of the twenties. In East Germany, partly for political and partly for economic reasons, many twenties buildings were simply stabilized and repaired only slightly. As a consequence, they have been left to deteriorate over the past four decades in what is essentially their original condition, their stucco sometimes even still pockmarked from shrapnel damage done to it in the course of wartime hostilities. The reunification of Germany prompts numerous questions about the future of these buildings. Some fear that they are ripe for demolition and speculative development, in other words, that they will suffer the same fate as their western counterparts in the fifties. Others are hopeful that, as in west German cities over the past few years, their destiny will be the more positive one of landmark designation and restoration. Whatever the outcome, their survival represents another dimension to the continuity of multifaceted modernism.

How does the hybridized nature of approaches to modernism in Germany from the twenties through the postwar era relate to tendencies within German society and culture? Gordon Craig's books *Germany: 1866-1945* (1978) and *The Germans* (1982) characterize Germans as having particularly strong conservative and sentimental or emotional tendencies. We should beware of attaching too much importance to such generalizations, but they undoubtedly contain a kernel of truth. Certainly, features of German architecture in the period under discussion can be adduced in support of Craig's thesis. The more conservative, eclectic modernist mainstream work that was built and published in the twenties far outweighs that of the radical moderns. Similarly, the emotionalism that Craig attributes to Germans may be reflected in the extremes of mood encountered in German architecture at this time, ranging from the dynamic expressionism characteristic of building in Hamburg and elsewhere in northern Germany, to the more radical and, perhaps, politicized work of some Berliners, to the extreme distortions of scale and proportion often found in the classically detailed structures erected by the Nazis. A basic trait of emotionalism may even help to explain the continued popularity of expressionism in the architecture of the postwar era: it informs the work of Scharoun and of the structural experimentalist Frei Otto, among others, and, in a current version, the deconstructivism of Günther Behnisch. By the same token, it may well have been this intensity of emotional commitment that enabled the Germans of the interwar years to develop such a diversity of strong architectural solutions, often more powerful and more memorable than contemporary designs in other European countries. Whatever the answers proposed to what is, in any scientific sense, certainly unanswerable, the importance of Germany's contribution to architectural design is not minimized by the pluralism of what was built there in the interwar years. Rather, the many expressions of modern design there confirm the country's place among the world leaders of twentieth-century architecture.

Selected Sources

Bauhaus Archiv (ed.), *Experiment Bauhaus* (Berlin, 1988); Fritz August Breuhaus de Groot, *Bauten und Räume* (Berlin, 1935); idem, *Das Haus eines Kunstfreundes* (Darmstadt, 1926); idem, *Das Haus in der Landschaft* (Stuttgart, 1926); idem, *Landhäuser, Bauten und Räume* (Tübingen, 1957); idem, *Landhäuser und Innenräume* (Düsseldorf, 1911); idem, *Neue Bauten und Räume* (Berlin, 1938; 2nd ed., 1941); idem, *Neue Werkkunst* (Berlin, 1929); Gordon A. Craig, *Germany, 1866-1945* (New York, 1978); idem, *The Germans* (New York, 1982); Ines Dresel (interviewer), *Werner Buch* (Chicago, 1990), audiotapes, transcript available at Ryerson and Burnham Libraries, The Art Institute of Chicago; Werner Durth, *Deutsche Architekten: Biographische Verflechtungen 1900-1970* (Braunschweig and Wiesbaden, 1986; 2nd ed., 1987; 3rd ed., 1988); Joachim Fest, *Cäsar Pinnau, Architekt*, ed. Ruth Irmgard Pinnau (Hamburg, 1982); Hartmut Frank (ed.), *Faschistische Architekturen: Planen und Bauen in Europa 1930 bis 1945* (Hamburg, 1985), esp. Gerhard Fehl, "Die Moderne unterm Hakenkreuz," pp. 88-122; idem, "Bridges: Paul Bonatz's Search for a Contemporary Monumental Style," in Brandon Taylor and Wilfried van der Will (eds.), *The Nazification of Art* (Winchester, England, 1989), pp. 144-57; idem, "Cäsar Pinnau: Ein Hamburger Architekt," *Architektur in Hamburg* 1 (1989), pp. 142-47; Wulf Herzogenrath, with Stefan Kraus, *Bauhaus Utopien* (Cologne, 1988); *Hitlers Sozialer Wohnungsbau, 1940-1945*, ed. Tilman Harlander and Gerhard Fehl (Hamburg, 1986); Elaine S. Hochman, *Architects of Fortune: Mies van der Rohe and the Third Reich* (New York, 1989); Barbara Miller Lane, *Architecture and Politics in Germany 1918-1945* (Cambridge, Mass., 1968; 2nd ed., 1985); Walter Müller-Wulckow, *Architektur der zwanziger Jahre in Deutschland: Neu-Ausgabe der vier Blauen Bücher* (Königstein-im-Taunus, 1975; first published 1929 and 1932); Winfried Nerdinger (ed.), *Bauhaus-Moderne im Nationalsozialismus: Zwischen Anbiederung und Verfolgung* (Munich, 1993); Wolfgang Pehnt, *Expressionist Architecture* (London, 1973); Detlev J. K. Peukert, *Inside Nazi Germany: Conformity, Opposition, and Racism in Everyday Life*, trans. Richard Deveson (New Haven, 1987; German ed., 1981); Richard Pommer and Christian F. Otto, *Weissenhof 1927 and the Modern Movement in Architecture* (Chicago, 1991); August Sarnitz, *Lois Welzenbacher, Architekt 1889-1955* (Vienna, 1989); Wolfgang Schäche, *Architektur und Städtebau in Berlin zwischen 1933 und 1945* (Berlin, 1991); Albert Speer, *Inside the Third Reich*, trans. Richard and Clara Winston (New York, 1970; German ed., 1969); Rainer Stommer (ed.), with Claudia Gabriele Philipp, *Reichsautobahn: Pyramiden des Dritten Reichs* (Marburg, 1982); Rainer Stommer, *Hochhaus: Der Beginn in Deutschland* (Marburg, 1990); Robert R. Taylor, *The Word in Stone: The Role of Architecture in the National Socialist Ideology* (Berkeley, 1974); Wolfgang Voigt, "Fortsetzung oder Ende der Moderne?" *Deutsches Architektenblatt* 19 (December 1987), pp. 174-77; idem, "Kontinuität oder Bruch? Zum Weg einiger Schüler und Mitarbeiter Karl Schneiders nach 1933," *Deutsches Architektenblatt* 20 (January 1988), pp. 6-11; Sabine Weissler, *Design in Deutschland 1933-45* (Berlin, 1990); Uwe Westphal, "Architecture and Advertising in Third Reich Germany," *Rassegna* 12, no. 43 (September 1990), pp. 58-69.

Regional Surveys

NORTH SEA

BALTIC SEA

Denmark

Poland

The Nether-lands

France

Switzerland

Austria

Czech Republic

KIEL
Laboe
Heikendorf
STRALSUND
ROSTOCK
Niendorf
LÜBECK
CUXHAVEN
HAMBURG
Reinbek
SZCZECIN (STETTIN)
WILHELMS-HAVEN
BREMER-HAVEN
Jesteburg
BREMEN
Delmenhorst
Elbe
Neuruppin
Oranienburg
Bernau
Elstal
BERLIN
Frank-furt an der Oder
Oder
CELLE
HANOVER
BRANDENBURG
POTSDAM
BRAUNSCHWEIG
MAGDEBURG

1 GELSENKIRCHEN
2 ESSEN
3 BOCHUM
4 DORTMUND
5 KREFELD
6 DÜSSELDORF
7 MÖNCHENGLADBACH
8 RHEYDT

DESSAU
KASSEL
HALLE
LEIPZIG
Löbau
ERFURT
Apolda
WEIMAR
JENA
DRESDEN
Freiberg
CHEMNITZ

COLOGNE
LEVERKUSEN
MARBURG
AACHEN
BONN
Bad Godesberg
Leversbach
Remagen
Rhine
Ruhr
Limburg
Kronberg
Coburg
Bad Schwalbach
SCHWEINFURT
WIESBADEN
Rüdesheim
FRANK-FURT
MAINZ
Main
WÜRZBURG
Bamberg
MANNHEIM
Bad Mergentheim
Fürth
NUREMBERG
St. Ingbert
PIRMASENS
Neckar

1 Maulbronn
2 Kornwestheim
3 STUTTGART
4 Esslingen
5 Salach
6 Wildbad
7 TÜBINGEN

REGENSBURG
KARLS-RUHE
Danube
Passau
Schliffkopf
Reutlingen
Bad Urach
AUGSBURG
Freiburg
Rhine
Fürstenfeldbruck
MUNICH
Utting
Herrsching
Diessen
Ammersee
Starnberger See
Wangen
Kochel

Poland

SZCZECIN (STETTIN)
Oborniki Ślgskie (Obernigk)
WROCŁAW (BRESLAU)
Gliwice (Gleiwitz)
Zabrze (Hindenburg)

A Note on the Compilation

The primary sources for many of the buildings in our survey were journals and books of the 1920s and 1930s held by the core library for our study, the Ryerson and Burnham Libraries of The Art Institute of Chicago. This major architectural library possesses a considerable number of relevant architectural books and periodicals. Although it continues to add volumes from this era to its stock, the library acquired many of the publications that we consulted soon after their appearance. They serve as a reference point for items available to a widespread audience at the time. The magazines frequently consulted range from conservative periodicals, such as the *Monatshefte für Baukunst und Städtebau, Der Baumeister*, and *Deutsche Bauzeitung*, to more balanced, mainstream magazines — for example, *Moderne Bauformen* — and even radical journals, such as *Die Form*. Of contemporary monographs and books, the most important in terms of breadth was the series *Neue Werkkunst*. The buildings of mainstream modernism published throughout these and other sources exist here in relation to the more obvious landmarks of the Modern Movement that have been documented in architectural publications from the twenties through the post-World War II era. A number of these are guidebooks. One of those consulted was Falk Jaeger's *Bauen in Deutschland* (Stuttgart, 1985), although it deals only with what was then West Germany. Fortunately, the East German *Architekturführer* series of guides, published from the 1970s through 1991, often provides corresponding data for the communist-ruled part of the country. We mention other local guides in the source listings after the various regional mini-essays and after the site descriptions within those regions.

Our focus relates to buildings published during the twenties and thirties and we have tried, wherever possible, to reproduce photographs of sites as they appear today. Photographs of many of the structures seen here were taken over the past five years. They thus document the relative condition of buildings in the former Deutsche Demokratische Republik, or German Democratic Republic (East Germany), before its union with the Bundesrepublik Deutschland, or Federal Republic of Germany (West Germany). One expects further alterations, even full-scale restorations, to be made to these buildings in both sectors, as well as changes to the names of the streets on which they are located. Every effort has been made to provide up-to-date information on the condition and use of buildings included here, but in general, alterations to the fabric and function of structures that have occurred since the end of 1992 could not be taken into consideration.

We discuss a number of buildings in cities which, though belonging to Germany in the twenties and thirties, became part of Poland after World War II. However, sites in the former German city of Königsberg (now Kaliningrad) could not be included, since the city served as a major Soviet naval base in the postwar era and its buildings were thus subject to limited access.

Our concentration in this book leans toward civil rather than military architecture, even though the same architects often built both types of structure. This focus resulted purely from practical considerations, not from the notion that military buildings are unworthy of historical study. Most surviving military installations are still occupied and hence, as we often discovered, usually off-limits to visitors. With the diminished threat of war in Central Europe, and the withdrawal from Germany of American and British troops, as well as those of the former Soviet Union, it is likely that a number of these military sites will remain in the hands of the German military forces, the Bundeswehr, while others will be recycled into different functions. In any case, our present survey usually does not include them. Politically sensitive and morally reprehensible sites, such as concentration camps, do not lie within the scope of this survey, despite the fact that their architectural imagery is modernist in its austerity and industrial orientation. We have also excluded such sites as the Hitler Youth buildings, the "Ordensburgen," or other paramilitary training camps that the Nazis established, in part, because of the Romantic, associative imagery evoked by these buildings, which are clearly not modernist in inspiration. Neither do we explore more potentially relevant sites, such as the ruined rocket installations at Peenemünde or the less well known concrete caves near Kahla. The latter housed jet aircraft assembly plants after Allied bombing forced the German war machine underground in 1943-44 (see the U. S. Army Air Force journal *Impact* [July 7, 1945], pp. 20-23). All buildings of Germany's military-industrial complex of the thirties, both modernist and conservative, deserve a study of their own. Occasionally, however, we do discuss structures related to civil defense in large urban areas, especially when they are still such a prominent presence as in Berlin and Hamburg (see p. 140).

Finally, this acknowledgment of urban defense brings us to the organization of our survey. We have arranged our sampling of buildings according to regional spheres of influence, focusing on the urban centers of Germany's various regions. After all, architecture is principally an urban art. These municipal clusters of influence usually predominate in their respective regions, or *Länder* (federal states). Following introductory remarks about the character and the architects of modernism in each of the six regions that we discuss, the reader will find illustrated and further explored extant examples of the many approaches to modern design that existed in Germany. We have arranged these structures in a variety of ways, sometimes according to building type, sometimes according to an architect's oeuvre. Books and articles given in the source listings are cited in abbreviated form after their first mention in each of the six regional sections.

Regardless of our different site choices and analytical approaches, it is our hope that some of the less well known or even previously overlooked buildings shown here will be again appreciated after a half-century and more of intellectual and, at times, physical neglect.

Berlin, Capital of the Modern Movements

John Zukowsky

Berlin is the German city most commonly associated with modern architecture. Since the last decades of the nineteenth century, it had striven to be Germany's world-class city, comparable to Paris or Rome, and this involved the erection of buildings by the best architects from throughout the country. The post-World War I republican government, a coalition dominated by Social Democrats and Catholic Centrists, was set up in 1919 in Weimar, far from the political agitation of socialist and communist factions in Berlin. Although the parliament briefly left Berlin, the city's cosmopolitan associations continued to be cultivated and, as the cultural capital of the new Weimar Republic, Berlin saw the development of an imaginative and liberal diversity of expressions in all the arts. Architecture was no exception. Radical arts organizations were formed, such as *Der Ring*, founded in 1925, and the *Novembergruppe* and the *Arbeitsrat für Kunst* (Workers' Council for Art), both founded in 1918. Among the Berlin architects included in the last of these were Walter Gropius, Hugo Häring, Ludwig Hilberseimer, Paul Mebes, Erich Mendelsohn, Ludwig Mies van der Rohe, Hans Poelzig, Hans Scharoun, and Bruno and Max Taut. Even these practiced distinctly diverse approaches to modernist design. When coupled with the impact of all the other famous architects from around Germany who built in Berlin, from German Bestelmeyer of Munich to Fritz Höger of Hamburg (see Fig. 1) and Emil Fahrenkamp of Düsseldorf (see Fig. 2), it should come as no surprise

that Berlin in the twenties was indeed the capital of the modern movements (plural).

Several other factors contributed to the plurality of building expressions in Berlin. Among them was the creation in 1920 of a larger, unified city from Old Berlin and its outlying areas. By the mid-thirties, with a population of some four-and-a-quarter million, this metropolis had become the fifth largest in the world. Because Greater Berlin remained a relatively decentralized city, with many of its constituent districts and towns possessing their own town hall (see Fig. 3), development in this large-scale urban structure was not usually dominated by one or two official architects, as in smaller German cities. Parallel to this patchwork-quilt heritage, all the architects named above, and many more, played equally important parts in adding to Berlin's urban fabric in the twenties. That said, those who specialized in particular building types, such as housing, played a slightly more prominent role than the others, since their work could be found in neighborhoods throughout the greater city. This is especially true of the most prolific of them: Bruno Taut (see Figs. 4-6) and Mebes and Emmerich (see Figs. 7-9). In all, this diverse group of twenties designers presented a bewildering variety of architectural expressions, which contrasts with the more refined and unified modernist forms found in some of the more famous and idealized Berlin Building Exposition spaces of 1931.

A small selection of the countless books, exhibition catalogues, and articles that have

been devoted to architecture and design of the twenties and thirties in Berlin appears at the end of this short essay. Since the architecture of Berlin is probably the most comprehensively published of any German city, only a handful of buildings erected in the interwar period have received little or no recognition since their construction. It is upon these less familiar elements of Berlin's urban fabric that the present chapter concentrates, only occasionally relating them to more famous structures. Thus, many renowned extant buildings by important architects, including Mendelsohn's Einstein Tower (Fig. 10), the apartment blocks by Hans Scharoun at Kaiserdamm 25 and on Hohenzollerndamm (Fig. 11), and Mies van der

Fig. 1   Fritz Höger. Evangelische Kirche (Protestant Church), Hohenzollernplatz, Berlin-Wilmersdorf, 1931-33. Photograph 1989.

Fig. 2   Emil Fahrenkamp. Shellhaus (now BEWAG building), Reichpietschufer 60-62, Berlin-Tiergarten, 1930-31 (facade rebuilt 1960 and later). Photograph 1989.

Fig. 3   Friedrich Hellwig. Wedding Rathaus, Müllerstrasse 146-47, Berlin-Wedding, 1928-30. Photograph 1989.

Fig. 4   Bruno Taut and Martin Wagner. Aerial view of the Hufeisensiedlung and adjacent properties, Berlin-Britz, 1924-27.

Fig. 5   Bruno Taut and Franz Hillinger. Carl-Legien-Siedlung, Erich-Weinert-Strasse, Sültstrasse, and Gubitzstrasse, Berlin-Prenzlauer Berg, 1928-30. Photograph 1989.

Fig. 6   Bruno Taut. Am Schillerpark Siedlung, Bristolstrasse 9-13, Berlin-Wedding, 1924-28. Photograph 1989.

1
2

Fig. 7   Mebes and Emmerich. Werra Block, Roseggerstrasse, Werrastrasse, Innstrasse, and Weserstrasse, Berlin-Neukölln, 1925-26. Photograph 1991.

Fig. 8   Mebes and Emmerich with Anton Brenner. Laubenganghaus (arcaded apartment house), Neuchateller Strasse 19-20, Berlin-Steglitz, 1929. Photograph 1989.

Fig. 9   Mebes and Emmerich. Spreesiedlung, Hainstrasse near Britzer Strasse, Berlin-Niederschöneweide, 1930-32. Photograph 1991.

Fig. 10 Erich Mendelsohn. Einstein Tower (now part of the Akademie der Wissenschaften), Einsteinstrasse at Telegrafenberg, Potsdam, 1920-24. Photograph 1991.

Fig. 11 Hans Scharoun and Georg Jacobowitz. Apartment building, Hohenzollerndamm 35-36, Berlin-Wilmersdorf, 1929-30. Photograph 1991.

Fig. 12 Werner March. Behringer House, Am Rupenhorn 16, Berlin-Charlottenburg, 1928 (demolished). From *Neues Bauen in Berlin* (1931).

Fig. 13 Mebes and Emmerich. Feuersozietät der Provinz Brandenburg building, Am Karlsbad 4-5, Berlin-Tiergarten, 1934-35. Photograph 1989.

Fig. 14 Otto Firle. Nordstern-Versicherungs-Bank building, east side of Fehrbelliner Platz, Berlin-Wilmersdorf, 1935-36. Photograph 1989.

Fig. 15 Friedrich Hetzelt. Former Italian Embassy building (now part of Italian Consulate), Tiergartenstrasse 21a-23, Berlin-Tiergarten, 1938-41. Photograph 1989.

Fig. 16 Ernst Sagebiel. Tempelhof airport, Platz der Luftbrücke, Berlin-Tempelhof, 1936-39. Photograph 1989.

15
16

Rohe's apartment building at Afrikanische Strasse 14-41, are not discussed here.

Two publications from the modernist era are notable for the variety of building types and styles that they treat. One is a standard work, *Berliner Architektur der Nachkriegszeit* of 1928, which provides a wide-ranging pictorial survey of office buildings and department stores, boutiques and showrooms, public housing and private homes, industrial and ecclesiastical structures, and even transportation facilities such as subways and Tempelhof airport. The second, rather rarer book is a 1931 guide, titled *Neues Bauen in Berlin*, that discusses 118 sites. Of the buildings surveyed in both books, approximately sixty percent still exist. They run the gamut from very radical looking sites by the Luckhardt brothers to Mendelsohn's expressionist works, from the hybridized modernism of Alfred Grenander's U- and S-Bahn structures (see p. 37) to conservative and radical housing projects at Siemensstadt (see pp. 50-51), and to private homes that were also hybrids of traditional and more modern forms (see Fig. 12). What both books and their era accepted was a pluralistic notion of which architectural styles could be considered "new" or appropriate to the modern times of the Weimar Republic.

The Nazis' accession to power in 1933 brought a new sense of mission to the "Weltstadt" Berlin. The hosting of the 1936 Olympics there and in Kiel acted as a catalyst for the new regime to display its architecture to the world. Through his architect Albert Speer, Hitler initiated a series of increasingly expansive plans intended to make Berlin the capital of a new Europe. These plans began on a comparatively small, simple scale and were implemented with specific structures in the mid- to late thirties, among them small corporate office buildings (see Fig. 13) and larger office structures (see Fig. 14), as well as embassies in the Tiergarten district (see Fig. 15). The buildings increased in size and scale according to their

governmental importance and to the image to be projected. The most publicized of them was the 1938 Reichskanzlei (Reich Chancellery), but even that would have been dwarfed by the buildings of megalomaniac scale that Speer and his associates planned, but never built, in the forties.

The eclectic appreciation of some modernist and more conservative forms in the thirties and even in the war years was by no means unique to Germany. A typical case is that of the Chicago architect Carl John Sterner, who visited Berlin in 1937 on a Plym Traveling Fellowship from the University of Illinois, his alma mater. Sterner, a 1927 graduate, was already an experienced architect, having designed historicist and Art Deco apartment houses in Chicago for the firm of McNally and Quinn in the late twenties. During the Great Depression and immediately afterward, he was the architect of a *moderne* remodeling of the Marshall Fields Store in Chicago in 1933, a senior Project Planner for the United States Public Housing Authority in Washington, D. C., from 1935 to 1941, and a part-time student of Mies in Chicago in 1941 before he entered the U. S. Army as a combat officer. The drawings he did while attending Mies's seminar show, almost predictably, an eclectic mixture of Wrightian, *moderne*, and Miesian elements. After service in the North African and European campaigns he spent most of his postwar career in Los Angeles and Santa Barbara, designing buildings on his own and with others, including Richard Neutra. He was an architect interested in various types of modernist architecture, so his impressions of modernism in Berlin, and of its role in the new regime, gained during a visit to the city on October 26 and 27, 1937, and written down in his as yet unpublished diary, are particularly noteworthy.

Sterner remarks that the radical modernism fostered throughout Germany during the Weimar Republic was not much in evidence in Ber-

lin: "The expected predominance of modern architecture was not an actuality. There is no doubt that much exists in Germany today but the examples are quite scattered so that no unified force is present; furthermore, all efforts in the direction of a more modern architecture have been stifled by the new government. New stadia, airports and other nationalistic structures were extremely interesting from an engineering standpoint due to much creative design of huge structural members in both steel and concrete." As with any architectural tourist to a major metropolis, Sterner could not see everything, but his overall impression of the urban fabric suggests an eclectic mixture of modernist buildings co-existing with other types. Thus, the "hype" about revolutionary modernism produced by post-World War II publications and exhibitions did not correspond to its actual impact on the streetscape, not even in this most radical of cities. Sterner's observation concerning the engineering focus of new buildings in the Third Reich corroborates the lingering and underlying role of modernism even in official buildings of the era, such as the Luftfahrtministerium (Air Ministry) building and Tempelhof airport (Fig. 16), both by Ernst Sagebiel. The Luftfahrtministerium featured a structurally expressive concrete basement garage reminiscent of designs by the famous engineer Pier Luigi Nervi, while Tempelhof's new terminal, which could handle up to 600 flights and 1,500 passengers daily, included spectacular open hangars on either side of the terminal building itself.

Unlike some American architects of the twenties and early thirties, whose chief goal was Onkel Toms Hütte in the Zehlendorf district (Fig. 17), Sterner visited a variety of buildings, and these reflect an eclectic appreciation of modern architecture common in the mid- to late thirties, as well as before: Fritz Höger's Hohenzollernplatz church (Fig. 1), the Europa Haus by Bielenberg and Moser with Otto Firle, Mendelsohn's Columbus Haus,

Fig. 17   Bruno Taut. Onkel Toms Hütte, Argentinische Allee, Berlin-Zehlendorf, 1930. Photograph 1989.

Fig. 18   Philipp Schaefer. Karstadt department store, Hermannplatz, Berlin, 1929 (largely destroyed). From *Neue Warenhaus-Bauten der Rudolph Karstadt von Architekt Philipp Schaefer*, Neue Werkkunst (1929).

Fig. 19   Erich Mendelsohn with Richard Neutra. Mosse Haus, Jerusalemer Strasse 46-47 and Reinhold-Huhn-Strasse, Berlin-Mitte, 1921-23 (remodeled). From *Berliner Architektur der Nachkriegszeit* (1928).

Fig. 20   Postwar renovation of the remains of the Mosse Haus. Photograph 1991.

ironically symbolic reuse of masonry from the Reichskanzlei, finally demolished completely in 1949, in the Soviet War Memorial in Treptower Park.

The postwar rebuilding of the city brought more than memorials. Berlin needed buildings quickly to replace the more than half the city's structures that had been either destroyed or severely damaged in the war. Partitioned into French, British, American, and Soviet sectors, it became a bipartite city held by the western allies and the Russians. Values of the victors became those of the vanquished, in architecture as well; yet the need for serviceable buildings, even if they were Nazi ones, led to repairs and reuse on both sides of the ideological fence, just as the Nazis themselves had utilized modernist buildings for their own purposes. Obviously, there is no need to demolish a useful building. For one thing, it is not as easy as burning a book or selling a painting when its social and political content is held to be unacceptable. Thus, Tempelhof airport in the American sector lost its swastikas, if not all its eagles, as it was repaired and even expanded; and the Luftfahrtministerium was reused and redecorated with socialist murals and emblems of the East German government, set up in 1949, when it was remodeled in the early fifties as the new state's House of Ministries. Some structures from the Nazi era were so well built compared with their modernist predecessors that it proved cost effective to retain rather than destroy them. This is particularly true of some air raid bunkers, one of which, constructed in 1942-43 in Humboldthain, has been incorporated in a park design as an observation platform. Likewise, modernist buildings damaged during the war — especially housing blocks — were repaired when possible; those rebuilt in the fifties often bear dated plaques to that effect, at least in what was once West Berlin.

Other structures were not so easily salvaged. The famous Karstadt department store

Fahrenkamp's Shellhaus (Fig. 2), and the Luftfahrtministerium building. Because of Sterner's background in government housing projects he was officially escorted to see apartments under construction. His notes refer to "bomb proof cellars" (air raid shelters) of thick reinforced concrete as parts of these new sites, a prefiguration of one role of modernism in the wartime years to follow. Sterner's notes afford a glimpse into the mind of an American visitor and into the attitude prevalent in the city itself. Both indicate an acceptance of various aspects of modernism, even in the capital of the new, Nazi Germany. The horrific wartime struggle of the forties was to change dramatically the face of the German capital in ways not predicted by the "Führer" and his henchmen.

Like Germany's other major cities, Berlin lay in ruins at the end of the war. It suffered heavy damage from both aerial bombardment and hand-to-hand fighting, as soldiers and citizens resisted the Soviet army's advance until the last days of the conflict. Some buildings still show the shrapnel scars incurred at the time. The districts to receive the heaviest damage were the city center (Mitte) and the areas adjacent to it, the parts east along the Spree River, and those to the southwest and just west of the Tiergarten. The dreams that Hitler and Speer had for the capital of the "thousand-year Reich" ended in the devastation of the city and the

19
20

on Hermannplatz had been designed by Philipp Schaefer, the Hamburg architect of many of that chain's buildings, in a style reminiscent of American modernist structures. Unfortunately, this spectacular 1929 structure (Fig. 18) was almost completely destroyed in the war. Only a stub remains — as part of a building dating from the fifties and later. This kind of thing happened in East Berlin, too. One of the best known examples is the postwar rebuilding of Mendelsohn's Mosse Haus of 1923 (Fig. 19): what we see today (Fig. 20) falls far short of a genuine reconstruction of this important commercial project.

Even more significant buildings survived the war only to be destroyed later. Such was the case with the famous 1931-32 Columbus Haus by Mendelsohn. Alan Balfour recounts its interesting history. Originally planned for a Galeries Lafayette department store, the structure, similar to Mendelsohn's Schocken store of 1928-29 in Chemnitz (see p. 220), became the most striking building on Potsdamer Platz, surpassing the curvilinear modernism of the nearby Telschowhaus by the Luckhardt brothers and Alfons Anker, which would also be destroyed in World War II. Columbus Haus served as an office and retail building. During 1935-36 the lower levels were used as retail facilities and services, with the spaces above housing various offices of German industry. The building survived the war with some damage, but not to its structure. In 1951 the

East German State Department Store was quartered there. The workers riots of June 17, 1953, took place near the building; it was subsequently abandoned and finally demolished in 1957. Balfour explains East German indifference to twenties modernism in the early fifties as the result of the regime's association of that style with the liberal capitalism of the Weimar Republic and, by extension, with the postwar West. Perhaps this attitude contributed to the demise of Columbus Haus, yet it was doomed in any case due to its location at the southwestern edge of East Berlin — the area that was, from 1961 to 1989, no man's land, adjacent to the Berlin Wall and the frontier of the communist world.

By contrast with early East German ambivalence, and even antagonism, toward Modern Movement masterpieces, America and the other western powers promoted modernism in books such as In USA erbaut, a 1948 German edition of the catalogue Built in USA since 1932, published by the Museum of Modern Art, New York, in 1944. The volume featured work by American architects with differing approaches to modernist design, such as Frank Lloyd Wright, already famous in Germany, and the firm of Skidmore, Owings and Merrill, soon to be highly influential there. Yet the book also included thirties buildings by the European émigrés Gropius, Mies, Neutra, and Marcel Breuer. In this way the many varieties of modern design that were accepted and

supported in America during the war years were encouraged to reemerge from their shell-shocked state in the western sector of postwar Germany.

Sources in Brief

Books on Berlin's architecture are too numerous to list here in full. Among the best are those in the series Berlin und seine Bauten, the volumes of which deal with various building types in the city. Three guidebooks that are still in print offer fairly comprehensive surveys: Rolf Rave and Hans-Joachim Knoefel, Bauen seit 1900 in Berlin (Berlin, 1968); Peter Güttler, Joachim Schulz, Ingrid Bartmann-Kompa, Klaus-Dieter Schulz, Karl Kohlschütter, and Arnold Jacoby, Berlin-Brandenburg: Ein Architekturführer (Berlin, 1990); and Martin Wörner, Doris Mollenschott, and Karl-Heinz Hüter, Architekturführer Berlin (Berlin, 1991). An East German survey of Berlin's monuments is Die Bau- und Kunstdenkmale in der DDR: Hauptstadt Berlin, 2 vols., ed. Institut für Denkmalpflege der DDR (Berlin, 1983). For general histories, see Karl-Heinz Hüter, Architektur in Berlin 1900-1933 (Dresden, 1988), 750 Jahre Architektur und Städtebau in Berlin, ed. Josef Paul Kleihues (Stuttgart, 1987), and Baumeister, Architekten, Stadtplaner: Biographien zur baulichen Entwicklung Berlins (Berlin, 1987). Sources used in the above text include E. M. Hajos and L. Zahn, Berliner Architektur der Nachkriegszeit (Berlin, 1928); Heinz Johannes, Neues Bauen in Berlin (Berlin, 1931); Alan Balfour, Berlin: The Politics of Order 1737-1989 (New York, 1990); In USA erbaut, ed. Elizabeth Mock (Wiesbaden, 1948); and Eberhard Steneberg, Arbeitsrat für Kunst Berlin 1919-1921 (Berlin, 1987).

Mies van der Rohe might have dreamt of creating an all-glass skyscraper in Berlin, but the city's commercial buildings of the mid- to late twenties were masonry structures. They evinced a wide range of modernist design; a selection from both the twenties and the thirties is illustrated here. Although these buildings have figured in some architectural guides, one example of comparable design tendencies that has been overlooked is the Loeser and Wolff building by Albert Biebendt. A self-effacing structure in comparison to the better known masonry ones just mentioned, this curvilinear building exists almost as constructed in 1929. The Potsdamer Strasse lobby has changed, but not the tiled courtyard entrance on Schöneberger Ufer. The eight-story structure is more than ninety-eight feet high, yet its scale is adapted to that of the buildings around it on its distinctive corner location near the Landwehr Canal. A similar curved-corner building was designed by Rudolf Kesseler on Kochstrasse and Charlottenstrasse, but this was rebuilt, extended, and rather differently resurfaced by Ferdinand Streb in 1951.

Ludwig Mies van der Rohe. Skyscraper project for Friedrichstrasse, Berlin, 1921.

bottom left: Hans Jessen. Deutsche Bau-und-Boden-Bank (later Liberal-Demokratische Partei Deutschlands) building, Johannes-Dieckmann-Strasse 48-49, Berlin-Mitte, 1928-29. Photograph 1989.

bottom right: Bruno Paul. Kathreiner Hochhaus, Potsdamer Strasse 186, Berlin-Schöneberg, 1929-30. Photograph 1990.

Selected Sources

Architekturführer Berlin, sites 1 (Lenz Haus), 4 (Feuer-sozietät building), 14 (Shellhaus), 195 (Haus Nürnberg), 202 (Kathreiner Hochhaus), 223 (Konsumgenossenschaft store), 524 (Reichsbank building), 543 (ADG building), 550 (Verkehrsbund building), and 554 (Alexanderplatz); *Berlin-Brandenburg*, pp. 22 (Alexanderplatz), 32 (ADG building), 57 (Shellhaus), 72 (Lenz Haus), 129 (Kathreiner Hochhaus), and 139 (Amerikahaus); *Berliner Architektur*, pp. 8 (Lenz Haus) and 76 (ADG building); *Neues Bauen in Berlin*, sites 3 (Salamander Hochhaus), 4 (Alexanderplatz), 6 (ADG building), 20 (Deutsche Bau-und-Boden-Bank), 22 (Kathreiner Hochhaus), 33 (Amerikahaus), 34 (Haus des Rundfunks), and 48 (Reichsknappschaftshaus); Julius Posener, *Hans Poelzig: Reflections on his Life and Work* (New York, 1992), pp. 227-29 (Haus des Rundfunks); *Der Schrei nach dem Turmhaus*, ed. Florian Zimmermann and Christian Wolsdorff (Berlin, 1988); Dietrich Naumann, "Deutsche Hochhäuser der zwanziger Jahre," Ph. D. diss. (Munich, 1989); Rainer Stommer, *Hochhaus: Der Beginn in Deutschland* (Marburg, 1990); "Geschäftshaus der Firma Loeser & Wolff an der Potsdamer Brücke in Berlin," *Deutsche Bauzeitung* (June 7, 1930), pp. 361-66; "Hauptverwaltungsgebäude der Iduna-Germania-Versicherungs-AG, Berlin," *Deutsche Bauzeitung* (August 5, 1931), pp. 373-76 (see also Karin von Behr, *Ferdinand Streb 1907-1970* [Hamburg, 1990], pp. 26-27).

Taut and Hoffmann. ADG building, Inselstrasse 6 and Wallstrasse 61-65, Berlin-Mitte, 1922-23 (addition and central tower by Walter Würzbach, 1930-31). Photograph 1989.

bottom left: Erich Mendelsohn with Rudolf Reichel. Deutscher Metallarbeiterverband (Union of German Metalworkers; now I. G. Metall) building, Alte Jacobstrasse 148-55, Berlin-Kreuzberg, 1929-30. Photograph 1988.

bottom right: Heinrich Wolff. Reichsbank building, facade on Kurstrasse near Hausvogteiplatz, Berlin-Mitte, 1932-40. Photograph 1989.

top left: Heinrich Straumer. Lenz Haus, Kurfürsten-strasse 87, Berlin-Tiergarten, 1928. Photograph 1989.

top right: Heinrich Straumer. Amerikahaus (later Naafi-Club), Theodor-Heuss-Platz, Berlin-Westend, 1929-31 (facade altered). Photograph 1991.

Taut and Hoffmann with Bruno Taut. Deutscher Verkehrsbund (German Transit Workers Federa-tion) building, Michaelkirchplatz, Berlin-Mitte, 1927-30. Photograph 1991.

opposite:
top left: Bielenberg and Moser. Haus Nürnberg, Nürnberger Strasse 50-55, Berlin-Schöneberg, 1928-31. Photograph 1989.

top right: Albert Biebendt. Loeser and Wolff building, Potsdamer Strasse 56, corner of Schöne-berger Ufer, Berlin-Tiergarten, 1929. Photograph 1989.

Taut and Hoffmann. Reichsknappschaftshaus (Imperial Miners' Society Building), Breitenbach-platz 2, Berlin-Wilmersdorf, 1929-30. Photograph 1991.

Werner and Walter March, and Georg Steinmetz. Community House, Olympic Village, near Elstal, 1936. Photograph 1991.

Speisehaus der Nationen, Olympic Village, near Elstal, 1936. From *Moderne Bauformen* (1936).

Hitler used the Olympic Games of 1936 in Kiel and especially Berlin as a means of promoting his new Germany to an international audience. Such public building projects as Tempelhof airport (Fig.16, p. 25) and the additions to the Messe (trade fair) grounds by Richard Ermisch were undertaken with this event in mind. Although these sites and the enormous stadium by Werner March are familiar to architectural historians and enthusiasts alike, another, more interesting complex has rarely been discussed, even though it was integral to the games. The Olympic Village of 1936 still stands in a rather dilapidated state on Heerstrasse (route 5), just southeast of Elstal to the west of Berlin. The village for Olympic

competitors, completed by Werner and Walter March after the death of its little-known designer Georg Steinmetz (a contributor to the modernist housing of Onkel Toms Hütte), was built on a Wehrmacht base more than nine miles from the Olympic sports facilities. The Wehrmacht was in charge of erecting the buildings, to ensure rapid construction and to enable their subsequent reuse as part of the base. The location well outside the city both insulated the athletes from urban diversions and assisted the authorities in surveillance of foreign participants. The buildings included housing in the form of simple, traditional cottages and larger, barrack-like structures. The designers intended these low-rise construc-

tions to blend in with the wooded landscape, complete with picturesque green and lake, in contrast with the more modernist, stark housing constructed for the 1932 Olympics in Los Angeles. The smaller homes still exist, but the barrack-like structures were replaced by even larger, prefabricated apartment blocks after the war, when the base was taken over by the Soviet army. The traditionally roofed community house survived with most of its interior detailing intact, becoming a Propaganda Center and the equivalent of an officers' club for the Soviet base.

Two other buildings in the Village, the entrance gate and the Speisehaus der Nationen (International Restaurant Pavilion), were more

Richard Ermisch. Ehrenhalle (Hall of Honor) addition to the Messe grounds, Hammarskjöldplatz, Berlin-Charlottenburg, 1935. Photograph 1989.

modernist in design and detail — curvilinear structures of reinforced concrete with steel balconies. The gate, which had a traditional tiled roof, no longer exists, though its telephone or communication room remains in the shape of a small, ruined brick and concrete structure. The Speisehaus, however, has survived, curved facade, balconies, and railings all apparently original. Its international function may well have induced the designers to use more overtly modernist forms for the facade. A smaller service building, more traditionally roofed, is situated to the rear of the Speisehaus so that the opposing concave curves of both buildings create a mandala-shaped court. Since late 1991, when the

Soviet army relinquished the base, the fate of the buildings has remained uncertain, yet in view of their importance to such a historic event as the 1936 Olympics, it is to be hoped that they will not be demolished.

Selected Sources

Architekturführer Berlin, sites 95 (Messe grounds) and 107-10 (Olympic buildings); "Das Olympische Dorf der Wehrmacht," *Deutsche Bauzeitung* (October 30, 1935), pp. 894-901; "Das Olympische Dorf, erbaut von der Deutschen Wehrmacht," *Moderne Bauformen* (1936), pp. 458-59.

Otto Bartning. Office building for Elektro-Thermit, Colditzstrasse 33, Berlin-Tempelhof, 1928. Photograph 1989.

Bruno Buch. Groterjan brewery, Prinzenallee 78-80, Berlin-Wedding, 1928-29. Photograph 1991.

Egon Eiermann. Auergesellschaft factory (now Berlin State Administration), Torfstrasse 34-35, Berlin-Moabit, 1937-38 (renovated 1987). Photograph 1991.

Berlin's industrial buildings have received frequent coverage in histories and guides. However, one area that has sometimes been overlooked is that of structures related to aviation. The German aircraft industry often benefited from state support, resulting in the construction of beautiful, modernist complexes to house its factories in the mid- to late thirties. These include Otto Biskaborn's brick structures for the Henschel aircraft company in Schönefeld, Berlin; Werner Issel's buildings for Junkers in Dessau and Magdeburg (see p. 239); Godber Nissen's work for Junkers in Stettin (now Szczecin, Poland); Wilhelm Wichtendahl and Bernhard Hermkes's Messerschmitt factory in Regensburg; and the Air Ministry's own

experimental station at Johannistal in Berlin. Some of the Johannistal buildings may still survive within the former research complex that the East German government established there after the war. Of all the airplane factories in the Berlin area, the most extensive and consistently functionalist was the 1935 Heinkel company's plant of 1935 southwest of Oranienburg, near Annahof farm. Herbert Rimpl designed this large complex, which included recreational facilities (see Fig. 4, p. 12) and housing for the employees, the latter at Leegebruch, southeast of the factory itself. Spared destruction during the war, the plant was demolished by the Russians after 1945. All that remains are some housing units in Leegebruch

and, perhaps, a brick and steel hangar just north of Annahof, near Bärenklauer Weg, at the edge of what was the company's airfield and, later, part of a Soviet base. Its overall form is certainly similar to that of the other buildings in the complex.

Immediately after World War II, Rimpl worked in the Rhineland, restoring the historic Bassenheimer Hof in Mainz and designing housing in Bad Godesberg and Bonn which, like that at Leegebruch, combined modernist simplicity with more traditional roofs and gables. In 1953 he published *Die geistigen Grundlagen der Baukunst unserer Zeit* (The Spiritual Foundations of the Architecture of Our Time), in which he set forth his view of

evolving modernism. Although Rimpl created a notably functionalist warehouse, and offices, for a company in Nuremberg in the fifties, he never again built on the scale of the work he had done for Heinkel in Oranienburg and Rostock-Marienehe (see Fig. 3, p. 11, and p. 36).

Selected Sources

Architekturführer Berlin, sites 45 (Auergesellschaft factory), 241 (Buchdrucker building), 308 (Schwarzkopf factory), 309 (Ullstein building), and 410 (Groterjan brewery); *Berlin-Brandenburg*, pp. 107 (Groterjan brewery), 124 (Buchdrucker building), 125 (Ullstein building), and 126 (Schwarzkopf factory); *Berliner Architektur*, pp. 77 (Buchdrucker building) and 81 (Elektro-Thermit building); *Neues Bauen in Berlin*, sites 8 (Buchdrucker building) and 64 (Ullstein building); "Ein Verwaltungsgebäude," *Die Form* (1929), p. 431 (Elektro-Thermit building). For Rimpl's work at Oranienburg, see Hermann Mäckler, *Architekt Herbert Rimpl: Ein deutsches Flugzeugwerk* (Berlin, 1938); *Moderne Bauformen* (1942), pp. 1-13; and *Monatshefte für Baukunst und Städtebau* (1940),

pp. 289-300. For Rimpl's other work, see *Der Baumeister* (1950), pp. 653-54; (1953), pp. 169-84; (1956), pp. 470-75; and (1960), pp. 466-67. For other aircraft factories, see "Bauten der Junkerswerke," *Monatshefte für Baukunst und Städtebau* (1939), pp. 73-91; "Die Neubauten der Deutschen Versuchsanstalt für Luftfahrt, e. V. in Berlin-Adlershof," *Moderne Bauformen* (1936), pp. 537-57; Hartmut Frank, "Inseln am Grossen Strom: Der Architekt Godber Nissen," *Architektur in Hamburg* (1991), pp. 120-27; "Neue Bauten der Henschel Flugzeug-Werke," *Monatshefte für Baukunst und Städtebau* (1939), pp. 133-40; *Architektur in Regensburg, 1933–1945*, ed. Neuer Kunstverein (Regensburg, 1989), pp. 46-47, 51-54, 72, and 119-21; and Martin Middlebrook, *The Schweinfurt-Regensburg Mission* (London, 1983), pp. 32-34, 148, 153-65, 289-90 and figs. 1, 2, 9-14.

Herbert Rimpl. Heinkel factory, near Oranienburg, 1935 (demolished). From *Architekt Herbert Rimpl* (1938).

Herbert Rimpl. Houses for employees of the Heinkel factory, Leegebruch near Oranienburg, 1935 (partly demolished). From *Architekt Herbert Rimpl* (1938).

Hangar at Annahof, near Oranienburg, possibly part of the Heinkel factory. Photograph 1991.

Present-day Berlin boasts a highly efficient and comprehensive public transportation network that includes a number of buildings from the twenties and thirties. Although these small monuments of modernism seldom have been listed in recent architectural guides, their appearance in surveys and guides published at the time of their construction alerts us to their importance in the development of this "metropolis of villages," all connected by U- and S-Bahn lines. Two architects figure prominently in their design.

The better known is Alfred Grenander, a Swede who had studied in Stockholm prior to attending the Technische Hochschule (polytechnic) in Berlin-Charlottenburg. He worked with Paul Wallot on the Reichstag building before setting up his own architectural practice in 1896. From 1900 until his death in 1931 he was architect for the Berliner Hoch- und Untergrundbahn Gesellschaft (Elevated and Underground Railroad Authority). Among the structures he designed in this capacity were the famous modernist U-Bahn stations of Alexanderplatz, Krumme Lanke, and Olympia-Stadion, as well as the more historicist ones at Nollendorfplatz, Kottbusser Tor, Ruhleben, and Wittenbergplatz.

The work of Richard Brademann has been neglected by comparison with that of Grenander. Brademann was architect for the Reichsbahn, the German railroad. The small, brick, somewhat expressionist-inspired structures that he designed for the railroad and S-Bahn during the twenties can still be seen throughout Berlin: the switching stations Halensee (between Halensee and Westkreuz stations), Markgrafendamm (near Ostkreuz station), and Eberstrasse (at the Schöneberg S-Bahn station), the Westkreuz station, and the transformer buildings at Treptow (at Treptower Park station) and Friedrichstrasse (at Georgstrasse and Planckstrasse) are all by Brademann. Most have been altered only in minor details. In the mid-thirties he designed Humboldthain station and, in 1933, erected simple, yet striking little brick structures at the Feuerbachstrasse and Sundgauer Strasse stops on the S-Bahn line to

Alfred Grenander. Krumme Lanke U-Bahn station, Berlin-Zehlendorf, 1929 (rebuilt 1988). Photograph 1989.

Alfred Grenander. Olympia-Stadion U-Bahn station, Berlin-Charlottenburg, 1929-30. Photograph 1989.

Wannsee. The Wannsee stop itself is a Brademann design of the twenties. In the later thirties he continued to design eclectic modernist buildings, including the additions to the Reichsbahn offices in Kreuzberg. Brademann's structures, though perhaps less prominent than the 1928 cylindrical electrical station by Hans Heinrich Müller on Mauerstrasse in Berlin-Mitte, deserve to be more widely recognized.

Selected Sources

Architekturführer Berlin, sites 111 (Olympia-Stadion station), 197 (Wittenbergplatz station), 199 (Nollendorfplatz station), 371 (Krumme Lanke station), 389 (Wannsee station), 553 (Alexanderplatz station), and 612 (Markgrafendamm switching station); *Berlin-Brandenburg*, p. 73 (Wittenbergplatz station); *Berliner Architektur*, pp. 69-72 (Nollendorfplatz station); *Neues Bauen in Berlin*, sites 5 (Alexanderplatz station), 7 (Kottbusser Tor station), 23 (Nollendorfpatz station), and 58 (Krumme Lanke station); Peter Bley, *Berliner S-Bahn* (Berlin, 1980; new ed., 1991), pp. 71, 84-85; *Alfred Grenander*, Neue Werkkunst (Berlin, Leipzig, and Vienna, 1930); "Hochbauten der Reichsbahn-Direktion Berlin für die Elektrisierung der Berliner Stadt-und Vorortbahn," *Wasmuths Monatshefte für Baukunst und Städtebau* (1929), pp. 481-93; Paul Kahlfeldt, *Hans Heinrich Müller, 1879-1951: Berliner Industriebauten* (Basel, 1992), pp. 87 and 90.

Richard Brademann. Service building for the S-Bahn, Treptower Park station, Berlin, 1926-27. Photograph 1991.

Richard Brademann. Feuerbachstrasse S-Bahn station, Berlin-Zehlendorf, 1933. Photograph 1991.

Richard Brademann. Sundgauer Strasse S-Bahn station, Berlin-Zehlendorf, 1933. Photograph 1991.

Hans Ratzlow. Omnibushof, Winfriedstrasse and
Berliner Strasse, Berlin-Zehlendorf, 1936-37.
Photographs 1991.

The best known modernist building relating to
street transportation in Berlin is the 1930
garage at Kantstrasse 128 in Charlottenburg,
originally called the Kant-Garagen-Palast. Its
facade was designed by Zweigenthal and
Paulik, the layout and spiral ramp by engineer
Louis Serlin.

There are, however, more significant
garages in Berlin in terms of size, planning,
and service to the community. These are the
streetcar and bus service areas situated in the
courts of large apartment complexes. Jean
Krämer, one of Peter Behrens's more important
assistants and the head of his atelier, created
two, in Charlottenburg (at Knobelsdorffstrasse
94-122) and Wedding, in the late twenties.
The former was reconstructed in the fifties, but
the latter, designed in conjunction with the
surrounding housing by Otto R. Salvisberg, still
functions almost as intended: planned for
streetcars, it now serves their successors,
buses. The apartment blocks around the

service court have remained essentially unchanged, but the small, curved streetcar
station in the court has disappeared. The
streetcar/bus hall exists as built, with the exception of slightly different doors.

The same planning solution of placing a
public transportation service facility in the
middle of a housing complex appears a decade later in the Omnibushof in Zehlendorf by
Hans Ratzlow. The entrance to this was hit in a
1944 bombing raid and reconstructed without
its upper story and roof, yet much of the areas
behind, including a gas station and bus hall
(the latter obviously resurfaced later), remains
as erected in 1936-37. It is interesting to note
that this was one of several industrial and
transportation facilities surveyed in a 1939
book on steel construction that was in the library of Ludwig Mies van der Rohe in Chicago.
He would no doubt have appreciated the 200-
foot-wide clear-span roof that originally
covered the bus hall.

Selected Sources

Architekturführer Berlin, sites 89 (Charlottenburg
service building) and 405 (Wedding service building); *Berlin-Brandenburg*, p. 155 (Wedding service
building); *Berliner Architektur*, p. 73 (Wedding service building); *Neues Bauen in Berlin*, site 30 (Kantstrasse garage); "Garagenhochhaus Kantstrasse in
Charlottenburg," *Deutsche Bauzeitung* (May 6,
1931), pp. 226-28; Ulf Dietrich,"Neuer Betriebsbahn-
hof und Wohnbauten der Berliner Strassenbahn,"
Wasmuths Monatshefte für Baukunst und Städtebau
(1930), pp. 570-79; *Architektur und Städtebau in
Berlin zwischen 1933 und 1945*, Die Bauwerke und
Kunstdenkmäler von Berlin (Berlin, 1991), pp. 457-59
(Zehlendorf Omnibushof); Dieter Gammrath and
Hans Jung, *Berliner Omnibusse* (Berlin, 1988); *Vom
Werdegang der Stahlbauwerke*, ed. Deutscher Stahl-
bau-Verband (Berlin, 1939), vol. I, pp. 19-26 (Zehlen-
dorf Omnibushof).

Several police facilities were built in Berlin during the Weimar years to ensure the safety and control of a population that increased enormously with the creation of Greater Berlin in 1920. Two such neighborhood police buildings appeared in the 1931 guide *Neues Bauen in Berlin* but have received scant attention since. The former Polizeidienstgebäude in Köpenick, its expressive, concave, stucco and brick form following the curve of the street, has been altered by the addition of a projecting story in the middle of the facade east of the tower that marks its entrance. The building now houses Berlin city offices. The small *moderne* stucco and brick building for the 123 Polizeirevier (123rd Police District), near the Olympic Stadium, included a barrack-type room among its facilities. With the exception of an eagle emblem that has been removed from its rounded corner, it stands more or less as built.

Selected Sources

Berlin-Brandenburg, pp. 141 and 185; *Neues Bauen in Berlin*, sites 36 and 91a.

Conrad Beckmann. Polizeidienstgebäude, Seelenbinderstrasse 83, Berlin-Köpenick, 1930-31 (altered). Photograph 1991.

Richard Scheibner. 123 Polizeirevier, Reichssportfeldstrasse 22, Berlin-Charlottenburg, 1930-31. Photograph 1989.

Along with structures for the police, new schools and related buildings for neighborhood children were needed in the twenties to meet the demands of a growing population. Two schools by Max Taut, the Dorotheen-Lyzeum and the complex Am Nöldnerplatz, have long been recognized as important examples of institutional design, though war damage and renovation have altered their appearance. A hitherto unpublished building, related in function, is the Jugendheim of 1929 by Fritz Freymüller, designer of the contemporary stadium in Berlin-Lichterfelde. Although this youth center, with kindergarten, has been resurfaced in smoother, uncoursed stucco and the color of its window trim changed, its overall appearance remains intact: a simple box only slightly ornamented with brick trim at the entrances and between the strip windows of its main facade. This is a minor monument that undeservedly has been overshadowed by larger, more elaborately planned educational complexes by Taut and others. Equally overlooked was the cylindrical Kinderkrippe (children's day care center) of 1931 on Dieselmeyerstrasse in Berlin-Friedrichshain. It was situated on the edge of a cemetery on the site of an unfinished crematorium. Only the entrance gate remains today.

Selected Sources

Architekturführer Berlin, sites 336 (Lichterfelde stadium), 649 (Am Nöldnerplatz schools), and 665 (Dorotheen-Lyzeum); *Berlin-Brandenburg*, pp. 179 (Am Nöldnerplatz schools) and 188 (Dorotheen-Lyzeum); "Fr. Freymüller, Berlin: Sportplatz und Jugendheim," *Moderne Bauformen* (1930), pp. 219-23; "Städt. Bauten und Aufgaben im Berliner Osten," *Deutsche Bauzeitung* (March 23, 1932), pp. 245-50, esp. 245-46 (Kinderkrippe).

Max Taut. Dorotheen-Lyzeum (now Alexander von Humboldt-Schule), Oberspreestrasse 173-78 and Menzelstrasse, Berlin-Köpenick, 1928-29. Photograph 1989.

Fritz Freymüller. Jugendheim, southeast corner of Herderstrasse and Paulsenstrasse, Berlin-Steglitz, 1929. Photograph 1989.

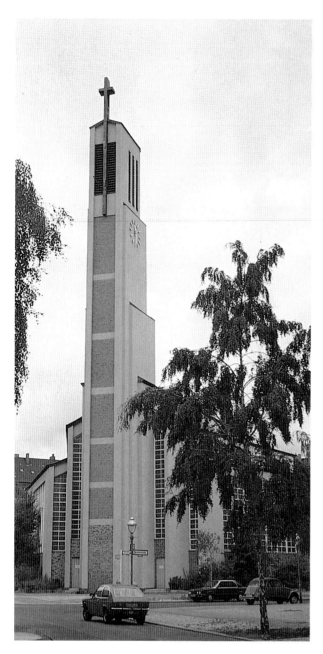

top left: Otto Bartning. Gustav-Adolf Church, Herschelstrasse 14-15, Berlin-Charlottenburg, 1932-34 (rebuilt 1950-51). Photograph 1991.

above: Josef Bachem and Heinrich Horvatin. Augustinuskirche, Dänenstrasse 17-18, Berlin-Prenzlauer Berg, 1927-28. Photograph 1989.

Alexander Beer. Synagogue, Prinzregenten-strasse, Berlin-Wilmersdorf, 1928-30 (demolished). From *Deutsche Bauzeitung* (September 10, 1930).

Ecclesiastical buildings take their place alongside schools and health care facilities in offering services to a neighborhood. Most of Berlin's extant ecclesiastical structures of the twenties have always been well known and widely published. With the possible exceptions of an ingenious courtyard design by Otto R. Salvisberg and an emotionally powerful church by Otto Bartning, none of these structures comes as much of a surprise: most accord with one's expectations of an ecclesiastical building in that they either carry spiritual associations or refer to accepted historical images. Solutions in Stuttgart, Tübingen, and Hamburg often seem more daring (see pp.141-42, 184). Less well known extant ecclesiastical buildings in Berlin also conform to traditional types. Some examples are the Ernst-Moritz-Arndt Church of 1934-35 by Diez Brandi in Zehlendorf, a stylized historicist village church; the Carolingian/Early Romanesque-style Friedhofkapelle (cemetery chapel) of 1930-33 by Otto Risse in Kleinschönebeck, northeast of Berlin; and the distinctive hybrid of Gothic and expressionist forms in the Augustinuskirche of 1927-28, in the Prenzlauer Berg district, by Josef Bachem and Heinrich Horvatin. The 1928-30 neo-Romanesque synagogue by Alexander Beer, which stood on Prinzregentenstrasse before the Nazis came to power, also evinces a very conservative approach to religious design, especially when compared with the slightly later synagogue in Hamburg, which is a strong modernist statement in stone. It is clear that the Modern Movement barely affected the planning, or even the detailing, of many religious buildings in Berlin. This is surprising in view of the wealth of modernist structures in other building types in the city. It must remain a point for speculation and further study as to why conservatism in ecclesiastical design was more prevalent here than elsewhere in Germany in the twenties.

Selected Sources

Architekturführer Berlin, sites 124 (Gustav-Adolf Church), 161 (Evangelische Kirche), 187 (Kreuzkirche), 323 (Matthäuskirche), 565 (St. Adalbert), 593 (Augustinuskirche), and 672 (St. Laurentius); "Friedhofkapelle Kleinschönebeck bei Berlin," *Deutsche Bauzeitung* (July 12, 1933), pp. 551-54; "Neubau der Synagoge Prinzregentenstrasse in Berlin," *Deutsche Bauzeitung* (September 10, 1930), pp. 521-25.

Heinrich Lassen, with Rietz, Scherler and Barfeld. Stadtbad-Schöneberg, Heinrich-Lassen-Park, near Eisenacher Strasse and Hauptstrasse, Berlin-Schöneberg, c. 1930. Photograph 1989.

Health care buildings in Berlin from the period under study are functionalist in appearance, particularly when compared with their ecclesiastical cousins. Two of the most famous are by Otto Bartning; both have been considerably altered. In addition to hospitals, public swimming pools and baths catered for the health and well-being of neighborhood inhabitants. Perhaps the most renowned is Heinrich Tessenow's Stadtbad-Mitte of 1929-30 at Gartenstrasse 5-6. Virtually unknown, however, is the Stadtbad-Schöneberg of 1930 by Heinrich Lassen, with assistance from Rietz, Scherler and Barfeld. New windows and doors are among the alterations that have

been made to its facade, and the interior has undergone comparable renovation; but the situation of the building in Heinrich-Lassen-Park provides the visitor with the same general experience as when it was new. Its red brick texture incorporates bricks of a lighter tone, giving a slightly mottled appearance to the exterior that recalls some industrial buildings of the period, such as the Heinkel factory of 1935 in Oranienburg (see Fig. 3, p.11, and p. 36). Lassen's Berlin work includes housing projects that also have industrial overtones.

Selected Sources

Architekturführer Berlin, site 578 (Stadtbad-Mitte); *Neues Bauen in Berlin*, sites 76 (Kinderkrankenhaus Lichterfelde) and 102 (Stadtbad-Mitte); "Die Landhausklinik vom Roten Kreuz Berlin-Wilmersdorf," *Die Form* (1932), pp. 44-46; *Neuzeitliche Hotels und Krankenhäuser*, ed. Hermann Gescheit (Berlin, 1933), pp. 322-27 (Kinderkrankenhaus Lichterfelde); "Stadtbad Berlin-Schöneberg," *Der Baumeister* (1931), pp. 82-83.

Erwin Gutkind. Apartment building, Ollenhauer-strasse 45-96a at Kienhorststrasse and Pfahler-strasse, Berlin-Reinickendorf, 1927-28. Photograph 1989.

Erwin Gutkind. Apartment building, Thulestrasse, Talstrasse, Hardangerstrasse, and Eschengraben, Berlin-Pankow, 1925. Photograph 1989.

opposite: Erwin Gutkind. Sonnenhof apartment building, Marie-Curie-Allee and Archenhold-strasse, Berlin-Friedrichsfelde, 1926-27. Photograph 1989.

Erwin Gutkind was almost as prolific a designer of apartment houses as Bruno Taut and Mebes and Emmerich. He, too, developed a characteristic appearance for his buildings. They are often bold combinations of stucco and exposed brick, with large windows and strikingly individual corners. Behind what are usually rather showy facades lie more uniform apartments. As with many other developments in Berlin, the complexes often have large courts. A native of Berlin, Gutkind graduated in 1913 from the Technische Hochschule (polytechnic) in the city's Charlottenburg district. He subsequently held positions with various building agencies, including the Reichskomissariat (state commission) for housing. When the Nazis came to power in 1933, the Jewish-born Gutkind emigrated to England, where, in 1940, he headed a demographic survey team. It was there that he began a second career as a city planner. He subsequently moved to the United States, living in Philadelphia from 1956 until his death in 1968. It is unfortunate that he chose not to practice architecture in this country, but he perhaps realized how difficult this would be for an immigrant and that his chances of designing large complexes, as he had done in Berlin, were limited (he did in fact return to Berlin in 1960, but only for a short visit). Throughout his English and American years Gutkind was, however, a prolific writer, his publications including *Creative Demobilization* (1943), *Our World from the Air* (1952), *The Twilight of Cities* (1962), and *The International History of City Development* (1964).

Selected Sources

Architekturführer Berlin, sites 419, 624, and 652; *Baumeister, Architekten, Stadtplaner*, p. 621; "Berliner Siedlungsbauten von Dr. Erwin Gutkind," *Moderne Bauformen* (1931), pp. 120-27; [Obituary], *Der Baumeister* (1968), p. 392; Rudolf Hierl, *Erwin Gutkind* (Basel, 1992).

opposite page:

top left: Peter Behrens. Apartment building, Bolivarallee 9, Berlin-Charlottenburg, 1930. Photograph 1991.

top right: Jacobus Goettel. Apartment building, Kraetkestrasse, Berlin-Treptow, 1929-31. Photograph 1989.

bottom left: Rudolf Fränkel. Apartment building, Freiherr-vom-Stein-Strasse and Meraner Strasse, Berlin-Schöneberg, 1931. Photograph 1989.

bottom right: Paul Zimmerreimer. Apartment building, Pommersche Strasse and Württembergische Strasse, Berlin-Wilmersdorf, 1926. Photograph 1991.

this page:
Georg Caro. Apartment building, Frankenallee corner Karolingerplatz, Berlin-Charlottenburg, 1931. Photograph 1991.

Kurt Heinrich Tischer. Apartment building, Teplitzer Strasse, Egerstrasse, and Karlsbader Strasse, Berlin-Schmargendorf, 1930-31. Photographs 1991.

Aside from the ubiquitous work of Bruno Taut, Mebes and Emmerich, and Erwin Gutkind, a variety of solutions to the design of multi-family dwellings were provided by numerous architects in Berlin. Two examples, both published in magazines of the twenties yet not discussed since, are Hans Jessen's Jeverstrasse apartments of c. 1927-29 (rebuilt in 1962) and Rudolf Fränkel's contemporaneous courtyard apartment building in Humboldthain. Another

Hans Jessen. Apartment building, Jeverstrasse,
Berlin-Steglitz, c. 1928-29 (rebuilt 1962). From
Moderne Bauformen (1929) and photograph
1989.

Rudolf Fränkel. Apartment building, Zingster-
strasse and Bellermannstrasse, Berlin-Humboldt-
hain, 1928. From *Moderne Bauformen* (1928).

site has been completely overlooked since its
publication in *Neues Bauen in Berlin* in 1931.
This is the low-rise, garden courtyard complex
of 1930-31 on Teplitzer Strasse by Kurt Heinrich Tischer. The courtyard perimeter contains
garages below grade, their entrances located
between the housing blocks.

Selected Sources

Architekturführer Berlin, sites 113 (Behrens), 193
(Buch), 415 (Ahrends), 557 (Poelzig), 654 (Goettel),
and 684 (Förster); *Neues Bauen in Berlin*, site 46
(Tischer); "Reg. Baumeister a. D. Hans Jessen: Wohn-
hausgruppe in Berlin-Steglitz Jeverstrasse," *Moderne
Bauformen* (1929), p. 320; "Neue Arbeiten von
Rudolf Fränkel, Berlin," *Moderne Bauformen* (1928),
pp. 249-53.

Paul Baumgarten is a good example of a second-tier Berlin architect who maintained his own sense of modern architecture before, during, and after World War II. He was born in 1900 in Tilsit, East Prussia (now Sovetsk, Russia), the son of a well-known architect of the same name. After serving in World War I, he studied at the Technische Hochschule (polytechnic) in Danzig (now Gdansk, Poland) in 1919-20 and at that in Berlin-Charlottenburg from 1920 to 1924. From 1924 to 1929 he worked in the office of Mebes and Emmerich, continuing to act as a free-lance designer for them until 1934, five years after he had established his own practice. In this period he planned some homes that blend traditional and modern design elements in a way that he also employed for the 1929-35 offices of Berlin's trash collection agency, BEMAG, in the Mitte district. Baumgarten's best known building from this time is the 1932-36 Müllver-ladeanlagen, where BEMAG stored and loaded rubbish for shipment on the river. It juts into the Spree River like a *moderne* machine or ship, rounded prow and all. These two BEMAG structures led to other commissions from that agency, including the design of their *Fuhrhof* (dispatching yard) at Ilsenburger Strasse 18-22 and 20-21. In the thirties he designed larger jobs, too, among them an apartment building on Hohenzollerndamm which, though traditionally roofed, has boldly massed towers, containing bedrooms, on the curved

rear facade. Baumgarten's skeletal information booth for the 1936 Olympics gave overt expression to his modernist inclinations. During the war he worked for Philipp Holzmann and for Berlin agencies dealing with industrial spaces and health care structures for the military. His career truly flourished after the war. His finest work of this period, well known to all students of Berlin architecture, represents an extension of the eclectic range of modern design that he had practiced in the twenties and thirties. Some of the more famous examples are the 1950-73 renovation of the Hotel am Zoo; the renovation of the Reichstag, 1961-69; and the BEWAG offices of 1962-68 at Stauf-fenbergstrasse 27-34, next to Emil Fahren-kamp's renowned Shellhaus (Fig. 2, p. 22). Baumgarten's career is thus comparable to Cäsar Pinnau's (see pp. 14-16) in that it spanned several decades of intensive modernist design work.

Selected Sources

Architekturführer Berlin, site 141 (Müllverladean-lagen); Barbara Volkmann, with Elisabeth Lux, Rose-France Raddatz, and Martin Wiedemann, *Paul Baumgarten: Bauten und Projekte 1924-1981* (Berlin, 1988).

Paul Baumgarten. BEMAG offices (later GDR Staatsbank), Poststrasse 13-14, Berlin-Mitte, 1929-35 (renovated 1987). Photograph 1989.

Paul Baumgarten. BEMAG Müllverladeanlagen, Helmholtzstrasse 42, Berlin-Charlottenburg, 1932-36 (renovated 1974).

Paul Baumgarten. Apartment building, Hohen-zollerndamm 67-76 and Flinsberger Platz, Berlin-Wilmersdorf, 1933-36. Photograph 1991.

top left: Otto Bartning. Ringsiedlung, Siemensstadt, south side of Goebelstrasse east of Jung-
fernheideweg, Berlin-Charlottenburg, 1929-31.
Photograph 1991.

top right: Hugo Häring. Ringsiedlung, Siemensstadt, Goebelstrasse, Berlin-Charlottenburg,
1929-31. Photograph 1991.

Hans Hertlein. Siemensstadt, Im Eichengrund,
Berlin-Charlottenburg, 1922-25. Photograph
1991.

top left: Hans Hertlein. Siemensstadt Church, Schuckertdamm 336-40, Berlin-Charlottenburg, 1929-31. Photograph 1991.

top right: Hans Hertlein. Erholungsheim (rest home), Siemensstadt, Goebelstrasse and Lenther Steig, Berlin-Charlottenburg, 1928. Photograph 1991.

Hans Hertlein. Heimatsiedlung, Siemensstadt, Schuckertdamm, Berlin-Charlottenburg, 1930-34. Photograph 1991.

In the minds of professionals and laymen alike, Siemensstadt is virtually synonymous with modernist housing, almost equal in importance to the Weissenhof Siedlung in Stuttgart. Architecturally inclined visitors to Berlin flock to Siemensstadt's Ringsiedlung to see the 1929-31 buildings by such famous designers as Walter Gropius, Otto Bartning, Hugo Häring, and Hans Scharoun. Yet those same architectural tourists forget what their counterparts in the twenties and thirties knew, and could see in a book like *Neues Bauen in Berlin* (1931): that Hans Hertlein, with his conservative and eclectically modernist Siemensstadt housing, paved the way for the Ringsiedlung expansion. Hertlein, born in Regensburg and a student at schools in Dresden, Berlin-Charlottenburg, and Munich, became an architect with the Siemens company in 1912. Within three years he had become director of their building department and, as such, was responsible for a number of their research and indus-

trial facilities erected in Berlin over the next thirty years. As mentioned, he designed the original Siemensstadt, situated to the northwest of the famed modernist housing complex, just east of Rohrdamm. This "company town" came to consist not only of the historicist apartment buildings from the early to mid-twenties, but also of various neighborhood facilities and the later, more eclectically modernist housing of the adjacent Heimatsiedlung. All were the work of Hertlein, and all were accorded as much space in the 1931 guide as the more radical Ringsiedlung buildings. Recent guidebooks have included a few of the earlier structures, but omit some of the brick neighborhood buildings.

Selected Sources
Architekturführer Berlin, sites 115-21, 446, and 447; *Berlin-Brandenburg*, pp. 146-47; *Neues Bauen in Berlin*, sites 112-16; Wolfgang Ribbe and Wolfgang Schäche, *Die Siemensstadt: Geschichte und Architek-*

tur eines Industriestandorts (Berlin, 1985); "Neue Bauten der Siedlung Siemensstadt," *Wasmuths Monatshefte für Baukunst und Städtebau* (1930), pp. 186-88; "Neue Wohlfahrtsanlagen in Siemensstadt," *Wasmuths Monatshefte für Baukunst und Städtebau* (1930), pp. 222-25; "Siedlung 'Heimat' in Berlin-Siemensstadt," *Wasmuths Monatshefte für Baukunst und Städtebau* (1930), pp. 537-41.

Ludwig Mies van der Rohe was one of the great architects of the twentieth century. Born in Aachen, he apprenticed as a stone mason with his father before designing furniture in Bruno Paul's Berlin office from 1905 to 1907. The latter year witnessed Mies's first constructed design, the Riehl House, which still exists at Spitzweggasse 3 in Babelsberg, near Potsdam, though it has been altered somewhat. In 1908 he went to work with Peter Behrens, for whom he is said to have designed the German Embassy building of 1912 in St. Petersburg, Russia. Homes created by Mies in Berlin during this pre-World War I period include the Perls House of 1911 at Hermannstrasse 14 in Zehlendorf and the nearby Werner House project of 1913 at Quermatenweg 2, the designs for which are in the Bauhaus Archiv. It was after World War I, however, that Mies's career skyrocketed, as he produced plans for large complexes and buildings (see pp. 28, 108-9). In the end, he established a practice creating modernist homes of consistently beautiful proportions. The last of these to be built, the Lemke House of 1932, has survived.

Occupying a mere 1,725 square feet, the Lemke House is a simple brick structure on an L-shaped plan that is related to the "courthouse" compositions developed by Mies and Ludwig Hilberseimer in the thirties. Although the building was relatively undamaged in World War II, it was seized by the Soviet occupation force and used as a garage until, in the fifties, it became part of a complex of houses and service buildings administered by the feared Staatssicherheitsdienst ("Stasi"; State Security Service) of the East German government. Numerous postwar alterations have affected interior spaces, floor surfaces, and the fenestration of the facades facing the court and Oberseestrasse. With the reunification of Germany and the abolition of the secret police, the house reverted to neighborhood administration. It is now being turned into a museum. Visitors should note that some of its original wood furnishings are in the Kunstgewerbemuseum in the Tiergarten district.

Selected Sources
Architekturführer Berlin, sites 373 (Perls House) and 636 (Lemke House); *Mies Reconsidered*, ed. John Zukowsky (Chicago, 1986); Franz Schulze, *Mies van der Rohe* (Chicago and London, 1986).

Private homes in Berlin during the twenties and

opposite:
Ludwig Mies van der Rohe. Lemke House, Oberseestrasse 60, Berlin-Weissensee, 1932. Photograph as originally built and furnished.

Ludwig Mies van der Rohe. Lemke House, Oberseestrasse 60, Berlin-Weissensee, 1932. Photograph 1991.

above: Ludwig Hilberseimer. Blumenthal House, Wilskistrasse 66, Berlin-Zehlendorf, 1932. Photograph 1989.

below: Luckhardt brothers with Alfons Anker. Row houses, Schorlemerallee 12, Berlin-Dahlem, 1930. Photograph 1989.

Hugo Häring. Ziegler House, Lepsiusstrasse 112, Berlin-Steglitz, 1936. Photograph 1989.

Herbert (Hans) Ruhl. Paret House, Am Vogelsang 12, Berlin-Dahlem, 1929. Photograph 1991.

thirties run the gamut from traditional to avant-garde designs. A great many of them survived the war intact. Indeed, a mere list of the extant examples would require a separate volume, but many figure in the guides to Berlin published over the past sixty years or so. A selection is illustrated here. A rather unfamiliar, though not unknown, example of modernist architecture by one of Berlin's lesser lights is the Paret House of 1929 by Herbert Ruhl with landscaping by Gustav Allinger. Virtually unknown, yet almost completely intact, is a tile-roofed modernist house by Gustav Hassen-pflug in a wooded site at Gross-Glienicke near Potsdam. *Moderne Bauformen* described it in 1939 as "severe," adding that it nonetheless "harmonizes pleasingly with the scenery." Urban and suburban villas constructed during the Third Reich combine aspects of the large traditional homes built in the early twenties by an architect such as Oscar Kaufmann with the simple, severe wall planes of modernist houses

from the later twenties. Fritz August Breuhaus de Groot designed several such large residences in the thirties, and they appear today much as they did half a century ago. His Haus am Wannsee is particularly interesting in its union of the kind of formal front elevation found in any grand suburban villa with less formal, curved, *moderne* windows at the rear. Essentially, such hybridization is not so very different from, and possibly even more advanced than, the combination of traditional materials and modern forms found in the famous Marlene Poelzig house of 1930 in Charlottenburg.

Selected Sources

Architekturführer Berlin, 322 (Häring), 344 (Luckhardt brothers), 369 (Mendelsohn/Neutra), and 370 (Hilberseimer); *Berlin-Brandenburg*, p. 200 (Ruhl); *Neues Bauen in Berlin*, site 53 (Ruhl); *Architektur und Städtebau in Berlin zwischen 1933 und 1945*, pp. 495 (Breuhaus) and 498 (Häring); *Neue Bauten und Räume: Fritz August Breuhaus de Groot* (Berlin, 1941), pp. 112-15 (Wannsee) and 76-80 (Dahlem); *Bauten und Räume* (Berlin, 1935), pp. 97-101 (Wannsee); "Wohnhaus in Gross-Glienicke bei Berlin," *Moderne Bauformen* (1939), pp. 373-77.

Gustav Hassenpflug. House, Waldfrieden 7,
Gross-Glienicke, c. 1937-39. Photograph 1992.

Fritz August Breuhaus de Groot. Haus am Wannsee (Bauer House), Am Sandwerder 27, Berlin-
Wannsee, 1934. From *Bauten und Räume* (1935)
and photograph 1991.

Fritz August Breuhaus de Groot. "W" House,
Dohnenstieg 12, Berlin-Dahlem, c. 1934. Photograph 1992.

"Das Neue Frankfurt"

John Zukowsky

"Das Neue Frankfurt" (The New Frankfurt) commonly denotes the revolution in housing that took place in Frankfurt am Main in the mid- and late 1920s, in particular the large residential planning projects of Ernst May. May trained with Theodor Fischer in Munich. He was in charge of Frankfurt's city department dealing with high-rise and apartment house development from 1925 to 1930, in which year he moved to the Soviet Union, where he practiced city planning until 1933. After living in South Africa from 1934 to 1954, he returned to Germany to head the Neue Heimat housing program of postwar reconstruction.

An equally important person in Frankfurt's urban development was Martin Elsaesser. Tübingen-born Elsaesser was a student of Fischer in Munich and of Paul Bonatz in Stuttgart. From 1925 to 1932 he was City Architect of Frankfurt. In the thirties he lived in Berlin and practiced there. International projects of his from this era are the Sumerbank in Ankara, Turkey (1932-34), and a competitive entry for the Bruckner Concert Hall in Linz, Austria (1943-44). After the war, he moved to Stuttgart and participated in reconstruction there and in Frankfurt.

In the years between the world wars, Elsaesser and May shaped Frankfurt's urban character and pushed the city into the forefront of modernist design. May's coordination of various architects, as well as his own designs, made possible the widespread construction of major apartment blocks throughout the city, providing more than 12,000 living units between 1925 and 1930. These were financed in a public/private partnership, with more than half the funds coming from the city and city building agencies, and the rest from private cooperatives and building societies. The housing units themselves provided a variety of square footage for their occupants: approximately 1,500 to 1,600 square feet for single-family row houses and 600 to 700 square feet for two-bedroom apartments. The famous Frankfurt Kitchen, developed by Viennese architect Grete Schütte-Lihotzky, graced many of the apartments. This industrialized and ergonomic kitchen, intended to modernize and simplify household chores, was constructed in some 10,000 units. From 1926 to 1931, Frankfurt's creative new housing program was promoted in the city's own monthly magazine, *Das Neue Frankfurt*. A number of architects participated in the design of these multi-family housing complexes, including the less well known Franz Roeckle and Anton Brenner and the famous Walter Gropius (see pp. 59-60).

Many of the houses are what one would term starkly radical in design, though a few combined modernist forms with such traditional elements as pitched roofs (see Fig. 1).

As City Architect, Elsaesser contributed designs for public buildings in Frankfurt that ranged in scale from his famous Grossmarkthalle (market hall) of 1926-28 to smaller individual buildings, such as the Ludwig Richter School of 1928-29 (rebuilt by him in 1951; see p. 62). Although some of his work remains, much has disappeared as a result of war destruction or of subsequent alteration. Gone are his hospital buildings, such as the Röntgeninstitut (X-ray station) of the Städtisches Krankenhaus (city hospital) from 1929 and the slightly earlier Kinderbeobachtungsstation (children's observation ward) of 1927-28 (Fig. 2), both in the city's Sachsenhausen district.

In addition to May, Elsaesser, and their colleagues and collaborators, other architects made their mark on Frankfurt's cityscape. J. W. Lehr's 1929 *Volksstimme* (Voice of the People) office building for the publisher of the newspaper of that name, Union Druckerei (Fig. 4), is among the least known. In its time it was highly esteemed, even figuring in the famous 1932 book *The International Style* (p. 171) by Henry Russell Hitchcock and Philip Johnson. Its strong, simple modernist masses contrast, on the one hand, with the more expressionist and historicist ecclesiastical work of Martin Weber and others (see p. 66) and, on the other, with the individual approach to modern design of Ernst Balser. Balser's various approaches include the brick, somewhat expressionist apartments on Grethenweg from 1926 (see p. 68) and the like-styled Mannesmann-Mulag offices and garage of 1922-23 (Fig. 3). But he also designed the modernist masonry Allgemeine Ortskrankenkasse (AOK; General Health Insurance Fund) building of 1928-30 (renovated and added to by him after the war) and the small, functionalist gasoline station on the north bank of the Main River at Friedensbrücke from 1936 (Fig. 5). Other structures, by such architects as Max Taut and Franz Hoffmann, Hans Poelzig (see p. 65), Hermann Senf, Fritz Nathan (see p. 67), and Franz Thyriot, rounded out the variety of expressions within modern design, even though the image of the stark housing blocks of the New Frankfurt has determined our notion of modernism in the city.

It is instructive to compare Frankfurt's modernist buildings with those in the more northern towns of Celle in Lower Saxony and Kassel in Hesse, even though, geographically, these are not directly within Frankfurt's sphere of in-

fluence. The strongest of these buildings were designed by Otto Haesler. Haesler, in fact, worked in Frankfurt with architect Ludwig Bernouilly, before moving further south, to Karlsruhe on the Rhine, to practice with Hermann Billing. Haesler finally settled in the small, conservative town of Celle in 1906. He is best remembered by architectural historians for his brightly colored Italienischer Garten housing of 1923-24 in Celle, said to have been the first flat-roofed (actually, low-profiled, tile-roofed) simple-planed housing in Germany. He made his mark on this little town with housing and public projects that were even more avant-garde in character (see p. 70), spreading his design formulas to other cities, such as Kassel and Karlsruhe. In many ways, his functionalist buildings seem somewhat out of place in the conservative environments of half-timbered Celle and classicistic Kassel. They certainly appear as intruders in the brick and half-timbered rural atmosphere of Lower Saxony, whose regional modern tradition of brick expressionism had virtually no impact on Celle. Haesler's buildings there, like their New Frankfurt counterparts, best represent the International Style housing that symbolized the new Germany of the Weimar Republic. As with their Frankfurt cousins, Haesler's housing projects were extensively published both in Germany and abroad. Haesler spent the years of the Third Reich in Eutin, Schleswig-Holstein, and, after the war, he practiced in East Germany. His autobiography, *Mein Lebensweg als Architekt*, was published in Berlin in 1957.

Sources in Brief

Frankfurt is fortunate to have Heike Risse, *Frühe Moderne in Frankfurt am Main 1920-1933* (Frankfurt am Main, 1984), which presents a thorough picture of the modernist buildings in the city.

Fig. 1   Ernst May assisted by Herbert Boehm with Otto and Eduard Fucker and Franz Thyriot. Design for the courtyard elevation of housing in Riederwald, Am Erlenbruch and Schäfflestrasse, Frankfurt am Main, 1926.

Fig. 2   Martin Elsaesser with Walter Körte. Cutaway view of the Kinderbeobachtungsstation, Frankfurt-Sachsenhausen, 1927-28 (replaced). From *Der Baumeister* (1930).

Fig. 3   Ernst Balser. Bird's-eye view of the Mannesmann-Mulag garage and office building, Hersfelder Strasse 21-23, Frankfurt am Main, 1922-23. From Gustav Lampmann, *Ernst Balser: Ein Baumeister unserer Zeit* (Munich, 1953).

Fig. 4   J. W. Lehr. Office building for the *Volksstimme* newspaper of the Union Druckerei, Zeppelinallee and Bockenheimer Landstrasse, Frankfurt am Main, 1929 (demolished). From *Der Baumeister* (1930).

Fig. 5   Ernst Balser. Gasoline station on the North Bank of the Main River at Friedensbrücke, Frankfurt am Main, 1936 (demolished). From Lampmann, *Ernst Balser: Ein Baumeister unserer Zeit*.

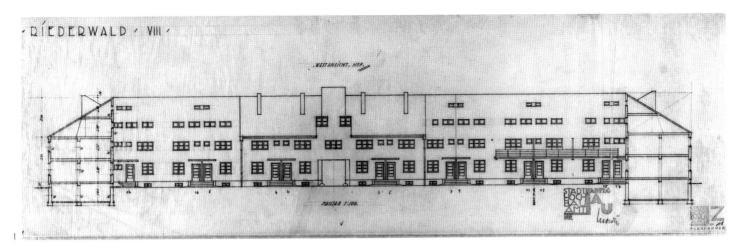

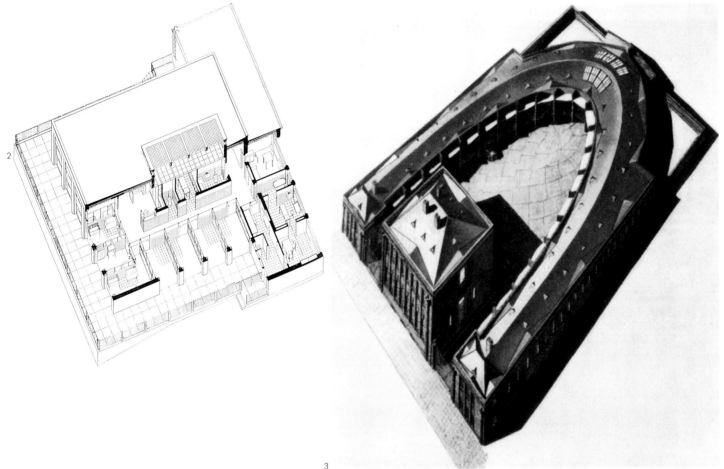

Ernst May assisted by Herbert Boehm and Wolfgang Bangert, for planning, and Carl Hermann
Rudloff and Blattner, Schaupp and Schuster, for
architecture. Römerstadt housing estate, Hadrianstrasse and In der Römerstadt, Frankfurt am
Main, 1927-28. Photographs 1988.

opposite:
Ernst May assisted by Herbert Boehm, for
planning, and by C. H. Rudloff. Niederrad
housing estate, Breubergstrasse, Frankfurt am
Main, 1926-27. Photograph 1991.

Walter Gropius. Am Lindenbaum housing estate,
near Nusszeil, Frankfurt am Main, 1930.
Photograph 1989.

From 1925 to 1930 Ernst May directed eight
major housing developments as part of the
New Frankfurt: Bornheimer Hang, Heimatsiedlung, Hellerhof, Niederrad, Praunheim, Riederwald, Römerstadt, and Westhausen. He
worked with a variety of architects within and
outside his city building office to execute these
buildings. The angular plan of the Heimatsiedlung, the zigzag configuration of the housing
blocks of Niederrad, and the curvilinear, ship-
like buildings of Römerstadt remain the most
striking of urbanistic statements. Not only the
street names of Römerstadt — Mithrasstrasse,
Hadrianstrasse, and Forum, for example —
carry Roman associations: the planning of the
complex evokes the rounded bastions of
Antique military structures. These contrast with

the no-nonsense rectilinear blocks of West-hausen. The housing here and at Praunheim appears today to be among the most severe examples of modernist design, making the Römerstadt buildings seem lush by comparison. In addition to the massive blocks in these developments, the building program of the New Frankfurt included smaller scale housing by such local architects as Karl Ollson and Franz Roeckle and by such an internationally renowned designer as Walter Gropius.

Selected Sources

Risse, *Frühe Moderne in Frankfurt*, pp. 227-29 and 243-99; D. W. Dreysse, *May-Siedlungen: Architektur-führer durch acht Siedlungen des Neuen Frankfurt 1926-1930* (Frankfurt, 1986); Rosemarie Höpfner and Volker Fischer (eds.), *Ernst May und das Neue Frank-furt 1925-1930* (Frankfurt, 1986). Additional illustrations can be found in the journals *Der Baumeister* (1929), pp. 29-35 and 97-125, and *Die Form* (1931), pp. 128-29.

Karl Ollson. Apartment building, Burnitz-strasse 2-8, Frankfurt am Main, 1926-29. Photograph 1989.

Franz Roeckle. Apartment buildings, Fontane-strasse 8-64 and 15-35, Frankfurt am Main, 1929. Photographs 1988.

Martin Elsaesser. Grossmarkthalle, Sonnemann-strasse, Frankfurt am Main, 1926-28. Photograph 1987.

Werner Hebebrand. Hauptzollamt, Domstrasse and Braubachstrasse, Frankfurt am Main, 1927 (rebuilt with a different roof profile after World War II). Photograph 1989.

Public building needs of the twenties enabled Martin Elsaesser to provide spectacular solutions to a number of sites and structures in Frankfurt. Most historians immediately think of the massive, expressively detailed Grossmarkt-halle (market hall) of 1926-28 as his master-piece. Others focus on his work with Ernst May in the elegant Gesellschafthaus of 1929 in the Palmengarten, a pleasant restaurant pavilion. Although only slightly damaged in the war, it has been extensively rebuilt. Yet, in addition to these prominent sites, Elsaesser designed a number of schools related to the new housing projects planned by May and his collaborators. Foremost among those that survived the war and alteration during recon-

struction is the Ludwig Richter School, which was built shortly before Walter Gropius constructed the nearby housing on Am Linden-baum. Although the school was damaged in World War II, Elsaesser rebuilt it to essentially the same design between 1951 and 1954. It compares favorably with his similarly styled Römerstadt School from the same period, near the curved Hadrianstrasse apartments. Both were featured in contemporary surveys of school design. Other architects contributed to the design of Frankfurt's public buildings in a variety of modernist styles. These include the hybridized, conservative and yet modernist, Hauptzollamt (Customs Headquarters) of 1927 by Werner Hebebrand, complete with art

glass in its windowed corner staircase. Another, more striking example is the 1929-30 Haus der Jugend by Franz Thyriot, an architect who specialized in schools and other institutions. The U. S. Army occupied this youth home and hostel after the war, but in 1937 it had already been somewhat altered by an addition.

Selected Sources
Martin Elsaesser, Bauten und Entwürfe aus den Jahren 1924-1932 (Berlin, 1933), vol. 2, pp. 164-85,

vol. 3, pp. 284-94, 310-26, and 341-48; "Haus der Jugend in Frankfurt am Main," *Wasmuths Monatshefte für Baukunst und Städtebau* (1931), pp. 251-54; Rainer Meyer, "Martin Elsaesser, 1925-32: Zum Werk eines avantgardistischen Baukünstlers," Ph. D. diss., University of Bremen, 1988; W. Schürmeyer, "Die Grossmarkthalle in Frankfurt a. Main," *Deutsche Bauzeitung* (November 24, 1928), pp. 797-801; "Frankfurter Volksschulbauten," *Deutsche Bauzeitung* (January 4, 1930), pp. 14-22; Julius Vischer, *Der neue Schulbau* (Stuttgart, 1931), pp. 72-73; Risse, *Frühe Moderne in Frankfurt*, pp. 36-53, 69-74, 115, 206-9, and 223-24.

Martin Elsaesser and Walter Schütte. Ludwig Richter School, Am Lindenbaum, northeast of Eschersheimer Landstrasse, Frankfurt am Main, 1928 and 1954. Photograph 1989.

Franz Thyriot. Haus der Jugend, Hansa-Allee 132, Frankfurt am Main, 1929-30. Photograph 1989.

Ernst May. The architect's house, Ludwig-Tieck-Strasse 11, Frankfurt am Main, 1925. From *Die Form* (1926-27).

Martin Elsaesser. The architect's house, Höhenblick 37, Frankfurt am Main, 1925-26. From *Moderne Bauformen* (1929).

The homes of Martin Elsaesser and Ernst May still exist. They provide fine counterpoints to the more public, large-scale work of these designers. Both houses appeared in journals of the time. The whitewashed brick home of May, with its clean-lined furnishings, received extensive coverage in the radical magazine *Die Form* (1926-27, pp. 293-98). By contrast, Elsaesser's unpainted brick house, modern in design but furnished rather more conservatively, was published briefly in the pages of *Moderne Bauformen* (1929, pp. 184-85).

Selected Source
Risse, *Frühe Moderne in Frankfurt*, pp. 218-20.

Fritz Mouson, with architects Geitner, Wollmann and Hirsch. J. G. Mouson factory, Waldschmidt-strasse 4, Frankfurt am Main, 1926. Photograph 1989.

opposite:
Taut and Hoffmann. Gewerkschaftsbund building, Wilhelm-Leuschner-Strasse 69-77, Frankfurt am Main, 1931. Photograph 1989.

Hans Poelzig. I. G. Farben headquarters (now Creighton W. Abrams Building), Fürstenberger Strasse on Grüneburgplatz, Frankfurt am Main, 1928-31.

Although the most famous industrial complex in this region is not in Frankfurt, but in Höchst, there are a number of interesting industrial structures still extant in Frankfurt itself. One is by well-known architect Adolf Meyer, who was in partnership with Walter Gropius from 1911 to 1925. Meyer's Prüfamt 6 on Gutleut-strasse is a simple, poured concrete building that was originally part of the power plant generating the city's electricity. The facility in-cluded offices, coal storage, and laboratory space. Unfortunately, later constructions and additions to the ever-changing site have altered its original pristine appearance. A less famil-iar, but perhaps more interesting, example of a recycled industrial building is the Mouson

soap and perfume factory, an expressionist brick addition of 1921-26 to a nineteenth-century industrial plant. The 1925-26 tower by Robert Wollmann was said to be Frankfurt's first high-rise. The building recently has been cleaned and refurbished as a multi-use cultural center, school, and café.

Selected Source
Risse, *Frühe Moderne in Frankfurt*, pp. 150-58.

Frankfurt's two most famous office buildings are by Berliners: Max Taut and Franz Hoff-mann designed the Deutscher Gewerkschafts-bund (German Federation of Labor Unions) building of 1931, while Hans Poelzig was responsible for the I. G. Farben headquarters (1928-31). At the time of its construction, the Gewerkschaftsbund building was the city's fourth skyscraper, after the Mouson tower, the Grossmarkthalle (see p. 61), and the I. G. Far-ben headquarters. It became the offices of the Deutsche Arbeitsfront (German Labor Service) in the Third Reich and, although an extension was planned then, in a somewhat official style, it was never realized. Postwar additions by Taut (1946-49) are on the river side of the complex. Poelzig's famous I. G. Farben offices, executed in a more restrained modernism than the Gewerkschaftsbund building, is a massive structure situated in Grüneberg park, northwest of the city center. It sits within a landscaped green designed by Max Bromme. Its scale and form remind one of other corporate headquar-ters, notably the General Motors Building in Detroit from 1922 by Albert Kahn. After World War II the building served as General Eisen-hower's headquarters and, at the time of this writing, it is still occupied by the U. S. Army.

Selected Sources
Risse, *Frühe Moderne in Frankfurt*, pp. 125-30 and 132-35; Rainer Stommer, *Hochhaus: Der Beginn in Deutschland* (Marburg, 1990), pp. 158-59; Matthias Schirren (ed.), *Hans Poelzig* (Berlin, 1989) pp. 138-41; Julius Posener, *Hans Poelzig: Reflections on his Life and Work* (New York, 1992), pp. 229-38.

Martin Weber was Frankfurt's most important church architect. A native of the city, Weber worked with renowned ecclesiastical designer Dominikus Böhm (see pp. 77-79) from 1922 to 1925. Two representative examples of churches designed by Weber after his apprenticeship with Böhm are the brick, somewhat expressionist, neo-Gothic St. Boniface of 1926-32, which was won in competition, and the stylized neo-Romanesque Heiligkreuzkirche (Church of the Holy Cross) of 1929, also a winning competition entry. Although heavily damaged in World War II, the latter church was partly restored in 1946, and completely renovated by Harald Greiner in 1951-52. It was originally built to serve the occupants of the newly constructed housing complex at

Bornheimer Hang. Hugo Herkommer, whose entry achieved second place in the St. Boniface competition, submitted a competitive design for the Frauenfriedenskirche (Church of Our Lady of Peace) in 1927. The distinguished jury of Peter Behrens, Ernst May, and Paul Bonatz favored the entry by Böhm, but Herkommer proved more flexible in the design process and was given the commission. Constructed in 1929, the church includes an elaborate complex of buildings around a World War I memorial cloister. The church's triple-arched entrance houses an enormous mosaic by Josef Eberz of Munich. After damage in World War II, the church was rebuilt in the fifties to the same design and has been renovated subsequently.

Selected Sources

Risse, *Frühe Moderne in Frankfurt*, pp. 167-80; Walter Schürmeyer, "Die Kath. Frauenfriedenskirche in Frankfurt a. M. ," *Deutsche Bauzeitung* (July 3, 1929), pp. 457-62.

top left: Martin Weber. St. Boniface Church, Oppenheimer Landstrasse and Heddrichstrasse, Frankfurt am Main, 1926-32. Photograph 1989.

right: Martin Weber. Heiligkreuzkirche, Bornheimer Hang and Kettelerallee, Frankfurt am Main, 1928-29. Photograph 1989.

bottom left: Hugo Herkommer. Frauenfriedenskirche, Franz-Rücker-Allee and Zeppelinallee, Frankfurt am Main, 1927-29. Photograph 1992.

Frankfurt's Hauptfriedhof (main cemetery) contains numerous commemorative monuments and tombstones from the 1920s and 1930s, but two architectural structures stand out as worthy of particular consideration. The first is the city's World War I memorial at the eastern side of the cemetery, near the Giessener Strasse entrance. Designed by Hermann Senf in 1928, it is sited in a field of 1,500 graves for victims of the war. Dead from World War II were later buried nearby. The entrance to this dramatic, open-domed cylindrical space contains inscriptions and memorials to soldiers from both wars. Although Risse likens it to the monumental forms in designs by such eighteenth-century revolutionary architects as Claude-Nicolas Ledoux and Etienne-Louis Boullée, its cylindrical form within a moat recalls a miniaturized fort or even a bastion or gun emplacement from a fortress.

At the northern end of the cemetery, with a separate entrance off Eckenheimer Landstrasse, is the New Jewish Cemetery complex and mourning hall designed by Fritz Nathan in 1928-29. This severe, somber brick building contains mourning chapels as well as support spaces, all off a central courtyard. Risse compares the building's clarity of design and visual strength favorably with the work of Martin Elsaesser. As the area around the War Memorial contains tombs of the fallen from World War II, the space behind this funerary complex has numerous monuments to victims of the Holocaust.

Hermann Senf. War Memorial, Main Cemetery, Frankfurt am Main, 1928. Photograph 1992.

Fritz Nathan. Mourning hall in the New Jewish Cemetery, Frankfurt am Main, 1929. Photograph 1992.

Selected Sources

Risse, *Frühe Moderne in Frankfurt*, pp. 201-3; Karl Schwarz, "Der Israelitische Friedhof in Frankfurt a. M.," *Deutsche Bauzeitung* (May 13, 1931), pp. 229-33; Hermann Senf, "Das Ehrenmal der Stadt Frankfurt a. M.," *Deutsche Bauzeitung* (November 26, 1930), pp. 645-48.

Ernst Balser was the son of a joiner in Neu-Isenburg, near Frankfurt. Balser studied at the Kunstgewerbeschule (arts and crafts school) in Offenbach, also near Frankfurt, under Hugo Eberhard. After service in World War I, Balser returned to his hometown to open an architectural practice. His most famous work of the twenties is the Allgemeine Ortskrankenkasse (AOK; General Health Insurance Fund) building of 1928-30 on Gartenstrasse near Stresemannallee. Although it was damaged only slightly in the war, Balser repaired, expanded, and altered it in 1949-50. It was then incorporated into the adjacent AEG corporate complex of 1949-51 by Adolf H. Assmann and Hans Bartolmes. Balser's large AOK building led to similar modernist expressions in masonry for AOK buildings in Mannheim (1928-30) and Reutlingen (1932). Modernist masonry massing continues in his 1939 design of a naval observatory near Cuxhaven, albeit

with some classicistic details, as well as in the postwar Chemag building of 1952 in Frankfurt. Aside from these large corporate or institutional structures, Balser designed some interesting residential buildings. They range from the distinctively sited and brick-detailed apartments of 1926 at the corner of Frankfurt's Grethenweg and Kranichsteiner Strasse to homes in a hybridized modernist style from the early thirties in the Niederrad district. Two of these, on Schwarzwaldstrasse 138 and 142, date from 1933 and 1934, respectively. They are surfaced with glazed ceramic tiles, similar to model homes shown at the World's Fairs in Chicago (1933) and New York (1939). Unfortunately, the house at number 138, published in the 1953 monograph on Balser, has been so much altered as to make it unrecognizable. That at number 142, however, is more or less in its original condition.

Selected Sources

Risse, *Frühe Moderne in Frankfurt*, pp. 131-32 and 241-42; Werner Hegemann, "Die Ortskrankenkasse in Frankfurt am Main," *Wasmuths Monatshefte für Baukunst und Städtebau* (1931), pp. 49-54; Gustav Lampmann, *Ernst Balser: Ein Baumeister unserer Zeit* (Munich, 1953).

Ernst Balser. Apartment buildings, Grethenweg 22, Frankfurt am Main, 1926. Photograph 1989.

bottom left: Ernst Balser. Bangert House, Neuwiesenstrasse 10, Frankfurt am Main, 1933. Photograph 1992.

bottom right: Ernst Balser. Ceramic tile house, Schwarzwaldstrasse 142, Frankfurt am Main, 1934. Photograph 1992.

Otto Haesler. Volksschule (now Altstädter Schule) and headmaster's house, Sägemühlenstrasse and Kanonerstrasse, Celle, 1928. Photographs 1989.

Otto Haesler's housing projects of the 1920s represent the modernist scene in Celle, as do his 1927-28 school and adjacent headmaster's house. The town is so small that these avant-garde projects, built to the southeast of its old center, are within some six or seven hundred feet of each other. Haesler's work spread to other places in this central area of Germany, such as Kassel, where his Rothenburg housing development of 1929-31 gained him world-wide fame after its inclusion in the 1932 exhibition of modern architecture at New York's Museum of Modern Art and in the book *The International Style* published in conjunction with that exhibition. Also featured in the book is the home for the elderly that Haesler designed with Karl Völker in 1930 in Kassel. The stark, sometimes skeletal modernism of Haesler's work here contrasts with the more restrained, stucco planes of Heinrich Tessenow's Heinrich Schütz School of 1927-30 nearby. Both are a far cry from the almost adjacent classicistic building of the later 1930s, which originally housed the local military administration.

Yet, of Kassel's modernist buildings, perhaps the most surprising is a small service

station of 1930 for the Dapolin company. This tiny, streamlined, red and white gem appeared in *The International Style* alongside the more famous Haesler buildings. Historians who have written on buildings included in that book and in the related exhibition have overlooked the fact that a truncated version of this station still exists *in situ*, its elegant skeletal window replaced by a differently proportioned one with no glass at base level. Despite such alterations, the station serves as a reminder that even the most modest of buildings from this time can have some kind of afterlife, this one having been converted into an art gallery.

Selected Sources

"Altersheim der Marie-von-Boschan-Aschrott-Stiftung in Kassel," *Moderne Bauformen* (March 1932), pp. 133-49; H. De Fries, "Organisation eines Baugedankens," *Die Form* (1926-27), pp. 193-201; Henry Russell Hitchcock and Philip Johnson, *The International Style* (New York, 1932), pp. 104-5 and 152-55; Gerdy Troost, *Das Bauen im neuen Reich* (Bayreuth, 1941), p. 92; Vischer, *Der neue Schulbau*, p. 71. Additional works by Haesler in Celle are illustrated in the journals *Die Form* (June 1932), pp. 173-75, and *Moderne Bauformen* (1928), pp. 364-65.

opposite page:
top: Otto Haesler. Italienischer Garten housing estate, Celle, 1924. Photograph 1989.

bottom left: Otto Haesler. Georgsgarten housing estate, Celle, 1927. Photograph 1989.

bottom right: Otto Haesler. Blumlagerfeld housing estate, Galgenberg and Weisses Feld to Blumlage, Celle, 1931. Photograph 1989.

this page:
top left: Otto Haesler. Rothenburg housing estate, Hersfelder Strasse, Gudensberger Strasse, Fritzlarer Strasse, and Marburger Strasse, Kassel, 1929-31. Photograph 1989.

top right: Otto Haesler and Karl Völker. Marie von Boschan Aschrott home for the elderly, Friedrich-Ebert-Strasse and Tannenkuppenstrasse, Kassel, 1930. Photograph 1989.

center: Hans Borkowsky. Service station, Karlstrasse and Wilhelmshöher Allee, Kassel, 1930 (substantially altered). Photograph 1989.

bottom left: Heinrich Tessenow. Heinrich Schütz School, Freiherr-vom-Stein-Strasse 11, Kassel, 1927-30. Photograph 1989.

bottom right: Kurt Schönfeld and Ernst Wendel. Former local military administration building, Graf-Bernadotte-Platz near Wilhelmshöher Allee and Heerstrasse, Kassel, c.1938. Photograph 1989.

The West: Rhine and Ruhr

Kennie Ann Laney-Lupton

"The Rhine is swift as the Rhone, wide as the Loire, deeply embanked like the Meuse, winding as the Seine, limpid and green as the Somme, historic as the Tiber, royal as the Danube, mysterious as the Nile, spangled with gold like a river of America, covered with fables and phantoms like a river of Asia." Written by Victor Hugo in 1838, this description of one of the most important waterways in the world testifies to the power that the Rhine has held over the European imagination for centuries. It has been valued not only as a major transportation route for commerce and industry, but also as a potent stimulus to composers, painters, writers, philosophers, and architects. Like their predecessors, architects of the 1920s evoked the turrets of the historic castles and the lighthouses on the Rhine (see Fig. 1) or sited their structures to take full advantage of the picturesque views along the river (see Figs. 2, 3).

Beyond the Rhine and its associations with artistic and national romanticism lies the harsh reality of the Ruhrgebiet (Ruhr District), commonly referred to simply as the Ruhr. The key to the industrialization of the Ruhr, an area particularly rich in mineral deposits, was the excavation of coal mines, which began here in the Middle Ages. During the industrial revolution, towns, factories, and workers' housing multiplied rapidly, eventually merging into what today seems one large, undifferentiated mass.

The contrasting geography of the Rhine and the Ruhr, together with their very different socio-economic conditions, provides a framework for comparing the architecture of the two regions. In the essay "Neue Arbeiten von H. H. Lüttgen, Köln," published in *Moderne Bauformen* in 1929, Wilhelm Kreis discussed the architecture of the Rhine and the Ruhr as a reflection of the spirit of the areas' surrounding countryside and of their inhabitants. He characterized the Rhinelanders as fun-loving and as imbued with a strong sense of freedom. This, Kreis claimed, had given rise to architecture that was both cozy and adventurous. The inhabitants of the industrial Ruhr, however, he described as serious, preoccupied with work and the struggle for existence — a mentality that, he felt, inhibited the free, shaping hand of design to produce harsh architecture. Whatever the rights and wrongs of Kreis's interpretation, differences can indeed be recognized between the architecture of the two regions.

The Rhine and the Ruhr had a common history during the period between the two world wars. When Germany embarked on World War I in 1914 it was one of the most highly industrialized countries in Europe. Industry, centered in the Ruhr, was modern and highly concentrated, unequaled in Europe in the production of steel, chemicals, drugs, electrical machinery, and gasoline engines. After Imperial Germany's defeat in 1918, the Treaty of Versailles, signed the following year, left Germany in a severely weakened state. Alsace-Lorraine was ceded to France, and parts of Silesia and Prussia to Poland; a fifty-kilometer (thirty-one-mile) strip of land on the right bank of the Rhine was declared a demilitarized zone; and the Saarland, the region bordering France some 130 miles south of the Ruhrgebiet, was to be controlled by the League of Nations, its coal mines assigned to France as compensation for damage done to that country's mining industry during the war. Reparations to be paid to the victors included sixty percent of the Ruhr's coal production and twenty-five percent of pharmaceuticals produced in Germany, in addition to railway stock, construction material, and shipping. The left bank of the Rhine was to be occupied by Allied troops (Belgian soldiers had begun to arrive as early as November 1918). In March 1921, due to an alleged default in payment of reparations, French troops moved into the right bank of the Rhine, occupying Düsseldorf, Duisburg, Mülheim, and Oberhausen.

The economic crisis of 1923, combined with inflation, made it all but impossible for the Germans to pay war reparations. The French refused concessions and joined the Belgian army in marching into the Ruhr to enforce industrial deliveries. Workers went on strike, and organized resistance led to problems throughout the country. Since eighty-five percent of German coal came from the Ruhr, there was a shortage of vital raw materials, causing widespread disruption in production and, eventually, increased unemployment. Between 1924 and 1929, Gustav Stresemann, the German foreign minister, negotiated a reduction in war reparations and the withdrawal of French forces from the Rhineland. He also attempted to put the Ruhr back on its feet by streamlining industrial production. His efforts, together with the resistance of the population, led to the complete withdrawal of Allied troops in 1930. By the time the Nazis came to power in 1933 only the Saarland remained under Allied control. It was returned to Germany by plebiscite in January 1935.

During the interwar years, the cities of Düsseldorf and Cologne enjoyed relative prosperity, primarily owing to the leadership of two men, Robert Lehr in Düsseldorf and Konrad Adenauer in Cologne. Lehr became mayor of Düsseldorf in 1924. For a decade progress had come to a standstill due to World War I, but under Lehr the city experienced a period of growth despite the general economic gloom.

Early in his term of office Lehr supervised a national health care exhibition titled "Gesolei" — a contraction of *GEsundheitspflege* (health care), *SOziale Fürsorge* (social welfare), and *LEIbesübungen* (physical exercise). Housed in the Ehrenhof (Court of Honor), it was built to plans by Wilhelm Kreis (see p. 93). One of the region's prominent architects, Kreis was born in Eltville near Wiesbaden in 1873 and, with varying degrees of success and creativity, survived three consecutive political regimes. After studying in Munich and Berlin, he began his career with a brief association with the architects Paul Wallot and Hugo Licht. Later he taught in Düsseldorf. In Imperial Germany, before the outbreak of World War I, he won commissions for numerous monuments to Bismarck, for commercial buildings, and for the Museum für Vorgeschichte (Museum of Prehistory) in Halle. His massive structures of rough-cut masonry were initially reminiscent of the work of the highly successful architect Bruno Schmitz, but he later moved away from the latter's historicist style toward simple geometric forms. Kreis developed this approach further during the Weimar Republic, when his designs, such as that for the Deutsches Hygiene-Museum in Dresden (see p. 242), were influenced by the austere aesthetic of the International Style. He received a full professorship at the Dresden Technische Hochschule (polytechnic) in 1926 and, the following year, became president of the Bund Deutscher Architekten (Union of German Architects). Kreis held official posts in the Third Reich, too, serving as president of the Reichskammer der bildenden Künste (Reich Chamber of Visual Arts) under Joseph Goebbels. His work in the thirties and forties reflected the Nazis' favored style of "stripped classicism," as demonstrated by his plan for the Soldatenhalle in Berlin and by the various large-scale monuments to the German war dead that he designed for the occupied territories.

In 1929 communal restructuring resulted in suburban communities being fused with Düsseldorf, increasing the city's area by a third and the number of its inhabitants by 36,000 to 473,000. Lehr used the brief boom before the world economic crisis to strengthen Düsseldorf's position. Yet during the Depression the number of unemployed increased from 15,700 in 1927 to a staggering 64,000 in 1932, when the city had to spend 35.5 million marks in unemployment benefits. When Hitler came to power in 1933, the number of those sympathetic to his aims was considerable in Düsseldorf. Following the national elections in March 1933, the local Nazis, led by Gauleiter Friedrich Karl Florian, forced Lehr out of office.

Fig. 1   Heinrich Jungst. Youth hostel, Rüdesheim, c.1931. Photograph 1989.

Fig. 2   Ernst Huhn, Hotel, Niederbreisig, c.1938. Photograph 1989.

Fig. 3   Theodor Merrill, St. Kanisius school, Remagen, c.1931. Photograph 1990.

In 1937 Düsseldorf hosted the exhibition "Schaffendes Volk" (A People at Work). Devoted to the achievements of industry, craftsmanship, social organizations, and art, it contained both a model colony with communal buildings and a residential town composed of sixty one-family houses designed by individual architects. The center of the exhibition was occupied by a building containing studios and by ten one-story houses for artists, designed by Hans Junghanns of Düsseldorf and constructed of whitewashed brick. The exhibition was surrounded by public gardens that had been landscaped as part of the development. The idea behind the exhibition was that builders

Fig. 4   Emil Fahrenkamp. Main restaurant, "Schaffendes Volk" exhibition, Düsseldorf, 1937 (destroyed). From *Monatshefte für Baukunst und Städtebau* (1937).

Fig. 5   Emil Fahrenkamp. Refreshment kiosk ("Kaffeemonument"), "Schaffendes Volk" exhibition, Düsseldorf, 1937 (destroyed). From *Monatshefte für Baukunst und Städtebau* (1937).

and planners should acquire information that would inform their own designs. The exhibition's artistic director was architect Peter Grund. He had served as director of the Düsseldorf Kunstakademie in 1933 and, that year, had produced one of six prizewinning entries for the Reichsbank building in Berlin (which was executed by another architect; see p. 29). After World War II, although he had been a member of the Nazi party, Grund continued to design acclaimed buildings in a variety of styles, including stripped classicism in the 1947 Parkhotel Aachener Hof in Darmstadt and uncompromising modernism in the Kaufhof department store of 1950 in Frankfurt am Main.

Grund himself was responsible for the entrance structures of the 1937 exhibition, while the monumental plaza and the modernist exhibition hall and refreshment kiosk (Figs. 4, 5) were the work of Emil Fahrenkamp, a very successful architect throughout the interwar period. He studied at the Technische Hochschule in Aachen and became assistant to Wilhelm Kreis at the Kunstgewerbeschule (arts and crafts school) in Düsseldorf, later succeeding Kreis as professor. He also taught at the Kunstakademie in Düsseldorf. During the Weimar Republic he received numerous commissions for modernist industrial, hotel, and office buildings in the Rhineland. In the Third Reich he continued to practice, but gave up teaching (to which he was to return after World War II). The buildings he designed for the Düsseldorf exhibition demonstrate the slightly more conservative modern style that he cultivated in the mid- to late thirties. In an article published in *Moderne Bauformen* in July 1937 Fahrenkamp wrote that he considered the exhibition to be a complete "exhibition town," consisting of detached buildings arranged in groups. He noted that, although the design of its buildings took into account

Fig. 6   Emil Fahrenkamp. Palast-Hotel Breidenbacher Hof, intersection of Flinger Strasse and Heinrich-Heine-Allee, Düsseldorf, 1927-28, From Hoff, *Emil Fahrenkamp* (1928).

Fig. 7   Adolf Abel. Mülheimer Rheinbrücke, Cologne, c.1930. From *Wasmuths Monatshefte für Baukunst und Städtebau* (1930).

Fig. 8   Adolf Abel. Exposition buildings, Cologne, 1926-28. From *Moderne Bauformen* (1929).

the surrounding country, there had been no reason to imitate rural roofs and housefronts.

None of the buildings from the "Schaffendes Volk" exhibition survived the war. On New Year's Eve, 1942, Düsseldorf suffered an intensive bombing attack by the British. By the break of day 3,900 buildings had been reduced to rubble and 1,200 people killed. Among the architectural casualties was Fahrenkamp's Breidenbacher Hof hotel of 1927-28 (Fig. 6). Totally destroyed, it was rebuilt in 1949-50, again to designs by Fahrenkamp. This second version reflected the influence of the classicism favored during and immediately after the Third Reich: it is far heavier than the 1927-28 building, monumen-

tal and rather overpowering in its massive solidity.

Cologne, occupied by the British until 1926, also enjoyed an extraordinary recovery from World War I, flourishing under the expert leadership of Konrad Adenauer, mayor of the city from 1917 to 1933. Adenauer not only redirected urban planning in Cologne, using the parks of Düsseldorf as a model for the inner and outer "green belts" that were designed, in part, by the famous Hamburg architect and planner Fritz Schumacher, but he also encouraged growth by bringing industry to the city — at this time, with 674,000 inhabitants, the fifth largest in Germany. In 1922 Adenauer made provisions for an industrial-

ized settlement to be built north of Cologne and also convinced the American Ford Motor Company to open a factory in the city's Niehl area. Under Adenauer's direction, Cologne experienced a boom in innovative architecture, with buildings being designed by Dominikus Böhm, Manfred Faber, Caspar Maria Grod, Jacob Koerfer, Wilhelm Kreis, Hans Heinz Lüttgen, and Wilhelm Riphahn. In addition, Adenauer was largely responsible for the construction of the Cologne-Bonn autobahn in 1932 and for the erection of several bridges across the Rhine (see Fig. 7).

In 1924 Adenauer succeeded in establishing Cologne as a host of important trade fairs in the Rheinpark, where the Werkbund exhibition

Fig. 9   Wilhelm Riphahn and Caspar Maria Grod. *Kölnische Zeitung* pavilion, "Pressa" exhibition, Cologne, 1928 (demolished). From *Wasmuths Monatshefte für Baukunst und Städtebau* (1929).

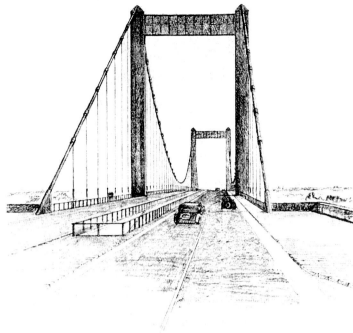

Fig.10 Wilhelm Riphahn. Die Bastei, Cologne, 1924. From *Gaststätten*, ed. Hubert Hoffmann (Stuttgart, 1939).

Fig.11 Paul Bonatz. Drawing for the Rodenkirchen autobahn bridge, Cologne, 1938-41. From Friedrich Tamms, *Paul Bonatz* (Stuttgart, 1937).

had been held a decade before. The following year, he organized a large exhibition celebrating the historical, political, and artistic development of the Rhineland over the past thousand years. The first international exhibition, "Pressa," devoted to journalism and newscasting, was held in 1928. The landscaping of the exhibition area, and the design of permanent exhibition buildings, took place under the aegis of architect Adolf Abel (see Fig. 8). One of the most interesting structures was the pavilion of the newspaper *Kölnische Zeitung* by Wilhelm Riphahn and Caspar Maria Grod of Cologne (see Fig. 9). A variation of an expressionist form, its shape, like that of a ship's bow, acknowledged the proximity of the Rhine. Riphahn had previous experience of building on the Rhine: in 1924 he had designed Die Bastei (Fig.10), a restaurant erected on the remains of an old Prussian artillery stand on the bank of the Rhine. The star-shaped structure, almost completely destroyed in World War II, was rebuilt in 1958.

With the advent of the Nazis in 1933, Adenauer was asked to step down as mayor. Cologne became a city of repression and persecution; many of its citizens involved in opposing the regime were murdered. Nonetheless, some modernist architects, such as Paul Bonatz, continued to build there (see Fig.11).

Destruction in Cologne during World War II was vast. Air attacks began with the large RAF raid of May 10, 1942, which was followed on May 30 by the launching of Operation Millennium. In this, the first "thousand bomber raid," the British dropped 1,455 tons of bombs on Cologne in ninety minutes.

Although portions of the Rhineland and the Ruhrgebiet were occupied by Belgium, Britain, and France during the twenties, contemporary architecture in these areas betrays little influence from those countries. While the occupying forces officially played only a policing role, the unspoken agenda of the occupation was to separate Rhine and Ruhr from the rest of Germany. The German response to this was one of national outrage, and this indignation found expression in the goverment's declared policy of "passive resistance," which was intended to ensure the failure of the "productive guarantees" that the occupation sought to enforce. Naturally, German architects practicing in the region at the time were determined not to acknowledge visually the presence of the occupying forces. Thus, while the architecture of the Rhine and Ruhr during the interwar years was eclectic in its mixture of *Rheinromantik*, international modernism, and self-celebrating indigenous styles, it remained very much a German architecture.

Sources in Brief

Sources consulted for overviews of the Ruhr and the Rhine in the context of economic and political developments in Germany through the post-World War II period include: Gordon Martel (ed.), *Modern Germany Reconsidered, 1870-1945* (London, 1992); Peter J. Katzenstein (ed.), *Industry and Politics in West Germany* (Ithaca, 1989); Detlev J. K. Peukert, *The Weimar Republic* (New York, 1989); Martin Gilbert, *The Second World War* (New York, 1989); George L. Mosse, *The Nationalization of the Masses* (New York, 1975); Jeffrey Herf, *Reactionary Modernism* (Cambridge, 1984); and George L. Mosse, *Nazi Culture* (New York, 1966). For Wilhelm Kreis, see Hans F. Mayer and Gerhard Rehder, *Wilhelm Kreis, Architekt in dieser Zeit: Leben und Werk* (Essen, 1953); Hans Stephan, *Wilhelm Kreis* (Oldenburg, 1944); Carl Meissner, *Wilhelm Kreis* (Essen, 1925); and Wilhelm Kreis, "Neue Arbeiten von

H. H. Lüttgen, Köln," *Moderne Bauformen* (1929). For Emil Fahrenkamp, see "Schaffendes Volk: Die Düsseldorfer Ausstellung," *Monatshefte für Baukunst und Städtebau* (1937), pp. 205-16, and August Hoff, *Emil Fahrenkamp: Ein Ausschnitt seines Schaffens aus den Jahren 1924-1927* (Stuttgart, 1928). Other sources used: Herbert Hoffmann, "Schaffendes Volk: Reichsausstellung Düsseldorf 1937," *Moderne Bauformen* (1937), pp. 337-70; Willehad Paul Eckert, *Kölner Stadtführer* (Cologne, 1990); Wolfgang Pehnt, *Expressionist Architecture* (London, 1973); "Wohnhaus Professor Hussmann" and "Zwei Wohnhäuser von Hans Schumacher," *Moderne Bauformen* (1932), pp. 40-42 and 555-58; "Hotel und Gasträume: Arbeiten von Ernst Huhn," *Moderne Bauformen* (1938), pp. 613-21; "Gymnasium und Internat St. Kanisius in Remagen," *Der Baumeister* (1931), pp. 95-98; Julius Vischer, *Der neue Schulbau im In- und Ausland: Grundlagen, Technik, Gestaltung* (Stuttgart, 1931); "Jugendherberge Rüdesheim," *Deutsche Bauzeitung* (April 22, 1931), pp. 205-8; "Die neue Köln-Mülheim-Brücke," *Wasmuths Monatshefte für Baukunst und Städtebau* (1930), p. 567; Hartmut Frank, "The Metropolis as a Comprehensive Work of Art: Fritz Schumacher's Plan for Cologne, Document of a Forgotten Modernity," in *The 1920s: Age of the Metropolis*, ed. Jean Clair, exhibition catalogue (Montreal, 1991), pp. 321-35; Hartwig Beseler and Niels Gutschow, *Kriegsschicksale Deutscher Architektur* (Neumünster, 1988); *Neue Deutsche Biographie*, vol. 12 (Berlin, 1980), pp. 381-82; Rudolf Pérard and Paul Girkon, *Der Architekt Peter Grund* (Darmstadt, 1952); Werner Durth, *Deutsche Architekten: Biographische Verflechtungen 1900-1970* (Braunschweig and Wiesbaden, 1987), p. 360; Klemens Klemmer, *Jacob Koerfer (1895-1930): Ein Architekt zwischen Tradition und Moderne*, Beiträge zur Kunstwissenschaft 13 (Munich, 1987); Alfred Ziffer, *Bruno Paul* (Munich, 1992), p. 312; and Wilhelm Busch, *Bauten der 20er Jahre an Rhein und Ruhr* (Cologne, 1993).

top left: Dominikus Böhm. Christkönigskirche, Bischofsheim, near Rüsselsheim, 1926. From Hoff et al., *Dominikus Böhm* (1962).

center left: Dominikus Böhm and Rudolf Schwarz. Prizewinning entry to the competition for the Frauenfriedenskirche, Frankfurt am Main, 1927. From Habbel (ed.), *Dominikus Böhm* (1943).

right: Dominikus Böhm. Immakulatakapelle, "Pressa" exhibition, Cologne, 1928 (destroyed). From Habbel (ed.), *Dominikus Böhm* (1943).

Dominikus Böhm. St. Franziskus, Franziskusstrasse, Rheydt-Geneicken, 1930. Photograph 1990. From Hoff et al., *Dominikus Böhm* (1962).

Dominikus Böhm. St. Kamillus asthma hospital and monastery church, Kamillianerstrasse, Mönchengladbach, 1928. Photograph 1990.

Churches built in the Rhine and Ruhr areas between the world wars laid the foundation for a tradition of experimentation in ecclesiastical architecture that would continue in Germany long after World War II. While hundreds of projects were designed by expressionist architects in the teens and early twenties, the majority of buildings actually constructed in what might be termed a conservative expressionist style were churches. These structures were designed with an essentially pragmatic attitude to traditional church architecture. They did, however, embody a new concept of the symbolism and function of churches. The utopian notions espoused by the visionary architects of the *Gläserne Kette* (Glass Chain) group and of the Bauhaus were catalysts in the evolution of a notion of the church as a cathedral of socialism. In his book *Vom neuen Kirchenbau* (On the New Church Architecture), published in 1919, Otto Bartning (see p. 81) advocated a new approach to church building. The book describes his vision of the church as a "holy melting pot" of the community of the future.

Dominikus Böhm was the leading pioneer of modern Roman Catholic church architecture in Germany. He was born in the Swabian town of Jettingen. His father was an architect and his mother a creative exponent of traditional rural handicrafts. Böhm studied under Theodor Fischer at the Technische Hochschule (polytechnic) in Stuttgart, and Fischer's teaching, together with his own family background, provided him with a wide-ranging appreciation of building materials and methods. Böhm's churches combined expressionist forms with a highly personal interpretation of the symbolic and liturgical meanings of the church. Publications, and his participation in competitions abroad, ensured that Böhm's architecture became internationally influential.

Böhm taught at the Kunstgewerbeschule (arts and crafts school) in Offenbach am Main from 1914 to 1926. During this time he was influenced by the Liturgical Movement, which led him to regard churches as the visible expression of the mystery of Christian worship. His designs retained the traditional path of access for the congregation to the altar, which he saw as a symbolic path to salvation. Characteristic of Böhm's churches are a continuous open plan, stressing the unity of the interior as a whole; elevated sanctuaries; processional passages formed by projecting wall segments pierced by arches; and series of side chapels between the segments of wall. The primary purpose of these open plan churches was to allow the congregation to participate more actively in the Mass in accordance with the tenets of the Liturgical Movement. Architecturally, this meant bringing priest and congregation physically closer together around the focal point of the altar. It is not unusual to find Böhm emphasizing the altar dramatically by placing it at the point where natural light from several sources of converges. Another frequent feature of his designs is stacked tiers of brick arches that curtain the ambulatory behind the altar and provide an exterior motif.

Böhm's brick and concrete Christkönigskirche (Church of Christ the King) of 1926 in Bischofsheim, near Rüsselsheim in Hesse, combines expressionist forms with "brutalist" surfaces. The decorative surfaces of the entrance facade and the adjoining bell tower, consisting of alternating bands of brick and concrete, scarcely reflects the drama of the interior. The portal, an immense pointed arch, leads to a dark, unadorned space spanned by a continuous parabolic tunnel vault that merges nave and sanctuary. The interior wall surface of exposed reinforced concrete is more sculptural than architectural. A series of tall, narrow windows allows soft light to filter into the space, emphasizing its dramatic quality. The combination of dramatic massing and mystical lighting recalls Gothic cathedrals.

In 1927 Böhm collaborated with Rudolf Schwarz (see pp. 82, 94) on what became the

Dominikus Böhm. Christkönigskirche, Küppersteg, Leverkusen, 1927-28. Photograph 1991.

Dominikus Böhm. Catholic Seminary, Limburg an der Lahn, 1929-31. Photograph 1992.

above: Dominikus Böhm. St. Engelbert, Riehler Gürtel 12, Cologne-Riehl, 1930. Photograph 1990.

prizewinning entry to the competition for the Frauenfriedenskirche in Frankfurt (see p. 66). This radical design, which was never built, featured a rectangular room with the congregation oriented in a double column toward the sanctuary, which was essentially undifferentiated from the nave. This break with traditional church design signaled a turning point in Böhm's career. His designs now became steadily more simple, stressing pure geometric shapes and unified spaces.

In 1926 Böhm had been invited by Konrad Adenauer, mayor of Cologne, to become director of church art at the Cologne Werkschule. Böhm was extremely active in Cologne and the surrounding areas. He served as supervisor of Cologne's "Pressa" exhibition of 1928 (see pp. 74-75), for which he designed

the cylindrical Immakulatakapelle (Chapel of the Immaculate Conception). The structure is no longer standing.

In 1930 Böhm designed two rather unusual churches, St. Engelbert in the Riehl district of Cologne and St. Franziskus in Rheydt-Geneicken. In the circular plan of St. Engelbert, Böhm drew the congregation together under a ring of eight parabolic vaults that form a most ingenious roof composition on the exterior of the church. Small circular windows near the apex of each elevation let in a minimal amount of light, emphasizing the interior's sense of mystery.

The design for St. Franziskus is simple in comparison with St. Engelbert. One end of the rectangular box forming the church proper is linked at right angles to a bell tower. The space thus created is occupied by a small courtyard along the street side of the site. The brick structure, pierced by a large rose window at one end, is unadorned.

In the Third Reich restrictions on modernist church building were increased and Böhm resorted in his designs to simplifying the forms of churches built during the Ottonian and Romanesque periods. His village church of 1935-36 at Ringenberg is considered one of his finest buildings of this almost historicist period. After World War II, Böhm was active in restoring churches and in designing new ones. He shared his practice in Cologne with his son Gottfried until his death in 1955.

Selected Sources

Josef Habbel (ed.), *Dominikus Böhm: Ein deutscher Baumeister* (Regensburg, 1943); August Hoff, Herbert Muck, and Raimund Thoma, *Dominikus Böhm* (Munich, 1962); Robert Maguire and Keith Murray, *Modern Churches of the World* (New York, 1965); Rudolf Schwarz, "Dominikus Böhm und sein Werk," *Moderne Bauformen* (1927), pp. 226-40; Rudolf Schwarz, "Dominikus Böhm: Kirchbauten aus vier Jahrzehnten", *Baukunst und Werkform* 8 (1955), pp. 72-83; Gesine Stalling, *Studien zu Dominikus Böhm* (Bern, 1974); "Vier Kirchen von Dominikus Böhm," *Moderne Bauformen* (1933), pp. 455-74; "Kleine Kirchen von Dominikus Böhm in Köln a. Rh.," *Moderne Bauformen* (1936), pp. 141-53.

Otto Bartning. Model of the Sternkirche, 1921-22. From Pollak, *Der Baumeister Otto Bartning* (1926).

Otto Bartning. Stahlkirche, "Pressa" exhibition, Cologne, 1928 (demolished). From Mayer, *Der Baumeister Otto Bartning* (1951).

above: Otto Bartning. Auferstehungskirche, Manteuffelstrasse, Essen-Altstadt, 1929-30 (damaged 1945, rebuilt 1950). From Mayer, *Der Baumeister Otto Bartning* (1951).

Otto Bartning, educated at the Technische Hochschule (polytechnic) in Berlin-Charlottenburg and at that in Karlsruhe, built or reconstructed over fifty-five Protestant churches between 1906 and the end of World War II. In 1925, when the Bauhaus moved to Dessau, Bartning was appointed director of the successor school in Weimar, the Bauhochschule, a post he held from 1926 to 1930.

The Sternkirche (Star Church), a project that Bartning designed in 1921-22, demonstrates his intense interest in expressionist church architecture. The structure's multifaceted exterior results from a complex parabolic structure of interlocking columns. The floor plan is a polygon with pulpit and altar in the center. In his book *Expressionist Architecture* Wolfgang Pehnt discusses this project as belonging among the most important architectural achievements of its period and as one of the most significant church designs of this century.

Bartning realized his Sternkirche project in modified form in the Stahlkirche (Steel Church) at the "Pressa" exhibition in Cologne in 1928 and in the Auferstehungskirche (Church of the Resurrection) of 1929-30 in Essen. The former,

a steel frame construction with stained-glass walls, is no longer extant, whereas the Auferstehungskirche, though damaged in World War II, was rebuilt in 1950. It shows Bartning's dramatic use of a central plan, the liturgical center being placed at the physical center of the building.

After World War II Bartning designed numerous temporary wooden churches throughout Germany, often within the ruins of their predecessors. The form of these churches owed much to the cultivation of vernacular traditions typical of the period and to postwar shortages.

Selected Sources

Otto Bartning, *Vom neuen Kirchbau* (Berlin, 1919); Otto Bartning, *Erdball* (Leipzig, 1947); Otto Bartning, *Mensch und Raum* (Darmstadt, 1952); Otto Bartning, *Kirchen,* Handbuch für den Kirchenbau 2 (Munich, 1959); Jürgen Bredow and Helmut Lerch, *Otto Bartning: Materialien zum Werk des Architekten* (Darmstadt, 1983); Hans Mayer, *Der Baumeister Otto Bartning und die Wiederentdeckung des Raumes* (Heidelberg, 1951; 2nd ed., 1958); Ernst Pollak, *Der Baumeister Otto Bartning: Unser Lebensgefühl gestaltet in seinem Werk* (Berlin, 1926); Alfred Siemon (ed.), *Otto Bartning* (Bramsche bei Osnabrück, 1958).

Rudolf Schwarz and Hans Schwippert. Fronleichnamskirche, Leipziger Strasse 19, Aachen, 1928-31. From *Der Baumeister* (1932).

Rudolf Schwarz and Johannes Krahn. St. Albert Chapel, Leversbach (Eifel), 1932-33. From *Der Baumeister* (1933).

The Fronleichnamskirche (Corpus Christi Church) of 1928-31 in Aachen included elements from one of the designs that Schwarz had produced with Böhm for the Frauenfriedenskirche competition in Frankfurt. The Aachen design, a collaboration with architect Hans Schwippert, stressed industrial building techniques. International Style influence is apparent on its exterior.

In 1932-33 Schwarz, together with his pupil Johannes Krahn, designed the St. Albert Chapel at Leversbach in the Eifel region, some sixty miles south of Cologne. Although it, too, is a rectangular, boxlike structure, it is far more traditional than the Aachen church in its use of local stone.

Although Rudolf Schwarz was influential in the development of modern church architecture in Germany in the twenties and thirties, he did not achieve real fame until after World War II, when he restored or rebuilt many of Germany's damaged or destroyed churches. Schwarz was educated at the Berlin Akademie der Künste (Academy of Arts), where he studied under Hans Poelzig. He later taught for two years at the Kunstgewerbeschule (arts and crafts school) in Offenbach am Main alongside Dominikus Böhm.

Schwarz became director of the Kunstgewerbeschule in Aachen in 1927, and remained in this position until the school was closed in 1934 by the Nazis. Like his contemporary Böhm, Schwarz was a pioneer of the one-room, open plan church interior. During the thirties, his practical activities were limited by government restrictions on church building, but in 1938 he published the most influential of his many publications, *Vom Bau der Kirche* (*The Church Incarnate*). In this book he described six archetypal plans for church design, which he used to illustrate the mystical symbolism of various relationships between church architecture and the people it served. During World War II, Schwarz was engaged in regional planning in the Saarland. After the war, he was a city planner in Cologne until 1952, when he left to teach at the Kunstakademie in Düsseldorf. He remained there until his death in 1961.

Selected Sources

Peter Hammond (ed.), *Towards a Church Architecture* (London, 1962); Maria Schwarz and Ulrich Conrads, *Rudolf Schwarz: Wegweisung der Technik und andere Schriften zum neuen Bauen 1921-1961* (Wiesbaden, 1979); Rudolf Schwarz, *Kirchenbau* (Heidelberg, 1960); G. E. Kidder, *The New Churches of Europe* (New York, 1964); Rudolf Bernhard, "In Memoriam Rudolf Schwarz," *Das Münster* 25 (1972), pp. 22-26; Frédéric D. Debuyst, "Vers une réévaluation des 'Classiques,'" *L'Architecture d'Aujourd'hui* 168 (July-August 1973), pp. 48-50; "Die Fronleichnamskirche in Aachen," *Der Baumeister* (1932), pp. 35-40; "Kleine Steinkirche in Leversbach (Eifel)," *Der Baumeister* (1933), pp. 325-26; Arnold Whittick, *European Architecture in the Twentieth Century* (New York, 1974).

Theodor Merrill. Melanchthonkirche, Zollstock Siedlung, Breniger Strasse 18, Cologne, 1929-30. Photograph 1990.

Karl Wach and Heinrich Rosskotten. Evangelisches Gemeindehaus, intersection of Pfalzstrasse and Collenbachstrasse, Düsseldorf, 1930-31. Photograph 1990.

In the new residential areas erected at this time on the outskirts of cities there was a widespread move to use the church building not only as a place of worship, but also as a social center. The Melanchthonkirche of 1929-30, designed by Theodor Merrill for the Zollstock Siedlung in Cologne, is an example of this. The building is extant, although, damaged during the war, it has undergone restoration with some changes to the original design.

The 1930-31 Evangelisches Gemeindehaus (Protestant parish hall) in Düsseldorf, by Karl Wach and Heinrich Rosskotten, shows the Church expanding its role as social focus by allocating an entire structure, physically separated from the church itself, to take on the functions associated with the "Volkshaus," the community center. This concept was closely allied with the aims of the socialist-oriented expressionist architects. The Gemeindehaus still exists, though it has been altered.

Additional churches of note built in the Rhine and Ruhr areas during the interwar period are the Matthäikirche in Düsseldorf and the St.-Nicolai-Kirche in Dortmund. The Matthäikirche, designed by Wach and Rosskotten, dates from 1930. Like other works by these architects, it is in a conservative modernist mode. Its design is akin to that of Rosskotten's own house in Düsseldorf from the early thirties. The St.-Nicolai-Kirche was designed by Pinno and Grund of Darmstadt (see p. 84). The church dates from 1929-30 and was con-

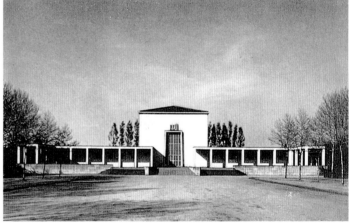

structed of reinforced concrete and glass on a plan in the shape of an angle which converges on the altar.

Other, less well known ecclesiastical structures were built in the Rhine and Ruhr areas by, among others, Bernhard Rotterdam and Josef Op Gen Oorth. One, the crematorium in Cologne's Westfriedhof (western cemetery), designed by architect Hans Heinz Lüttgen in the mid- to late 1930s, would seem to have been influenced both by the classicism prevalent in Scandinavia during the twenties and by the restrained classicism that was popular in Germany in the thirties. In its clarity and tranquillity, the structure, which still stands, is typical of Lüttgen's style.

Selected Sources

For Merrill, see *Der Baumeister* (1931), pp. 101-3. For Wach and Rosskotten, see "Bauten der Architekten BDA Prof. Karl Wach und Reg. Baurat Rosskotten, Düsseldorf," *Deutsche Bauzeitung* (August 5, 1931), pp. 371-84 (esp. pp. 380-3); "Ein Evangelisches Gemeindehaus in Düsseldorf," *Moderne Bauformen* (1930), pp. 513-15; "Baurat Rosskottens eigenes Wohnhaus in Düsseldorf," *Moderne Bauformen* (1935), pp. 193-96; and "Neue Evangelische Matthäikirche Düsseldorf," *Der Baumeister* (1932), pp. 189-93. For Pinno and Grund, see "Die neue Nicolai-Kirche in Dortmund," *Der Baumeister* (1931), pp. 28-31, and Rudolf Pérard and Paul Girkon, *Der Architekt Peter Grund* (Darmstadt, 1952). For Rotterdam, see Johannes Schumacher, *Bernhard Rotterdam* (Berlin, 1931). For Op Gen Oorth, see "Kirche zu Goch am Niederrhein," *Moderne Bauformen* (1935), pp. 453-63. For Lüttgen, see "Krematorium der Stadt Köln," *Moderne Bauformen* (1940), pp.123-25.

left: Karl Wach and Heinrich Rosskotten. Matthäikirche, Lindemannstrasse between Peter-Janssen-Strasse and Schumannstrasse, Düsseldorf, 1930. Photograph 1991.

top right: Pinno and Grund. St.-Nicolai-Kirche, Lindemannstrasse 72, Dortmund, 1929-30. From *Der Baumeister* (1931).

Hans Heinz Lüttgen. Crematorium, Westfriedhof, Venloer Strasse, Militärringstrasse, and Westendstrasse, Cologne-Mengenich, c.1935-39. From *Moderne Bauformen* (1940).

Fritz Nathan. Office and commercial building, Mannheim, c. 1929-30 (demolished). From *Deutsche Bauzeitung* (September 17, 1930).

Becker and Kutzner. Mannheimer Hof hotel, Augusta-Anlage 4, Mannheim, c.1928-29 (altered). From *Moderne Bauformen* (1929).

The city of Mannheim, situated at the confluence of the Rhine and Neckar rivers, barely rates a mention in accounts of twentieth-century architecture in Germany. Publications from the twenties show, however, that the city had several buildings of interest to architectural historians. Two of them still exist — and in a less altered state than the Mannheimer Hof hotel — even though they are located in the city's industrial area, north of the Neckar River. One is the almost Art Deco Capitol-theater from the late twenties by Paul Darius. Its exterior is essentially preserved as built, though the interior has been changed. The second site is the Erlenhof, a housing complex of 1926-27 near the industrial harbor. Designed

Paul Darius. Capitoltheater, Waldhofstrasse north of Lutherstrasse, Mannheim-Neckarstadt, c.1928. From *Moderne Bauformen* (1929).

Ferdinand Mündel. Entrance to the Erlenhof estate, Waldhofstrasse and Muhlaugrün, Mannheim-Industriehafen, 1926-27. From *Wasmuths Monatshefte für Baukunst und Städtebau* (1928).

in a restrained modernist mode by Ferdinand Mündel, the buildings bear classical cornices, and the elaborate fountain can still be seen near the entrance. The distinctive iron and masonry gates nearby, however, have been removed.

Selected Sources

"Zwei Warenhausbauten: Architekt BDA Reg.-Baumeister Fritz Nathan, Frankfurt a. M.," *Deutsche Bauzeitung* (September 17, 1930), pp. 529-32; "Architektur und Planung des Palasthotels Mannheimer Hof," *Moderne Bauformen* (1929), pp. 355-88; *Ein neuzeitlicher Grossbau: Palasthotel Mannheimer Hof* (Stuttgart, 1930); "Das Kapitoltheater in Mannheim," *Moderne Bauformen* (1929), pp. 133-36; "Siedlung Erlenhof in Mannheim," *Wasmuths Monatshefte für Baukunst und Städtebau* (1928), pp. 270-71.

Wilhelm Kreis. Wilhelm-Marx-Haus, Heinrich-Heine-Allee 53, Düsseldorf, 1921-24. Photograph 1991.

Paul Bonatz. Stumm building, Breite Strasse 69, Düsseldorf, 1922-24 (partly rebuilt). Photograph 1991.

Tower blocks built in the Rhine and Ruhr regions in the twenties and thirties demonstrate both the differences in design to be found at this time and a general inclination to stress the horizontal over the vertical. Some are internationally renowned; others, such as the Wilhelm-Marx-Haus by Wilhelm Kreis, the Stumm building by Paul Bonatz (both in Düsseldorf), and Jacob Koerfer's Hansa-Hochhaus in Cologne, are of more regional importance. At approximately 213 feet, the last of these was,

however, the tallest highrise in Europe when erected in 1925.

Only one third of the administrative building of the Vereinigte Stahlwerk A. G. (United Steelworks Corp.) in Düsseldorf, designed by local architects Ernst Petersen and Walter Köngeter, had been completed at the time of its publication in *Moderne Bauformen* in 1939. The building has received scant attention since. Representative of the architecture of the thirties, it contrasts with the tower block buildings just mentioned. Contemporaries praised the smooth, unadorned planes of its facade on Breite Strasse, a busy shopping street. The steel skeleton of the structure was covered on the exterior with polished limestone, with the exception of the base, which was left unpolished to simulate rustication. In the interior great importance was attached to well-lit rooms and flexible work areas separated by movable partitions. Of special interest at the time was the heating and cooling system,

top left: Ernst Petersen and Walter Köngeter. Vereinigte Stahlwerke A. G. (now Stahlhaus GmbH) building, Breite Strasse 69, Düsseldorf, c.1939. From *Moderne Bauformen* (1939).

top right: Jacob Koerfer. Hansa-Hochhaus, Hansaring 97, Cologne, 1924-25. From *Das Hochhaus am Hansaring* (1925).

Adolf Abel. Messebauten, Kennedyufer and Auenweg, Cologne, 1926-28. Photograph 1990.

88   The West: Rhine and Ruhr

which was supplied by a radiant heat plant. The building is extant and still in use.

In 1924 Konrad Adenauer initiated a program to strengthen Cologne's economy by attracting trade fairs to the city. Munich-trained architect Adolf Abel was commissioned in 1926 to design the Messebauten (exposition halls) along the banks of the Rhine. He produced three horseshoe-shaped exhibition structures terminated by a 262-foot-tall tower with the Panorama Restaurant at its top. The simple brick exterior of the tower shows the influence of Ragnar Østberg's Stockholm Town Hall of 1911-23. From 1941 to 1944 the Messe complex served as a holding station for prisoners who would later be transported to concentration camps in the east and as a jail for politicians of the Weimar period. Ironically, Adenauer himself was briefly imprisoned there. After World War II, the building was returned to its original function, which it continues to serve today.

Selected Sources

Lance Nobel, *Faber Guide to 20th-century Architecture* (London, 1985), p. 84; Falk Jaeger, *Bauen in Deutschland* (Stuttgart, 1985), pp. 103 (Wilhelm-Marx-Haus) and 102 (Stumm building); Pehnt, *Expressionist Architecture*; Barbara Miller Lane, *Architecture and Politics in Germany* (Cambridge, Mass., 1968), p. 36; "Bürohaus der Vereinigten Stahlwerke A. G. in Düsseldorf," *Moderne Bauformen* (1939), pp. 257-59; *Peter Behrens: Umbautes Licht*, ed. Bernhard Buderath (Munich, 1990); Peter Behrens, "Zur Frage des Hochhauses," *Stadtbaukunst alter und neuer Zeit* (Berlin, 1922); Paul Joseph Cremers, *Peter Behrens: Sein Werk von 1909 bis zur Gegenwart* (Essen, 1928); *Denkmälerverzeichnis Aachen*, ed. Landeskonservator Rheinland, 2 vols. (Cologne, 1977 and 1978); Klemmer, *Jacob Koerfer*, pp. 18-19 and 10-11; *Das Hochhaus am Hansaring in Köln* (Eschweiler, 1925).

Hans Herkommer. Becker brewery, St. Ingbert (Saarland), 1927. Photograph 1991.

Architect Hans Herkommer of Stuttgart was commissioned to work with a technical expert, Professor Ganzenmüller of the Weihenstephan brewery in Bavaria, on the design of a complex of buildings for the Becker brewery at St. Ingbert in the Saarland region. Built in 1927, the brewery, which still serves its original purpose, is composed of several buildings of different cubic masses and heights, and possesses the almost obligatory modernist tower.

Other modernist industrial facilities, in the Rhine and the Ruhr areas, by architects ranging from the renowned Dominikus Böhm to the little known Paul Pott, still exist and await historical analysis.

Selected Sources

"Bierbrauerei Gebr. Becker, St. Ingbert im Saargebiet," *Der Baumeister* (1933), pp. 85-87, and Jaeger, *Bauen in Deutschland*, p. 275; Hoff, Muck, and Thoma, *Dominikus Böhm*, pp. 280-81 and 508-9; "Ein Fabrikbau von Paul Pott, Köln," *Wasmuths Monatshefte für Baukunst und Städtebau* (1930), p. 256.

Wach and Rosskotten. Allianzhaus, Hermann-Becker-Strasse and Kaiser-Wilhelm-Ring, Cologne, 1931-33. Photograph 1991.

Bruno Paul. Dischhaus, Brückenstrasse 19, Cologne, 1929-30. Photograph 1991.

opposite: Hans Heinz Lüttgen. Prinzenhof, Aachener Strasse and Hohenzollernring, Cologne, 1935. Photograph 1991.

When building resumed in Germany after World War I, the commercial department store became an important building type. Erich Mendelsohn was commissioned to design large stores in several German towns (see Fig. 4, p.167, and pp. 220-21). A sound businessman and a prolific architect with, at times, as many as forty employees working in his office, Mendelsohn greatly admired the strong contours, layered masses, and organic unity of Henry van de Velde's Werkbund Theater in Cologne, an admiration apparent in the sculpturally molded forms and in the emphasis on the effect of movement produced by horizontal strips of windows that marked Mendelsohn's commercial style in the second half of the twenties.

His ideas concerning the image to be projected by modern commercial buildings were reflected in three thirties structures in Cologne: the Allianzhaus, the Prinzenhof, and the Dischhaus.

Düsseldorf architects Karl Wach and Heinrich Rosskotten collaborated on the new Allianzhaus of 1931-33. They designed a steel skeleton covered with 1½-inch-thick Gronsdorf limestone. Housing a bank, shops, and various offices, the new Allianzhaus was designed as a comfortable, quiet, and healthy work environment for approximately five hundred employees.

Local architect Hans Heinz Lüttgen, known among other buildings for his twenties villas in Wuppertal-Barmen, designed the Prinzenhof in 1935 for a site on the wide city ring road at the point where it intersected with the main road leading to Aachen. Working with a limited amount of very expensive space, Lüttgen met the challenge of designing a building that would exploit the maximum potential of the site. The ground floor was designed as a large restaurant with three hundred seats. The kitchens, offices, and a gallery with seating for 123 were located on the mezzanine, which projected from the building's facade over the restaurant space below. The interior design of the restaurant incorporated motifs reminiscent of an ocean liner, such as a balcony overlooking the lower dining area, curved walls, and porthole windows. The latter were used on the

facade of the building as well as in the restaurant. The entrances, one on each street facade, were set back in alcoves. Five of the levels above the mezzanine each contained three small, expensive flats with excellent views, while the sixth and final level, which was set back from the rest of the facade, housed one-room flats for maids and a laundry for the restaurant. Lüttgen designed the building with a soft curve at the point of intersection between the two streets, echoing the line of the Opera Restaurant, which at the time was located across the street. The facade of the building was faced with travertine stone, with the exception of the top story, where the facing was of Moselle slate. The iron window frames of the mezzanine were painted light and dark brown, whereas the wooden frames of the windows on the top level were given the same color as the facade's travertine. The facade was embellished with awnings, which added a dynamic element, and neon signage, a most unusual feature at the time. The building survives in an altered state.

The Dischhaus of 1928-30, named for art collector and amateur archaeologist Carl Damian Disch, was designed by Berlin architect Bruno Paul. The smooth, sweeping, sculptural curve of the building, with its continuous horizontal strips of glass alternating with bands of limestone, is closely related to Mendelsohn's department store in Chemnitz, which had been completed in 1929 (see p. 220). The

Dischhaus provided spaces for shops at street level and for offices above. The bands of windows running across the exterior, which is faced in limestone, stretch round the corner at the street intersection, giving an impression of continuous horizontal motion. The Dischhaus has been recognized as one of the finest modern structures in Cologne and, although destroyed in World War II, has been completely rebuilt to the original plans.

Other department stores with curved corners — by, for example, Jacob Koerfer's son Hanns — were erected in nearby towns in the thirties, and these testify to the continuing influence of Mendelsohn's sleek store designs of the previous decade.

Selected Sources

"Das neue Allianz-Verwaltungsgebäude in Köln am Rhein," *Der Baumeister* (1933), pp. 365-69; "Der neue 'Prinzenhof' in Köln," *Moderne Bauformen* (1937), pp. 551-57; Wilhelm Kreis, "Neue Arbeiten von H. H. Lüttgen, Köln," *Moderne Bauformen* (1929), pp. 97-115; "Hanns Koerfer, Köln: Der Königshof in Essen," *Moderne Bauformen* (1939), pp. 261-63; "Kolumbaviertel," *Kölner Stadtführer* (1990), p.119; *Bruno Paul: Deutsche Raumkunst und Architektur zwischen Jugendstil und Moderne* (Munich, 1992), p. 312.

Bernhard Pfau. Haus Ziem, Heinrich-Heine-Allee, Düsseldorf, c. 1932. Photograph 1991.

Wilhelm Kreis. Sparkasse Bochum, Dr.-Ruer-Platz, Grabenstrasse and Schützenbahn, Bochum, 1925-28. From *Wasmuths Monatshefte für Baukunst und Städtebau* (1929).

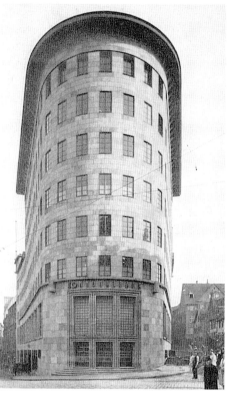

Düsseldorf architect Bernhard Pfau is best known for his Schauspielhaus (theater) of 1959-69 in that city, but he also received important commissions there before World War II, among them that for the Haus Ziem on a triangular site on Heinrich-Heine-Allee. He produced a different facade design for each of the three streets on which the building stood. The Haus Ziem originally functioned as both a commercial and a residential building, with apartments and offices occupying the upper levels and stores the ground floor. The structure still exists, but additions have been made to it and new buildings erected adjacent to it. The design is similar to other stores by Pfau, such as the tobacco shops on Königsallee and Schadowstrasse, the latter also on a triangular site.

Selected Sources

"Bernhard Pfau, Düsseldorf: Haus Ziem," *Moderne Bauformen* (1932), pp. 339-49; "Rheinische Läden," *Monatshefte für Baukunst und Städtebau* (1940), pp. 145-55.

The building housing the Sparkasse Bochum (formerly the Kommunalbank) was erected from 1925 to 1928 to designs by Wilhelm Kreis on Dr.-Ruer-Platz, at the intersection of Grabenstrasse and Schützenbahn in Bochum. In a sensitive solution to the problem posed by the site, Kreis created a curvilinear structure, whose exterior surfaces consist of smooth masonry. After suffering serious damage in the war, the building was reconstructed from 1946 to 1949 by Bernhard Wielers to a state very close to the original. It underwent remodeling in 1954-55, 1963-65, and 1980-82, yet to a large degree retains its twenties appearance.

Selected Sources

Bauen in Bochum, Architektur im Ruhrgebiet (Bochum, 1986), p. 86; *Wasmuths Monatshefte für Baukunst und Städtebau* (1929), pp. 246-49.

Wilhelm Kreis. Rheinhalle, Ehrenhof, Düsseldorf,
1925-26. Photograph 1990.

Wilhelm Kreis. Pavilion, Ehrenhof, Düsseldorf,
1925-26. Photograph 1990.

In 1925-26 Wilhelm Kreis designed a number of buildings for the "Gesolei" exhibition (see pp. 72-73), which opened on May 8, 1926, in the Ehrenhof area of Düsseldorf, immediately north of the Oberkasseler Brücke. While many of the structures have been demolished, several important buildings remain.

The Rheinhalle, at the south end of the Ehrenhof, was originally built to accommodate the health and sports section of the exhibition. The unique exterior form of Kreis's circular design was articulated with windows set in Gothic arches that evidenced his continued practice, here elegantly and subtly transformed, of drawing inspiration from historical styles. After the exhibition, the Rheinhalle was converted into a planetarium. Damage suffered during the war necessitated renovation, and the building finally reopened in 1978 as a concert hall with a seating capacity of two thousand.

Other buildings designed by Kreis for the "Gesolei" exhibition were the museums north

of the Rheinhalle, which originally contained exhibitions pertaining to social and economic life in various countries. The emphatic quality of the fluted columns of the pavilions between what are now the Kunstmuseum and Landesmuseum recurs a decade later in Nazi buildings, and indeed, in his book *Expressionist Architecture* Wolfgang Pehnt likens the pavilions to Paul Ludwig Troost's Temples of Honor, dedicated to the fallen heroes of the Nazi movement, near Munich's Königsplatz (demolished after World War II). He also compares the "marching rhythm" of the horizontal elevation of the Kunstmuseum with Albert Speer's grandstand on the Zeppelin Field in Nuremberg.

Selected Sources

Mayer and Rehder, *Wilhelm Kreis;* Stephan, *Wilhelm Kreis;* (Meissner, *Wilhelm Kreis;* Wilhelm Kreis, "Neue Arbeiten von H. H. Lüttgen, Köln," *Moderne Bauformen* (1929); Pehnt, *Expressionist Architecture.*

Alfred Fischer. Hans-Sachs-Haus, Ebertstrasse 17, Gelsenkirchen. From *Moderne Bauformen* (1930).

The brick Hans-Sachs-Haus, now the Rathaus (town hall), in the Old Town section of Gelsenkirchen was designed by Alfred Fischer of Essen. Fischer's structure was praised in a 1930 issue of *Moderne Bauformen* for the clarity of its horizontal form and for its kind of modern style, which was deemed appropriate to new civic architecture. The Hans-Sachs-Haus survives, though it was remodeled in 1958, and now houses the city council and the offices of city officials.

Selected Sources

Gelsenkirchen: Architekturführer, Architektur im Ruhrgebiet (Essen, 1985); Wilhelm Kästner, "Alfred Fischer, Essen," *Moderne Bauformen* (1930), pp.149-53.

The Soziale Frauenschule (school for women social workers) in Aachen, built in 1929-30 to designs by Rudolf Schwarz, is still used as a school. The stairwell leading to the building's upper level is encased by unadorned, industrial-type windows stretching the full height of the three stories. With a flat roof and facing of white stucco, the school, despite its far smaller dimensions, has much in common with the Bauhaus building in Dessau (Fig.1, p. 214).

A less well known school is the Volksschule (elementary school) in the Benrath district of Düsseldorf by local architect Georg Schmalz. A two-story building with three-story wings projecting from the front at each end and with a shorter, square structure attached to the rear, this school, too, was designed in the *Neues Bauen* style, its smooth, unadorned brick exterior pierced by horizontal strips of square windows. It could easily be mistaken for a factory. Originally, an open porch with square columns stretched across the front of the building; this has since been enclosed with glass windows. With this exception, the structure has remained relatively unchanged, and is still used as a school.

Selected Sources

"Soziale Frauenschule in Aachen," *Deutsche Bauzeitung* (July 22, 1931), pp. 357-60; *Denkmälerverzeichnis Aachen;* "Volksschule in Düsseldorf-Benrath," *Deutsche Bauzeitung* (June 7, 1933), pp. 455-58.

Rudolf Schwarz. Soziale Frauenschule, Robert-Schumann-Strasse 21, Aachen, 1929-30. From *Deutsche Bauzeitung* (July 22, 1931).

Georg Schmalz. Volksschule, Münchener Strasse and Hospitalstrasse, Düsseldorf-Benrath, 1931. Photograph 1991.

Richard Döcker. Hospital, Knittlinger Steige 205, Maulbronn, 1927-29. Photograph 1991.

The children's hospital at Maulbronn, some twenty miles east of Karlsruhe, is the work of Richard Döcker, recognized in the twenties as one of Stuttgart's leading architects and an exponent of *Neues Bauen* (see p.173). The hospital, built from 1927 to 1929 on a hillside overlooking the village of Maulbronn, is constructed from a quarry stone from the region, lending it a reserved appearance. The building was designed in two stages, but only the first was executed. Its terraced design gives all the rooms with large double windows along the south facade access to fresh air and sunlight. The interior is characterized by open spaces and unadorned wall planes, with large windows. An addition to the hospital, by Gerhard Aeckerle, was built in 1979.

Hebebrand and Kleinertz. Sonnenblick Sanatorium, Marburg an der Lahn, c.1932, Photograph 1992.

Selected Sources
Kurt and Gretl Hoffmann, *Architekturführer Stuttgart und Umgebung,* 3rd ed. (Stuttgart, 1983), p.109; *Der Baumeister* (1931), pp. 366-70.

The Sonnenblick Sanatorium in Marburg an der Lahn was built around 1932 for patients suffering from tuberculosis. The program for the new building was to combine a hospital with teaching facilities for the medical school of the nearby University of Marburg. Designed by architects Werner Hebebrand and Willy Kleinertz of Frankfurt, the building was located on a hilltop in the middle of a pine forest and brings to mind Alvar Aalto's tuberculosis sanatorium of 1929-33 at Paimio in Finland and the Zonnestraal tuberculosis sanatorium of 1926-28 by Johannes Duiker in Hilversum, Holland. All three hospitals were erected in accordance with twenties theories of tuberculosis, which decreed that the best treatment was isolation of the patients from the pollution of the city and plentiful rest, sunshine, and fresh air; location in a pine forest was supposed to have a special healing quality. The final design of the Sonnenblick Sanatorium was a T-shaped building of three levels with a central clock tower and flat roofs. The longest facade of the structure, on the south side, had a projecting pavilion at each end. These were enclosed by floor-to-ceiling sash windows that could be opened from the bottom to allow the beds to be pushed out onto the balconies, which were equipped with mechanical awnings. The north side of the hospital provided shadowed terraces for the patients. Attention was given to each surface of the interior: the floors, for example, were covered with linoleum to facilitate cleaning. The university's section of the structure, which was separated from the tuberculosis unit in order to guard against infection and contagious disease, contained a medical department with hospital beds and a surgical unit, as well as a lecture room and a laboratory. Although a new hospital has been built on the site, a portion of the original complex still exists.

Selected Source
"Sanatorium Sonnenblick in Marburg an der Lahn," *Der Baumeister* (1932), pp. 265-67.

Mehrtens, Mewes, Albert and Bartsch. Cologne airport, Butzweiler Hof, 1933-36 (demolished). From *Moderne Bauformen* (1937).

Although present-day travelers are familiar with Cologne's striking airport of 1970, few realize that the city previously had an equally important airport at Butzweiler Hof, northwest of the city proper. Dating from the twenties and thirties, this was the second busiest airport in Germany for freight and post in the early thirties, after Berlin's Tempelhof. In 1932 it served 16,348 passengers; the combined passenger figures of the other airports in the

region — Essen, Dortmund, and Düsseldorf — totaled less than 14,000 that year. This demand warranted new facilities, and a consortium of architects from the region designed the new terminal and hangars that were officially opened in 1936. The airport witnessed a huge increase in passenger traffic, with 37,279 using the facilities in 1938 alone. At the outbreak of World War II in 1939, the airport was commandeered by the Luftwaffe and served as a military base throughout the war. With the defeat of Germany in 1945, the Royal Air Force took over the site and planning began for a new civil airport to serve both Cologne and Bonn to the south — the current Köln-Bonn airport. The simplified classicist buildings of

the thirties at Butzweiler Hof no longer exist: the area is now an industrial park.

Selected Sources
"Der neue Kölner Verkehrsflughafen," *Moderne Bauformen* (1937), pp. 289-96; Werner Treibel, *Geschichte der deutschen Verkehrsflughäfen* (Bonn, 1992), pp. 287-313 et passim.

The "back to nature" ethos had long been widespread among German people, and the interwar period was no exception. In 1934 City Architect Härter designed a Hallen- und Freibad (indoor and outdoor swimming pools) at Pirmasens, a manufacturing town in the Rhineland-Palatinate between Karlsruhe and Saarbrücken. At the time of construction, the baths were located on the edge of the town in the vicinity of a large open field, sheltered from the wind by surrounding forests. The building, in the style that became known as international modernism or functionalism, consisted of three stucco-covered cubic forms. The

Härter. Hallen- und Freibad, Lemberger Strasse, Pirmasens, 1934. Photograph 1991.

largest of these, a three-story block with a two-story entrance chamber and a clock tower, recalls a composition frequently used by Walter Gropius in the twenties. The interior was arranged as an atrium, with the indoor pool placed in a two-story space at the center of the building block, directly beneath a glass roof. The roof could be opened mechanically, a novel feature at the time. The pool was surrounded on the first level by large windows, many of which functioned as sliding doors, and on the second level by a balcony bordered by ocean liner-type railings. The interior walls of the entrance structure were decorated at the top with murals, which have now been restored. The second level of the main section, its balcony lined with tables and chairs, contained a restaurant. The stairwell was placed inside the clock tower; the railings at the top recalled those of a ship. Between the building and the outdoor pool was a patio area for sunbathing and eating. After World War II, the Pirmasens facility was closed, owing to neglect that resulted in part from the fact that new bathing complexes had been constructed in the area. However, it has since been remodeled and additions have been made to it. It now thrives as a leisure center.

Selected Sources

"Das Hallen- und Freibad der Stadt Pirmasens," *Der Baumeister* (1936), pp. 181-87; *Wasmuths Lexikon der Baukunst*, pp. 52-54.

Franz Schuster and Edmund Fabry. Opel-Bad, Müllerweg, Wiesbaden-Neroberg, 1934. Photograph 1990.

In an effort to increase the well-being of the population, German politicians and architects between the world wars were concerned to create maximum opportunities for exposure to the healing properties of nature, and of water in particular. The Opel-Bad (Opel Baths) in Wiesbaden, designed by Franz Schuster and Edmund Fabry with landscape architect Wilhelm Hirsch, was among the many public bathing and spa facilities built at this time. Wiesbaden, situated between the Rhine and the Taunus hills, had been a health resort since Roman times; twenty-seven hot springs exist in the area. The Opel-Bad is situated on a wooded hilltop, the Neroberg, overlooking the city and is accessible by tram or on foot, up a rather steep incline. The site, its setting offering an escape from city life to the tranquillity of nature, was sheltered from the wind by forests to the north and the east. In addition to an open-air swimming pool, Schuster and Fabry designed other sports facilities and a restaurant in an attempt to attract visitors away from the renowned older spa. The terraces provided guests with a splendid view of the city of Wiesbaden. Much of the complex is extant and still serves its original purposes.

Selected Sources

"Opel-Bad Wiesbaden," *Moderne Bauformen* (1934), pp. 525-40; "Badeanlagen," *Wasmuths Lexikon der Baukunst*, ed. Ernst Wasmuth (Berlin, 1937),

Otto Bongartz. Changing rooms, Kölner Stadion, Aachener Strasse, Cologne, 1936. Photograph 1990.

The popularity of swimming facilities in the late twenties and early thirties was reflected in the expansion of the existing swimming pool in Cologne. Part of the Kölner Stadion (Cologne Stadium), this family bathing facility had be-

come so highly frequented by 1933-34 that a large-scale extension was necessary. Four new pools were added and the number of recreation areas increased. The additions, designed by architect Otto Bongartz in 1936 on a very tight budget and with a limited supply of materials, included a building containing changing rooms. This was an International Style, rectangular block with a flat roof. A

wide balcony, reached by curving staircases with carefully detailed railings, ran along the rear of the two-story structure, facing the swimming areas. The complex is still used as a swimming facility.

Selected Source
"Die neue Umkleidehalle im Schwimmbad des Kölner Stadions," *Der Baumeister* (1936), pp. 333-41.

The long tradition in Germany of taking spa cures continued unabated during the interwar years. Whenever possible, funds were made available for the renovation of old spas and the construction of new ones. In 1931, for example, a competition was held for an extension to the Kurhotel at Bad Schwalbach in the southwestern Taunus hills, not far from Wiesbaden. The resort is located at the entrance to a narrow, forested valley, with a view of the

mountains to the northeast and the southwest. The site was occupied by a hotel and a bathhouse dating from the mid-nineteenth century. Consideration was given to building a new bathhouse, but eventually it was decided that a hotel would be more successful. The winner of the competition, Wilhelm Kreis, designed the new structure, which was to be joined with the older hotel, such that it followed the curve of the valley to the south. Large windows and

balconies admitted a maximum amount of natural light to the building, whose roof consisted of a large terrace area with a magnificent view of the countryside. A tunnel connected the new hotel with the bathhouse. The Kurhotel was praised by contemporaries as offering peaceful, restive, and hygienic rehabilitation, a function that it continues to serve today.

Selected Source
"Staatliches Kurhotel in Bad Schwalbach," *Deutsche Bauzeitung* (April 1, 1932), pp. 268-73.

Wilhelm Kreis. Kurhotel, Neustrasse and Brunnenstrasse, Bad Schwalbach, 1931. From *Deutsche Bauzeitung* (April 1, 1932).

Sporting facilities became important commu- nity foci during the twenties and thirties. A stadium was erected in Cologne in the late twenties with the purpose not only of offering athletics facilities to adults, but also of provid- ing children with open green areas in which to play. The two matching buildings at the entrance to the stadium, flat-roofed, rectilinear structures, were designed by well-known local architect Adolf Abel. Their monumental porches, supported by colossal brick pillars, have much in common with what was later to be the official architectural style of the Third Reich. Also extant are several of the original lampposts, designed in an almost constructivist style with rectangular brick posts and glass- enclosed lamps.

Selected Source
"Grosskampfbahn, Bezirksstadion, oder Übungs- stätte?", *Der Baumeister* (1929), p. 18.

Adolf Abel. Entrance to Kölner Stadion, Aache- ner Strasse, Cologne, c.1928, Photograph 1990.

The connection between a healthy mind and healthy body, so important to Germans at this time, spurred the construction and improve- ment of sporting facilities. In Karlsruhe, for instance, a grandstand was added to the Hochschulstadion (college stadium). Designed by local architect Hermann Alker, the structure was noted for its innovative drainage system and for the construction of its projecting cement roof, thirty-three feet wide and unsup- ported. Alker, who also designed housing in Karlsruhe and Freiburg (see p. 102), was responsible for the gymnasium in the latter city's University Stadium complex on Schwarz- waldstrasse. Also dating from the twenties, the gymnasium has scarcely been altered since.

Selected Sources
"Der Tribühnenbau des Karlsruher Hochschulstadions und die Erneuerung der Stiftskirche in Neustadt," *Wasmuths Monatshefte für Baukunst und Städtebau* (1931), pp. 499-501; "Hochschulstadion Karlsruhe," *Wasmuths Monatshefte für Baukunst und Städtebau* (1929), pp. 414-15; "Stadion der Universität Freiburg i. Br.," ibid., p. 417.

Hermann Alker. Grandstand, Hochschulstadion (now Institut für Leibesübungen), Engesserstrasse, Karlsruhe, 1931. From *Wasmuths Monatshefte für Baukunst und Städtebau* (1931).

Walter Gropius. Row houses, Danziger Strasse, Dammerstock Siedlung, Karlsruhe, 1928. Photograph 1990.

H. D. Rösiger. Row houses, Falkenweg, Dammerstock Siedlung, Karlsruhe, 1928. Photograph 1990.

View of the Dammerstock Siedlung, Karlsruhe. Photograph c. 1927-28.

The government of the Weimar Republic regarded solving the postwar housing crisis as its responsibility. The Constitution of 1919 permitted government to acquire and control land and, with the end of inflation in 1923 and Germany's return to financial stability, the housing problem was addressed with renewed energy. Public money was made available at low interest rates to provide housing for those workers who were able to pay only minimal rents. The commitment to new social values embodied in such measures was reflected in the architecture of the large workers' *Siedlungen* (housing estates) that sprang up on the peripheries of many major German cities from the mid-

twenties to the mid-thirties. The idea was to place workers in an environment that allowed them to enjoy clean air, sunshine, and nature. The projects, which owed a great deal to the Garden City plan developed in Great Britain, often included communal facilities, such as schools, churches, playgrounds, and small areas that could be used for gardens.

One of the most famous of these housing developments was the Weissenhof Siedlung of 1927 in Stuttgart, a model exhibition designed as a prototype for future *Siedlungen* (see pp.171-72). The Dammerstock Siedlung in Karlsruhe, also conceived as a model exhibition, was designed in opposition to the precepts embodied by Weissenhof. It opened in September 1929 and was titled "Die Gebrauchswohnung" (The Practical Dwelling), indicating that it rejected the luxurious individual units of Weissenhof and their emphasis on stylishness in favor of the severe lines of rigorously structured, "minimalistic" housing that would deal with Germany's housing crisis in the most efficient manner. The terms of the competition, as enforced by the jury of Ludwig Mies van der Rohe, Ernst May, and Otto Völckers, stated that plans should follow the *Zeilenbau* system, straight, parallel rows of buildings aligned north-south and at right angles to major streets. First prize for site plan went to Walter Gropius of Berlin, who thus became director of the final project. Otto Haesler of Celle won second prize.

In implementing the *Zeilenbau* system, the architects embraced a rather inflexible vision of equality and efficiency, with regimented groups or blocks of structures, each designed by a number of architects. While the building blocks on the perimeter comprised three to six levels, containing up to eight single-family living units, most units were smaller. Alfred Fischer, for example, designed Le Corbusier-like, two-family structures with roof gardens. These were perhaps the most humane of all the estate's buildings.

At the time of its construction Dammerstock received mixed reviews. An article by Heinrich De Fries, a Berlin architect and critic, expressed concern that occupants would never shake off a feeling of depression in this monotonous complex. According to De Fries, the large distance between structures increased the feeling of alienation. In addition, there was anxiety that this type of building and site plan represented a continuation of the very kind of historical barrack-like design that architects were striving to overcome. De Fries suggested that, by being less insistent on arranging the structures in straight lines — by, say, staggering the rows — the architects would have made the buildings more open to natural light and fresh air. The Dammerstock Siedlung, which still functions as housing, has rightly received extensive coverage in architectural journals and guidebooks ever since its construction, but it should not be forgotten that other Karlsruhe

Otto Haesler. Restaurant, Nürnberger Strasse 1, Dammerstock Siedlung, Karlsruhe, 1928. Photograph 1990.

Alfred Fischer. Two-family house, Saarbrücken-strasse, Dammerstock Siedlung, Karlsruhe, 1928. Photograph 1991.

architects of the twenties and early thirties made their mark on the region's architecture. One of these was Hermann Alker, whose solid, rather conservative housing designs range from the 1930 apartments on Eberstrasse and Schwarzwaldstrasse in Karlsruhe itself to the contemporaneous, similarly styled, yet hipped-roofed housing blocks west of the University Stadium on Schwarzwaldstrasse in Freiburg, some seventy miles to the south.

Selected Sources

H. De Fries, "Problematik des Städtebaues," *Die Form* (April 1, 1930), pp. 189-93; "Die Dammerstock Siedlung bei Karlsruhe," *Moderne Bauformen* (1930), pp. 8-9; *Ausstellung Karlsruhe Dammerstock-Siedlung: Die Gebrauchswohnung*, exhibition catalogue (Karlsruhe, 1929); Paul Schültz, "Die Dammerstocksiedlung," *Werk, Bauen & Wohnen* 73, no. 11 (November 1986), pp. 56-64; Joachim Göricke, *Bauten in Karlsruhe: Ein Architekturführer* (Karlsruhe, 1980), pp. 649-55; Richard Pommer und Christian F. Otto, *Weissenhof 1927 and the Modern Movement in Architecture* (Chicago, 1991). For Alker, see Göricke, *Bauten in Karlsruhe*, p. 659, and "Wohnbauten in Freiburg und Karlsruhe: Architekt Hermann Alker, Karlsruhe," *Monatshefte für Baukunst und Städtebau* (1932), pp. 7-10.

Wilhelm Riphahn and Caspar Maria Grod. Weisse Stadt housing estate, Heidelberger Strasse, Waldecker Strasse, and Kopernikusstrasse, Cologne-Buchforst, 1926-29. Photograph 1990.

The Blauer Hof estate of 1926-28 in the Buchforst district of Cologne is the result of the combined talents of Wilhelm Riphahn and Caspar Maria Grod. After World War I, these two Cologne architects worked together to establish a new concept of the housing estate that emphasized light, air, and trees by including "green courtyards." Their initial designs for the Blauer Hof were based on an enclosed courtyard, but in the final version this was changed to an open courtyard in order to give the complex a more expansive feel and to relate the estate to a neighboring development by the same architects, the Weisse Stadt (White Town). Both complexes were part of an eastward city expansion plan. The Blauer Hof is unusual in being a block structure. More customary was the row-by-row layout of the Weisse Stadt, the preliminary plans for which were drawn up as early as 1926, though it was not built until 1929 to 1932. This estate is often referred to as the finest example of

Neues Bauen in Cologne. Its buildings were arranged at a slant to provide all apartments with optimum lighting.

Selected Source
Wohnreform in Köln, ed. Klaus Novy (Cologne, 1986), pp. 108-15.

Wilhelm Riphahn and Caspar Maria Grod. Zollstock Siedlung, Vorgebirgsstrasse, Gottesweg, and Zollstockgürtel, Cologne, 1927-28. Photograph 1990.

Another Cologne estate by Wilhelm Riphahn and Caspar Maria Grod, the Zollstock Siedlung of 1927-29, was intended primarily for middle-class civil servants and private sector employees, and the architects sought to reflect the occupants' shared social, economic, and political status in their design. Standardization was deemed necessary, with all the apartments, including those on the corners, having

certain basic elements in common. Each unit was equipped with a separate kitchenette, a matter of special interest to the architects and to critics. It was felt that combining the kitchen and living areas in one space, which was characteristic of the Rhineland tradition, reflected the lower social status of those who usually resided in housing estates. At Zollstock, the separation of the kitchen from the main living

room thus provided an indication of the higher social standing of the occupants while permitting a substantial improvement in the use of these two areas.

Selected Source
Moderne Bauformen (1929), pp. 313-17.

Cologne architect Otto Scheib's work in the Rhineland during the twenties ranged from expressionist commercial structures to more conservative housing. Among the latter are the apartment buildings of 1927-28 in the Riehl district of Cologne.

Otto Scheib. Housing estate, Ehrenbergstrasse and Barbarastrasse, Cologne-Riehl, 1927-28. From *Der Architekt Otto Scheib* (1931).

The structures were arranged in long horizontal rows with protruding square windows at the corner. The basement level and the entrances were constructed of dark stone, while the remainder of the buildings was painted white.

Selected Sources
Der Architekt Otto Scheib, Neue Werkkunst (Berlin, Leipzig, and Vienna, 1931); *Neuzeitliche Miethäuser und Siedlungen*, p. 111.

Fritz Toussaint. Apartment buildings, Guaita-strasse, Aachen, 1925. From *Moderne Bauformen* (1936).

In 1925 Fritz Toussaint designed housing blocks in Aachen that stretch along both sides of Guaitastrasse. Well preserved, the buildings continue to house apartments. Their conservative modernist forms were still appreciated a decade after construction, as is indicated by their publication in *Moderne Bauformen* in 1936.

Selected Sources

"Fritz Toussaint, Köln: Wohnblocks in Aachen," *Moderne Bauformen* (1936), p. 271-73; *Denkmäler-verzeichnis Aachen*.

The housing estate in the Gerresheim district of Düsseldorf was designed by Heinrich De Fries in reaction against the Dammerstock Siedlung (see pp.100-2). The development consisted of 101 four- or six-room single-family homes; half of them are oriented southward, the others on an almost exactly north-south axis. As opposed to the straight rows of Dammerstock, the Gerresheim houses, located on a steep incline facing southwest, follow the curve of the land from east to west. They were designed to echo the natural contours of the land and to take advantage of morning and evening sun.

Selected Source

H. De Fries, "Problematik des Städtebaues," *Die Form* (April 1, 1930) pp. 189-93.

Heinrich De Fries. Housing estate, Torfbruch-strasse and Dreherstrasse, Düsseldorf-Gerresheim, c.1930. From *Die Form* (March 15, 1931).

William Dunkel. Brückenkopfbauten, Kaiserswerther Strasse, Düsseldorf, c.1925-28. Photograph 1991.

The Brückenkopfbauten (bridgehead buildings) on Düsseldorf's Kaiserswerther Strasse were designed in the mid- to late twenties by William Dunkel, a New York-born architect who was raised in German-speaking Switzerland. The buildings, which were constructed in dark brick and recall north German expressionist architecture, still serve their original functions.

Selected Source
William Dunkel, Neue Werkkunst (Berlin, Leipzig, and Vienna, 1930).

Peter Behrens. Villa Ganz, Falkensteiner Strasse 19, Kronberg im Taunus, 1931. Photograph 1991.

In 1931 Peter Behrens designed one of his late works, the Villa Ganz, at Kronberg in the Taunus hills near Frankfurt. The structure, heavily influenced by the International Style, stands lengthwise on the southern slope of a hill. At the time of its construction, there were woods to the north and a wide sweep of undulating meadowland to the south. The house is constructed of brick, faced with slabs of light-colored Naumburg limestone. Its interior finishes were elaborate, with walls covered in parchment, moldings in rosewood, and an ample use of marble. The house was used by Eisenhower as his headquarters at the end of World War II. Today, the structure is divided into three apartments and the open staircase in the interior has recently been altered by architect Richard Meier. The horizontality of the building and its use of the latest technology, as in the hydraulic picture window facing the garden, recall Ludwig Mies van der Rohe's famous Tugendhat House of 1930 (Fig.2, p.10).

Selected Sources

"Peter Behrens: Landhaus einer Dame im Taunus," *Moderne Bauformen* (1932), pp.117-32; Tilmann Buddensieg, *Industriekultur: Peter Behrens and the AEG, 1907-1914* (Cambridge, Mass., 1984); Alan Windsor, *Peter Behrens: Architect and Designer* (London, 1981), p.168.

Dominikus Böhm, one of the most important church architects in Germany (see pp. 77-79), designed his own house and studio in 1931-32 in the Marienburg area of Cologne. The L-shaped structure is clearly influenced by Le Corbusier's projects of the early twenties, particularly the Villa Stein at Garches and the Planeix House in Paris. Today, the building functions as the studio of Dominikus Böhm's architect son, Gottfried.

Selected Source

"Dominikus Böhms eigenes Wohnhaus," *Moderne Bauformen* (1934), pp. 649-53.

Dominikus Böhm. The architect's house and studio, Römerberg 25, Cologne-Marienburg, 1931-32. Photograph 1991.

In 1927 Ludwig Mies van der Rohe was invited to design houses for two close friends, Hermann Lange and Josef Esters, managing directors of the state-owned Verseidag (Vereinigte Seidenwebereien AG; United Silk Weaving Mills Corp.) in Krefeld who had purchased adjoining lots on Wilhelmshofallee. The Lange and Esters families probably knew Mies through his associate, Lilly Reich, with whom he had designed a silk industry exhibition in 1926 in Frankfurt. The dark brick houses are marked by the austere International Style typical of Mies's work at the time. They are notable for their use of the latest design ideas in creating an open floor plan, something that Mies developed further in the German Pavilion at the World Exhibition in Barcelona and in the Tugendhat House (Fig. 2, p. 10). In 1968 a family member gave the Lange House to the city of Krefeld, which purchased the Esters House from heirs of the estate in 1976. The two buildings now belong to the Krefeld Kunstmuseen.

After completion of the residences in Krefeld, Mies was invited by the board of the Verseidag to design a new factory in the city. The resulting buildings were strongly influenced by the studies Mies had been conducting on the "skin" of his office building projects of 1928-29, by recent German factories, such as the Fagus-Werke of 1910-14 in Alfeld by Gropius & Meyer, and by Gropius's Bauhaus building of 1925 in Dessau (Fig. 1, p. 214). The Verseidag factory is extant, although the interiors have been changed and new structures added to the site.

Selected Sources

Wolf Tegethoff, *Mies van der Rohe: The Villas and Country Houses* (New York, 1985); Sandra Honey, *The Early Work of Mies van der Rohe* (London, 1978); *Mies van der Rohe: European Works*, ed. Sandra Honey (London, 1986); *Mies Reconsidered: His Career, Legacy, and Disciples*, ed. John Zukowsky (Chicago, 1986).

Ludwig Mies van der Rohe. Courtyard, Verseidag factory, Industriestrasse and Heimendahlstrasse, Krefeld, 1930-35. Photograph 1991.

Mies van der Rohe. Dyeing plant, Verseidag factory, Industriestrasse and Heimendahlstrasse, Krefeld, 1930-35. Photograph 1991.

opposite:
Ludwig Mies van der Rohe. Esters House, Wilhelmshofallee 91, Krefeld, 1927-30. Photograph 1984.

Ludwig Mies van der Rohe. Lange House, Wilhelmshofallee 93, Krefeld, 1927-30. Photograph 1984.

The park area bordering the Rhine in Cologne's Rodenkirchen district provided an expensive and difficult site for the erection of an ensemble of houses built in the radical *Neue Sachlichkeit* style. The economics of this much sought-after area meant that the rectangular lots were narrow and deep, the narrow sides facing the river. These proportions, and the location within the flood boundaries of the Rhine, forced the architects to stress verticality and to place the structures on pilings. The Rhine flows on the eastern, narrow side of each site and the houses are oriented to the south-east to capitalize on the view of the river and of the countryside of the Bergisches Land on the opposite bank.

The first villa, the Seewald House at Uferstrasse 11, was designed in 1927 by Theodor Merrill for the painter Richard Seewald. Faced in stucco, the building emphasized ship-type forms with an extensive use of railings and an open terrace facing the river on the upper level.

The Loosen House of 1929 by Hans Schumacher also acknowledges the presence of the Rhine: its form recalls that of a modern ocean liner and incorporates ship's motifs. The verticality of the structure is counterbalanced by continuous horizontal fenestration, the setback of the top floor, the curved treatment of the terrace on that floor, and the railings lining the terrace and roof garden. The large living room

on the second level was oriented toward the river to provide a view across it. The second house in the park by Schumacher was built in 1930 for a Professor Hussmann. This structure, now largely obscured by trees, has suffered few visible alterations.

Selected Sources

Kölner Stadtführer, p. 429; "Haus Seewald," *Der Baumeister* (1931), pp. 114-15; "Wohnhaus Professor Hussmann," *Moderne Bauformen* (1932), pp. 40-41; *Der Baumeister* (1932), pp. 200-1; "Alleinstehendes grosses Einfamilienhaus in der Grossstadt," *Der Baumeister* (1932), pp. 404-5; "Zwei Wohnhäuser von Hans Schumacher," *Moderne Bauformen* (1932), pp. 555-59.

top left: Theodor Merrill. Seewald House, Uferstrasse 11, Cologne-Rodenkirchen, 1927. From *Der Baumeister* (1932).

top right: Hans Schumacher. Hussmann House, Im Park 4, Cologne-Rodenkirchen, 1930. Photograph 1991.

Hans Schumacher. Loosen House, Im Park 7, Cologne-Rodenkirchen, 1929. From *Moderne Bauformen* (1932).

top left: G. Rüth. Rüth House, Henkelstrasse 5, Wiesbaden, 1930. Photograph 1991.

top right: Rudolf Dörr. Dr. Kl. House, Hohenlohe-strasse, Wiesbaden, c.1940. From *Moderne Bauformen* (1940).

Rudolf Dörr. Dr. N. K. House, Hohenlohestrasse, Wiesbaden, c.1940. From *Moderne Bauformen* (1940).

Houses built in Wiesbaden in the interwar period include one of 1930 designed by G. Rüth of Dresden. It has remained virtually unchanged and is still occupied by the Rüth family. Another well-known modernist villa in Wiesbaden was the Harnischmacher House of 1933, designed by Marcel Breuer in a style strongly influenced by Le Corbusier.

Two more traditional houses in Wiesbaden were designed around 1940 by local architect Rudolf Dörr for the same street in the city's Schöne Aussicht district, a residential area created in 1820 which contained structures in a wide variety of historicist and Art Nouveau styles. Dörr's "Dr. Kl." House is constructed of plastered brick and roofed with slate from

Kaub on the Rhine, while the "Dr. N. K." villa, also with slate roofing and plastered brick, makes additional use of local stone. Both houses are extant, but Dr. N. K.'s has undergone extensive renovation.

Selected Sources

"Eisenbetonskelettbau im Hochbau: G. Rüth, Dresden–Haus Rüth in Wiesbaden," *Moderne Bauformen* (1932), pp.101, 108; "Vier Wohnhäuser in Wiesbaden," *Moderne Bauformen* (1940), pp.163-65.

Hamburg, Hanover, and Expressionist Architecture in North Germany

John Zukowsky

When Henry Russell Hitchcock and Philip Johnson were preparing their famous 1932 book *The International Style* and the almost contemporaneous Museum of Modern Art exhibition, they met in Hamburg on July 7, 1930, with Alfred Barr, director of the Museum of Modern Art. But two years later, with the book published and the show opened, scant reference to that city could be found in either, except for a nod in the direction of Karl Schneider through the inclusion of one of his residences and his Kunstverein gallery of 1930 (Fig. 1). It was as if nothing else existed in this major metropolitan center, or, more likely, those three famous personalities spent little time outside the immediate city center to consider other buildings that might fit their narrow concept of modernism. Hamburg has much more to offer the architectural visitor, even within the restrictive categories imposed by Hitchcock and Johnson, and by subsequent writers who have confined their attention to radical modernism. But, in the end, radical modernism was not what the city and region were about in the twenties. More recent literature acknowledges this, but does not venture much beyond discussions of the famous Chilehaus by Fritz Höger and some other commercial buildings called *Kontorhäuser.*

The *Kontorhäuser,* expressive brick structures, are as integral to the architectural image of twentieth-century Hamburg as the skyscrapers of the Chicago School are to that U. S. city and Jugendstil buildings to Vienna. They establish a strong identity both for the city and for other sites throughout the region, which, politically and culturally, was as closely tied to Denmark as it was to Germany. Indeed, Altona, just west of Hamburg, was Danish territory until 1867, and it has always been a rival to its larger urban neighbor to the east. Hamburg, at times Danish, at times German in the Middle Ages and later, became a leading independent commercial city in the thirteenth century and a prominent member of the trading federation known as the Hanseatic League. In 1937, during the Third Reich, the city annexed its neighbors Altona, Harburg-Wilhelmsburg, and Wandsbek. The buildings erected in Hamburg between the world wars provide a notably homogeneous sample of a regional approach to twenties design in brick. This holds true, despite the variety of approaches taken, whether it be the dramatic, expressive works of Höger, the more eclectic combinations of masonry and brick by Elingius and Schramm, Distel and Grubitz, and the Gerson brothers, the so-called radical modernism of Schneider, or the functionalist public buildings,

principally schools, of Fritz Schumacher. Schneider made important contributions to the urban and suburban fabric (see pp. 128, 143), and his designs, perhaps owing to the influence of books and exhibitions like Hitchcock and Johnson's, have received rather more coverage than those of Hamburg's other architects. Yet Schneider is actually a relatively secondary figure to the development of urban environments in this region, especially when compared with Höger, the Gersons, and Schumacher.

Johann Friedrich (Fritz) Höger was important for the dramatic quality of his type of brick expressionism, which put Hamburg and Schleswig-Holstein on the map architecturally. His roots in the craft tradition of the area doubtless influenced his beautifully detailed buildings. More than any other Hamburg architect, he could make powerful sculptural forms and details simply by glazing and manipulating the bricks themselves with a virtuosity reminiscent of the medieval mason's art (see pp. 144, 159). As with the Chicago School of commercial buildings, whose main function was to cost little to construct and supply their investors with a profit, Höger's brick buildings provided beautifully decorative surfaces at a fraction of what an elaborately ornamented building would have cost if constructed in stone and marble. No doubt the inventive frugality of this pleased his commercial clients, especially in a city which, in an almost American way, prizes commerce above all else.

After studying at the Baugewerkschule (architecture school) in Hamburg, Höger joined the firm of Lund and Kallmorgen in 1901, remaining there until 1905. Two years later he set up his own practice. His early jobs included homes and, in 1910, the *Kontorhaus* Klosterhof and the Doberowsky department store, and in 1913 the Köpperhaus at Mönckebergstrasse 3 — three large commissions. Designs for other commercial buildings followed until the outbreak of World War I, in which he served. In 1918 he reestablished a practice in housing and office design. His most famous work, the Chilehaus of 1922-24 (see p. 116), became a landmark of the large commercial city of Hamburg, much as the Empire State Building represents New York or the Sears and Hancock towers, Chicago. In addition, Höger constructed distinctively designed minor masterpieces for other towns and cities in the region, from Delmenhorst, near Bremen (see p. 150), through Hanover (see p. 159) and the Rüstringen district of Wilhelmshaven (Fig. 2), and even for places as far away as Berlin. During the late twenties and the harsh

Depression years of the early thirties, his style became somewhat more closely aligned with the severe masonry and brick modernism of Schneider and other Hamburg architects. And, although studies for large projects exist, few of notable scale were realized, with the exception of occasional individual buildings. In the Third Reich he continued to produce designs that related to his earlier successes with commercial expressionism, as well as more conservative ones that returned him to the craft traditions of his youth. His most celebrated accomplishment of this later period was the 1943 completion of the Sprinkenhof *Kontorhaus* across the street from the Chilehaus, a project that had been begun in 1927 with the Gerson brothers.

If Höger was the best known and, perhaps, the most successful commercial architect in Hamburg, then the Gerson brothers were not far behind. Yet they have received only a fraction of the recognition they deserve for shaping the city, in part, because they were Jewish. The work of Hans and Oskar Gerson was featured in a *Neue Werkkunst* book of 1928. Major office buildings, such as the neo-Gothic-detailed Ballinhaus of 1923-24 (see p. 117) and the Thaliahof of 1922, were included in that volume alongside various conservatively expressionist and more functionalist apartments, many of which have been destroyed (see Fig. 3). After Hans's death in 1931, Oskar remained in Germany, but in the Third Reich jobs were few and far between for a Jewish architect, even a famous one: from 1933 Jews were excluded from private practice, as they could not become members of the Reichskulturkammer (Reich Chamber of Culture). Oskar Gerson's only work at this time was for the interior of a building on Hartungstrasse housing a Jewish cultural organization, the Jüdischer Kulturbund. Eventually realizing that he would receive no further commissions, he left Germany in 1939 for Northern California, where he practiced until his death. As an émigré architect in America, he never achieved the success that he had enjoyed in Germany. In this, his career was similar to that of Karl Schneider, who in 1938 also left his successful Hamburg practice for a new life in Chicago as a designer of home furnishings for Sears, Roebuck and Company. Their common plight was the typical one of immigrant professionals not acquiring a prominence in their adopted country comparable to that which they had attained in their homeland. Ludwig Mies van der Rohe, Walter Gropius, and a few others were the exceptions to this rule; their move to America enabled them, through supportive connections, to develop their careers further.

If Höger and the Gerson brothers were leaders in commercial and residential design in Hamburg in the twenties, their equivalent in the design of public buildings was Fritz Schumacher. Bremen-born Schumacher received his training from Gabriel von Seidl in Munich, and made his mark on Hamburg while serving

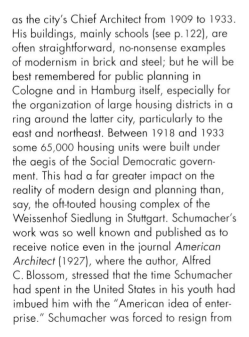

Fig. 1   Karl Schneider. Kunstverein gallery, Neue Rabenstrasse 25, Hamburg, 1930 (demolished). From *Moderne Bauformen* (1931).

Fig. 2   Fritz Höger. Town Hall, Wilhelmshaven-Rüstringen, 1928. From *Deutsche Bauzeitung* (May 10, 1930).

Fig. 3   Hans and Oskar Gerson. Housing block of 600 units, Hamburg-Barmbek, 1927 (demolished). From *Die Architekten-Brüder Gerson* (1928).

as the city's Chief Architect from 1909 to 1933. His buildings, mainly schools (see p. 122), are often straightforward, no-nonsense examples of modernism in brick and steel; but he will be best remembered for public planning in Cologne and in Hamburg itself, especially for the organization of large housing districts in a ring around the latter city, particularly to the east and northeast. Between 1918 and 1933 some 65,000 housing units were built under the aegis of the Social Democratic government. This had a far greater impact on the reality of modern design and planning than, say, the oft-touted housing complex of the Weissenhof Siedlung in Stuttgart. Schumacher's work was so well known and published as to receive notice even in the journal *American Architect* (1927), where the author, Alfred C. Blossom, stressed that the time Schumacher had spent in the United States in his youth had imbued him with the "American idea of enterprise." Schumacher was forced to resign from

his post when the Nazis came to power in 1933, after which he went into retirement. Gustav Oelsner, his counterpart in Altona (see pp. 126-27), also lost his post then for political reasons. When, in 1937, Hamburg, Altona, and other towns and districts were unified in a Greater Hamburg, this was very much a consequence of Schumacher's large-scale approach to planning around the city center.

After the change in government, a new personality eventually appeared on the scene to replace Schumacher in his leadership role among Hamburg architects. Konstanty Gutschow was educated from 1922 to 1924 at the Technische Hochschule (polytechnic) of Stuttgart under Heinz Wetzel, although his training was influenced by other faculty members, such as Paul Bonatz and Paul Schmitthenner. After graduation in 1926 and work in Stuttgart, Gutschow returned to his native Hamburg for a brief stint working for

Höger on the *Anzeiger* building in Hanover (see p. 159). Gutschow's own work in the late twenties evinced a modernist style similar to that of his modernist masonry mentors in Stuttgart (see pp. 188-89). A constructed example of his work from this period is the Göttsche apartment block of 1929 in Altona-Stellingen. However, like other architects of the time, such as Fritz August Breuhaus de Groot, Cäsar Pinnau, and Carl August Bembé (see pp. 14-16), Gutschow was flexible in his approach to design, responding equally well to a variety of situations. His 1932 single-family homes for the Stadtrand housing development demonstrate his versatility in designing either traditional or modernist residences. After the Nazis' accession to power in 1933, he continued to design both conservative and modernist buildings. He is famous for his 1937-41 masonry skyscraper design for the Gauhochhaus in Hamburg, which was based in part on American skyscrapers of the thirties. This project was a

Fig. 4   Konstanty Gutschow and Klaus Hoffmann. Cactus house, Zoologischer Garten, Am Dammtor, Hamburg, 1935 (demolished).

Fig. 5   Carl Winand. Schauburg, Am Millerntor, Hamburg-St. Pauli, 1926-27 (demolished). From *Moderne Bauformen* (1928).

Fig. 6   Carl Winand. Hanseatenhalle sport facility on the Elbe River, Rothenburgstrasse and Ausschläger Strasse, Ausschläger Elbdeich, Hamburg, 1934-35 (demolished). From *Der Baumeister* (1935).

direct result of the plan to unify Hamburg and Altona architecturally and make Greater Hamburg the equivalent of an American metropolis such as New York, but it did not progress much beyond the design stage. Gutschow also designed and built such smaller scale buildings as autobahn bridges and, in 1935, the appropriately all-glass cactus houses in the Zoologischer Garten (Fig. 4). The latter, as well as a range of buildings that included works by Höger, Schumacher, the Gersons, and Schneider, were published in an article by Gutschow himself, "Ein Architekt besucht Hamburg," in *Moderne Bauformen* in 1938 (pp. 569-74). Later, Gutschow headed a team of architects directed by Albert Speer to plan the reconstruction of Hamburg and other German cities after the devastation wrought by bombings in 1943. After the war, he continued in reconstruction work in Hamburg and maintained a thriving practice in institutional and health care design, planning postwar modernist hospital complexes in Tübingen (1952) and Düsseldorf (1961-78).

Alongside the prolific Höger, the Gersons, and the politically influential Schumacher and Gutschow, many architects practiced modernist design in Hamburg with approaches different both from those of these more famous designers and from that of Schneider. Elingius and Schramm, Distel and Grubitz, Dyrssen and Averhoff, Friedrich Ostermeyer, Hinsch and Deimling, and Bomhoff and Schöne are among those who are fairly well known to architectural historians. Carl Winand, however, has faded into obscurity. He was an active and versatile designer who could work in Art Deco (see Fig. 5), functionalist (see Fig. 6), and more traditional modes (see p. 138). Although there seemed to be some recognition of his architectural abilities in the twenties and thirties, he has not been acknowledged since. Comparable situations existed in Bremen, Kiel, Lübeck, and other cities in northern Germany, where local masters contributed to the cityscapes of these and like urban centers. Yet no other architects in the north could rival the impact of Schumacher, Höger, and Gutschow — with the possible exception of Karl Elkart (see pp. 157-58). Although his architecture was always more conservative than that of Schumacher and Gutschow, he shaped the appearance of Hanover much as they did that of Hamburg, especially as regards public parks, transportation facilities, housing developments, and such public buildings as schools and libraries. Elkart, however, practiced in an official capacity both before and after the Nazis took control in 1933.

In short, the major shipping and industrial centers of northern Germany contained — and contain — a variety of modern design expressions if one is prepared to look beyond preconceived notions of the term "modern," notions that exclude expressions of regionalism in favor of an internationalized modern style. Thus, there is far more to be seen than the works of Schneider or the all too frequently reproduced images of Hugo Häring's starkly massed barn at the Gut Garkau farm of 1924. These brick and concrete buildings are simply part of the larger pattern of brick expressionist and eclectically modernist buildings in northern Germany at this time.

It is interesting that expressionism, both in the fine arts and architecture, had supporters among the officials responsible for Nazi cultural programs, at least for a few years after the 1933 takeover. In part, this relates to the connection between expressionism and the search for a typically German modern style to oppose an international one that, in terms of Nazi ideology, was implicitly socialist and communist. In addition, the initial approbation, and later tolerance, of this mode of design, and of such practitioners of it as Höger and Elkart, was based on a respect for craft traditions that Nazi arts policy shared with the architects themselves. It was, perhaps, this very alliance of interests, however marginal, that condemned expressionist buildings in the

eyes of the immediate postwar period, when the vanquished needed to conform to the internationalist architecture of their Allied victors. Certainly, brick expressionism, and even prewar street patterns, received scant attention in the post-1945 rebuilding of Hamburg and, especially, Hanover, giving way to the kind of high-rise architecture and planning that typified fifties modernism throughout the world, even in countries behind the "iron curtain." This rejection, conscious or unconscious, of regional modern traditions has distorted our image of north German architecture in the twenties and thirties. It is only recently that brick expressionist and eclectic modernist traditions have come to be appreciated by architects in Hamburg, with several buildings from the eighties and early nineties evincing a creative response to the local architectural heritage of the twenties.

Sources in Brief

There is a wealth of literature on Höger and Schumacher. Among recent sources consulted were *Fritz Höger: Baumeister-Zeichnungen,* exhibition catalogue (Berlin, 1977); Piergiacomo Bucciarelli, *Fritz Höger* (Verona, 1991); Hartmut Frank, "The Metropolis as a Comprehensive Work of Art: Fritz Schumacher's Plan for Cologne, Document of a Forgotten Modernity," in *The 1920s: Age of the Metropolis,* ed. Jean Clair, exhibition catalogue (Montreal, 1991), pp. 321-35; Werner Kayser, *Fritz Schumacher, Architekt und Städtebauer: Eine Bibliographie,* Arbeitshefte zur Denkmalpflege in Hamburg 5 (Hamburg, 1984); Edward H. Teague, *Fritz Schumacher: A Bibliography,* Vance Bibliographies A 1469 (Monticello, Illinois, 1985); and Hermann Hipp, "Fritz Schumachers Hamburg: Die reformierte Grossstadt," in *Moderne Architektur in Deutschland 1900 bis 1950: Reform und Tradition,* ed. Vittorio Magnano Lampugnani and Romana Schneider (Stuttgart, 1992), pp. 151-84. Earlier literature consulted included *Fritz Höger: Der niederdeutsche Backstein-Baumeister* (Wolfshagen-Scharbeutz, 1938); Fritz Schumacher, *Das Werden einer Wohnstadt* (Hamburg, 1932; reprinted 1984); and Alfred C. Blossom, "German Municipal Architecture, Illustrating the Work of Fritz Schumacher," *American Architect* (1927), pp. 709-14.

By contrast, nothing has been published on the Gersons since *Die Architekten-Brüder Gerson,* Neue Werkkunst (Berlin, Leipzig, and Vienna, 1928). Information on them here has come from Hans Gerson's son, Hans Ulrich, who currently resides in El Cerrito, California.

An exhibition on Schneider's work, accompanied by a monograph entitled *Karl Schneider: Leben und Werk (1892-1945),* ed. Robert Koch and Eberhard Pook (Hamburg, 1992), was held while the present publication was being prepared; Schneider's papers are in the Getty Center in Santa Monica, California. See also Robert Koch, "Eine Episode mit Folgen: Karl Schneider und die Landeskunstschule," in *Nordlicht,* ed. Hartmut Frank (Hamburg, 1990), pp. 193-210, and Janis Hendrickson, "Karl Schneider: Leben und Werk," Ph. D. diss. (Hamburg, 1986).

Gutschow's career, though dealt with occasionally in the past, is currently being documented for publication and exhibition by Martina von Limont. Until the appearance of her book, see Werner Durth, *Deutsche Architekten: Biographische Verflechtungen 1900-1970,* 3rd ed. (Wiesbaden and Braunschweig, 1988), passim; Hartmut Frank, "Das Tor der Welt," in *Das ungebaute Hamburg,* ed. Ulrich Höhns (Hamburg, 1991), pp. 78-99; and idem, "Neues Bauen im Nazi-Deutschland," in *Giuseppe Terragni,* ed. Stefan Germer and Achim Preiss (Munich, 1990), pp. 57-72 (esp. 70-71).

For information on the creation and organization of the 1932 International Style exhibition and book, see Terrence Riley, *The International Style: Exhibition 15 and the Museum of Modern Art* (New York, 1991).

Buildings in northern Germany can be found in several local guidebooks: *Architektur in Bremen und Bremerhaven,* ed. Architektenkammer der Freien Hansestadt Bremen (Bremen, 1988); Wolfgang Voigt, *Das Bremer Haus* (Hamburg, 1992); Hartwig Beseler, Klaus Detlefsen, and Kurt Gelhaar, *Architektur in Schleswig-Holstein 1900-1980* (Neumünster, 1980); Hermann Hipp, *Hamburg,* DuMont Kunst-Reiseführer (Cologne, 1989); and Volkwin Marg and Gudrun Fleher, *Architektur in Hamburg seit 1900* (Hamburg, 1983). Of the books on Hamburg cited, Hipp's is the most valuable. Finally, Roland Jaeger and Cornelius Steckner, *Zinnober: Kunstszene Hamburg 1919-1933* (Hamburg, 1983), is a good brief survey of art and architecture in that city between the world wars.

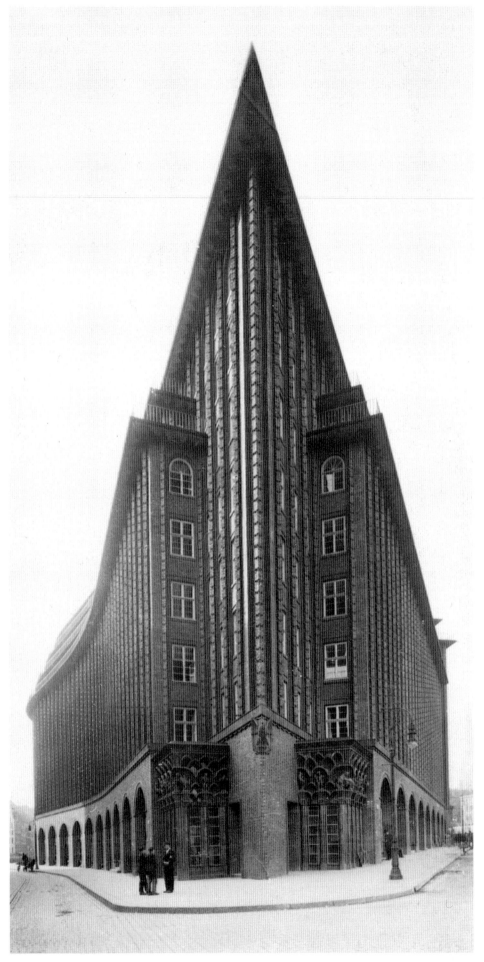

Fritz Höger. Chilehaus, Burchardplatz 1-2, Hamburg, 1922-24. Photographs by the Dransfeld brothers, 1925.

Fritz Höger with Hans and Oskar Gerson. Sprinkenhof, Burchardstrasse 6-14, Hamburg, 1927-43. Central section, 1927-28; west section, 1930-32; east section, 1939-43 (by Höger alone). The building on the left in the top illustration is Rudolf Klophaus's Bartholomay-Haus (1937-38) on Springelwiete. Photographs 1989.

bottom left: Hans and Oskar Gerson. Ballinhaus, or Messberghof, Messberg 1, Hamburg, 1923-24. Photograph 1989.

A walk through Hamburg's *Kontorhaus* quarter is a spectacular experience. Although commercial buildings serving various importers and exporters had been constructed there earlier, especially in the nineteenth and early twentieth centuries, the type reached its summit in the twenties, with major buildings by Fritz Höger, the Gersons, and others. From the late nineteenth century to the beginning of World War II, some three hundred office buildings were constructed in various neighborhoods near the harbor. The jewels among them are the Chilehaus of 1922-24, the Ballinhaus, or Messeberghof, of 1923-24, and the Sprinkenhof of 1927-43, all situated on adjacent blocks. Near to them, however, are examples almost as powerful in impact, from the Montanhof of

top left: Hans and Oskar Gerson. Thaliahof, Alstertor 1, Hamburg, 1921-22. Photograph 1989.

center left: Klophaus, Schoch and zu Putlitz. Mohlenhof, Burchardplatz, Hamburg, 1928-29. Photograph 1989.

right: Distel and Grubitz. Montanhof, Kattrepel 2, Hamburg, 1924-26. Photograph 1989.

bottom: Philipp Schaefer. Karstadt headquarters, Steinstrasse 16-20, Hamburg, 1921-24. Photograph 1989.

Zauleck and Hormann. Stella-Haus, Schaartors-brücke, Hamburg, 1922. Photograph 1991.

Geisler and Wilkening. Hotel Alsterhof, Esplanade 12, Hamburg, 1930. Photograph 1991.

1924-26 by Distel and Grubitz, with its angular bay windows reminiscent of skeletal Chicago School work of the late 1890s and expressionist crystal forms of the 1920s, to the conservative modernism of the Mohlenhof of 1928-29 by Klophaus, Schoch and zu Putlitz. Most of these *Kontorhäuser,* including the Chilehaus, Ballinhaus, and Sprinkenhof, have spectacular staircases and striking courts, the latter feature perhaps related to the open courts in some turn-of-the-century Chicago School buildings by Daniel H. Burnham. Progressing beyond this compact core in the old city center, one encounters a variety of twenties commercial designs. These include examples as disparate as the monumentally classical, yet highly fenestrated, facade of the Karstadt department store headquarters; exuberantly sculpted buildings, such as the Stella-Haus, that bridge the gap between the masonry buildings erected before World War I and the expressionist ones constructed after it;

and such restrained brick boxes as the Hotel Alsterhof and Höger's famed Leder-Schüler Werke of 1927-28. All these were built within a decade of one another. Luckily, some buildings in the *Kontorhaus* district were spared extensive damage during World War II, thus escaping demolition and replacement.

Selected Sources

Architektur in Hamburg seit 1900, sites 42, 43, and 59; Hipp, *Hamburg,* pp. 67-69, 178, 182-86, and 193; "Ein Architekt besucht Hamburg," *Moderne Bauformen* (1938), pp. 569-74 (p. 573 for Hotel Alsterhof); Hans Meyer-Veden and Hermann Hipp, *Hamburger Kontorhäuser* (Berlin, 1988); Rainer Stommer, *Hochhaus: Der Beginn in Deutschland* (Marburg, 1990), pp. 79-99. Selected early articles on the *Kontorhäuser* are: "Der Sprinkenhof in Hamburg," *Deutsche Bauzeitung* (July 13, 1929), pp. 481-86; *Wasmuths Monatshefte für Baukunst und Städtebau* (1929), pp. 225-30; "Hamburgs neues Büroviertel," ibid., p. 137; and "Kontorhaus-Neubau der Mohlenhof in Hamburg," *Deutsche Bauzeitung* (September 28, 1929), pp. 665-67.

opposite: Fritz Schumacher. Finanzbehörde building (left), Dammtorstrasse and Gänsemarkt, Hamburg, 1918-26. The building on the right is the Deutschlandhaus by Block and Hochfeld, 1929. Photograph 1989.

Fritz Schumacher. Ziviljustizgebäude addition, Sievekingplatz, Hamburg, 1927-30. Photograph 1989.

Fritz Schumacher. Gerichtsvollzieheramt building, Drehbahnstrasse west of Dammtorstrasse, Hamburg, 1926-28. Photograph 1989.

Fritz Schumacher's public buildings in the Neustadt (New City) of Hamburg include some of the more prominent examples of modern expressionist brick design in the city, namely, the Finanzbehörde (revenue offices) building of 1918-26 and the 1927-30 additions to the Ziviljustizgebäude (civil courts). Both received extensive coverage in their day as important public buildings, and both were well restored and maintained after the war. A less well

known example of Schumacher's municipal work, near the Finanzbehörde, is the Gerichtsvollzieheramt (bailiff's department) building of 1926-28. The image of this structure, with its decorative repeating towers, is almost that of a fortress, appropriate, in some ways, to the agency within. These municipal buildings represent Schumacher at three stages of his design career in the twenties, as his architecture became progressively more simple. The extent of his achievement is indicated by Block and Hochfeld's curved, *moderne* Deutschlandhaus of 1929 (now refaced) across the street from the Finanzbehörde: in its massing and detailing the latter is in every way superior to the Deutschlandhaus.

Selected Sources

Architektur in Hamburg seit 1900, sites 49, 68, and 73; Hipp, *Hamburg*, p.192; Fritz Schumacher, "Das Gerichtsvollzieheramt an der Drehbahn in Hamburg," *Deutsche Bauzeitung* (April 20, 1929), pp. 289-92; "Der Bau des Deutschlandhauses in Hamburg," *Die Form* (1930), pp.118-19. For several illustrations of the impressive spaces in the civil courts addition, see "Erweiterungsbau des Ziviljustizgebäudes in Hamburg," *Wasmuths Monatshefte für Baukunst und Städtebau* (1930), pp. 468-73, and "Zwei neue Bauten von Oberbaudirektor Fritz Schumacher, Hamburg," *Deutsche Bauzeitung* (January 14, 1931), pp. 37-41.

Of Fritz Schumacher's public buildings, the schools are the most avant-garde or industrial in appearance. Integrating a great deal of glass and steel within the framework of the regional brick style, they were built throughout the twenties to serve the increasing population of those areas formed by Schumacher's own belt of new housing developments around the city center. Although some have received attention — for example, the Meerweinstrasse school, owing to its proximity to the famous Jarrestadt housing — others have gone virtually unnoticed. Important examples still function as schools on Wendenstrasse in Hammerbrook, Adlerstrasse in Barmbek-Ost, near Dulsberg, and Schaudinnstwiete in Barmbek-Nord. Other architects, from Höger to Hinsch and Deimling, Bomhoff and Schöne, and Distel and Grubitz, built public and private or specialized schools in Hamburg, all constructed of unornamented brick and many of them soberly functional in appearance.

Selected Sources

Architektur in Hamburg seit 1900, sites 58, 59, 67, and 75; Hipp, *Hamburg,* pp. 272, 364, 392, 426, 442, and 496; "Ein Architekt besucht Hamburg," pp. 573-74; "Hamburger Schulbauten nach dem Kriege," *Der Baumeister* (1930), pp. 333-39, esp. 336 (Adlerstrasse School); "Hinsch and Deimling: Kaufmännische Berufsschule für Mädchen in Hamburg-Eimsbüttel," *Moderne Bauformen* (1932), pp. 73-75; "Volksschule am Schaudinnsweg in Hamburg," *Deutsche Bauzeitung* (January 20, 1932), pp. 65-70; "Volksschule an der Wendenstrasse," *Der Baumeister* (1930), pp. 484-85; "Zwei neue Hamburger Schulen," *Moderne Bauformen* (1931), pp. 404-11, esp. 404-7 (Wendenstrasse School).

Fritz Schumacher. Meerweinstrasse school, Meerweinstrasse 20-24, Hamburg-Winterhude, 1928-30. Photograph 1989.

Fritz Schumacher. Volksschule, Adlerstrasse, Elise-Lensing-Weg, and Habichtstrasse, Hamburg-Barmbek, 1929-30. Photograph 1989.

opposite:
top left: Distel and Grubitz. Luisenschule, Reinbeker Weg, Hamburg-Bergedorf, 1932. Photograph 1990.

top right: Fritz Höger. Curschmannstrasse Gymnasium, Curschmannstrasse 39 and Breitenfelder Strasse, Hamburg-Hoheluft, 1926-28. Photograph 1989.

Bomhoff and Schöne. Former Kirchenpauer Realgymnasium, Hammer Steindamm 129, Hamburg-Hamm, 1929. Photograph 1991.

bottom left: Fritz Schumacher. Volksschule, Wendenstrasse 162-64, Hamburg-Hammerbrook, 1928-29. Photograph 1989.

bottom right: Hinsch and Deimling. Schlankreye business school, Bundesstrasse 88, Hamburg-Eimsbüttel, 1928-29. Photograph 1989.

The district of Veddel, across the Elbe River just south of Hamburg-Hammerbrook, contains an interesting cluster of apartment buildings by various architects. As in other parts of Hamburg, Schumacher designed public buildings to provide services for residents. His Volksschule Veddel has the glass and steel staircase that was almost his signature in educational buildings. At the southern edge of the housing units on Müggenberg Hafen, next to the police barracks (1926), is the more official-looking Feuerwache (fire station) by him. While its main facade projects an almost historicist image, other parts of the building are more severely modernist in appearance. It has been altered somewhat, particularly in its fenestration and in the garage doors, above which the title "Feuerwache 12" originally appeared. A later addition is on the east side of the building. In spite of these changes, the fire station is still used as such. A similar, yet more functionalist, fire station by Schumacher stood in Finkenwerder, but it was demolished several years ago.

Selected Sources
Architektur in Hamburg seit 1900, site 57; Hipp, *Hamburg,* pp. 278-79; "Ein Architekt besucht Hamburg," pp. 571 and 574; "Die Feuerwache an der Veddel in Hamburg," *Deutsche Bauzeitung* (January 1-2, 1929, pp. 2-7; "Feuerwache im Hamburger Hafen," *Deutsche Bauzeitung* (April 26, 1933), p. 333.

Fritz Schumacher. Volksschule, Wilhelmsburger Strasse, Slomanstieg, and Slomanstrasse, Hamburg-Veddel, 1930. Photograph 1991.

Fritz Schumacher. Feuerwache12 (now Feuerwache Veddel), Zollhafen, Hamburg-Veddel, 1927-28. Photograph 1991.

When the works of Hans and Oskar Gerson appeared in the *Neue Werkkunst* series in 1928 these architects were at the peak of their career. Most of the buildings published were apartment houses, and a number of them still can be seen in Hamburg. They range from the more traditional downtown living units placed atop stores on Steinstrasse to the larger housing blocks of the twenties in Eppendorf. In the first decade of the century, before building their conservative examples of expressionist work, the Gersons specialized in rather historicist villas and houses, some of which still exist in the affluent western suburbs of Hamburg. Other apartment houses built by a variety of architects not so very long after the Gersons' show how much things had changed since the conservatism of the early twenties. Yet those by the Gerson brothers have proven to be better integrated in their residential surroundings than some more radical design solutions from the end of the twenties.

Selected Sources
Architektur in Hamburg seit 1900, site 45; Hipp, *Hamburg,* esp. pp. 338-40 (the Gersons' houses in the western suburbs) and 396 (their Haynstrasse project).

opposite:
top left: Hans and Oskar Gerson. Apartments, offices, and stores, Steinstrasse 12-14, Hamburg, 1923. Photograph 1989.

top right: Hans and Oskar Gerson. Apartment house, Breitenfelder Strasse and Husumer Strasse, Hamburg-Eppendorf, 1924-25. Photograph 1989.

bottom left: Hans and Oskar Gerson. Apartment house, Löhrsweg 1, Hamburg-Eppendorf, 1925. Photograph 1989.

bottom right: Hans and Oskar Gerson. Apartment house, Haynstrasse 2-4 and Löhrsweg, Hamburg-Eppendorf 1923. Photograph 1989.

Gustav Oelsner was Fritz Schumacher's
counterpart in Altona, the town just west of
Hamburg where he served as the senator in
charge of building from 1923 to 1933. He had
previously occupied official posts in Breslau
(now Wrocław, Poland), as Regierungsbau-
meister from 1904 to 1911, and Kattowitz
(now Katowice), as Stadtbaurat from 1911 to
1922. Much of his work in Altona from the late
twenties has survived, from various housing
projects and the famous Haus der Jugend
(youth center) to the court of the Arbeitsamt
(employment office) building. All these structures employ light-colored bricks or ceramic
tiles, often within a skeletal framework of reinforced concrete. After Oelsner's departure
from Altona in 1933, he traveled to the United
States in 1937 and, in 1939, taught in Istanbul.

He remained abroad until after World War II,
returning to his native country in 1949 to work
on Hamburg's reconstruction plan (through
1952). He died in Hamburg and is buried near
Schumacher in Ohlsdorf Cemetery.

Selected Sources

Architektur in Hamburg seit 1900, sites 52, 54, 55,
77, and 79; "Haus der Jugend Altona" and "Arbeitsamt Altona," *Der Baumeister* (1930), pp. 337-39;
Christoph Timm, *Altona: Altstadt und Nord,* Denk-
maltopographie Bundesrepublik Deutschland, Hamburg Inventar: Bezirk Altona (Hamburg, 1987),
pp. 55, 70-71, and 90-91; idem, *Gustav Oelsner und
das neue Altona* (Hamburg, 1989).

Other architects contributed to the extensive
program of housing construction in Hamburg
and towns nearby in the twenties. Fritz
Höger's Lilienthalblock of 1927-28, tucked
away near the airport on Hans-Grade-Weg,
was well known in its day, though it receives
little attention today, perhaps because it is so
far from the city center. Carl Winand's contemporaneous apartment building at Am Hasen-
berg 45, also built on the periphery of the city,
near the main cemetery, is largely ignored too,
despite its dramatic siting near water that
flows into the city lake, the Alster. Of housing
published in the twenties, one urbanistically
interesting, but now overlooked, block
deserves particular notice. This is the development by Walter Hinsch and Erwin Deimling
published in *Der Baumeister* in 1930. Its
curved facades on Alsterdorfer Strasse and
Buchsbaumweg present a dramatic, sweeping
front in both yellow and red brick — a hom-
age, it would seem, to the two types of brick
building popularized in the twenties by Gustav
Oelsner and Fritz Schumacher, respectively.
The main, raised section in the center has seen
some reconstruction.

Selected Sources

Hipp, *Hamburg,* pp. 461-62; Hans Harms and Dirk
Schubert, *Wohnen in Hamburg: Ein Stadtführer*
(Hamburg, 1989), pp. 266-68.

Hinsch and Deimling. Apartment building, Alsterdorfer Strasse, Braamkamp, and Buchsbaumweg,
Hamburg-Winterhude, c. 1929. Photograph 1989.

top left: Hermann and Paul Frank. Apartment building, Dulsberg housing estate, Oberschlesische Strasse, Hamburg-Barmbek, 1929-33. Photograph 1989.

top right: Karl Schneider. Apartment building, Habichtplatz, Hamburg-Barmbek (Nord), 1928 (rebuilt 1950). Photograph 1990.

Karl Schneider with Elingius and Schramm. Apartment building, Possmoorweg and Barmbeker Strasse, Hamburg-Winterhude, 1928. Photograph 1989.

Hamburg's most famous apartment buildings are in the Jarrestadt and the Dulsberg estates, for both of which a variety of architects designed blocks within Fritz Schumacher's overall plan. At Dulsberg, the most dramatic blocks, completed around 1933 to the designs of Hermann and Paul Frank, are those whose curved corners line Oberschlesische Strasse. An article on the Barmbek district in the *Hamburger Fremdenblatt* (January 8, 1944) prominently featured a photograph of these blocks in its history of the site in the twenties and thirties — published at a time when housing blocks in Barmbek and the Dulsberg estate had already been heavily damaged by the bombing raids of 1943.

Perhaps the most striking of the Jarrestadt blocks are the great gateway buildings at the center of the complex. These were designed by Karl Schneider, with dramatically sweeping balconies highlighting the corners in much the same way as in his Wiesendamm flats nearby and his Possmoorweg and Habichtplatz apartment buildings. The last of these, though destroyed in 1943, was rebuilt as before in 1950.

Selected Sources

Architektur in Hamburg seit 1900, sites 74, 82, and 84; *Hamburg und seine Bauten,* p. 150; Harms and Schubert, *Wohnen in Hamburg,* pp. 238-41 and 244-48; Hipp, *Hamburg,* pp. 425-27 and 435-37; idem, *Wohnstadt Hamburg* (Hamburg, 1982); Rolf Spörhase, "Vom Hamburg-Altonaer Wohnungsbau," *Moderne Bauformen* (1929), pp. 489-507.

Friedrich Ostermeyer was one of Hamburg's most prolific designers of housing, working from the twenties through the post-World War II period. His most famous works are the Friedrich-Ebert-Hof and the Hohenzollernring apartment buildings, but his other late twenties projects, though less publicized, are equally interesting. They run the gamut from structures that employ brick sculpturally, and have actual sculptures attached, to more plainly designed facades and masses. A good example of the former is the Fuhlsbüttler Strasse apartment block, curving down an irregular street with sculpted brick courts on the inside and sculpture itself on the building. Comparable in scale to the Friedrich-Ebert-Hof, and commissioned by the same self-help organization, is the somewhat simpler Selbsthilfe block on Pinneberger Chaussee (now Kieler Strasse). Much of this complex of five irregularly planned, open-court buildings still survives, with only one of the five structures destroyed (block V on the northwest corner of Kieler Strasse and Langenfelder Strasse). At the uppermost stories of some of the buildings, large windows have replaced the far smaller originals.

Selected Sources

Architektur in Hamburg seit 1900, sites 71 and 78; Hipp, *Hamburg,* pp. 307 and 331; *Moderne Bauformen* (1929), pp. 508-9 (Fuhlsbüttler Strasse and Pinneberger Chaussee apartment buildings).

Friedrich Ostermeyer. Apartment building, Fuhlsbüttler Strasse and Dennerstrasse, near Habichtplatz, Hamburg-Barmbek (Nord), 1928. Photographs 1990.

Friedrich Ostermeyer. Apartment building, Kieler Strasse and Waidmannstrasse, Hamburg-Altona, 1926-28. Photograph 1991.

Elingius and Schramm. Kinderkrankenhaus addition, Bülowstrasse east of Grünebergstrasse, Hamburg-Altona, 1929-31. Photographs 1991.

Aside from Gustav Oelsner's Schwesternhaus (nursing home) of 1926 and Karl Lembke's Stadtbad (municipal baths) of 1928-29 in the Harburg district, Hamburg's health care buildings have been published only in Hermann Hipp's comprehensive guide to the city. The most dramatic and, perhaps, least eclectically modernist of these is the addition to the Kinderkrankenhaus (children's hospital) in Altona by Elingius and Schramm. Its highly symmetrical plan, low-rise scale, and brick and masonry details relate to comparable features in the older hospital buildings that surround it. More historicist in detailing are the hospitals and related buildings designed by Hermann Distel and August Grubitz, architects who had been partners since 1911 and who, although they built large housing and office (see p.118) complexes, were really specialists in hospital design. Much of their work still exists as published in the twenties and early thirties, despite the minor alterations to be expected in buildings that are some sixty years old. The hospital they designed for the German-Jewish community in 1929-30 is perhaps the most modernist of their health care structures. Forced to fulfill another function during the Third Reich, it nonetheless still stands on Hein-Hoyer-Strasse between Clemens-Schultz-Strasse and Simon-von-Utrecht-Strasse. In contrast with the work of Elingius and Schramm, which has received considerable coverage, that of Distel and Grubitz, equally influential in the twenties and thirties, still awaits monographic treatment.

Selected Sources

"Ein Architekt besucht Hamburg," p. 573 (Bethanien Hospital and Kinderkrankenhaus, Altona); Hipp, *Hamburg,* pp. 329, 398, and 487; *Hermann Distel: Krankenhäuser,* ed. Werner Hegemann (Hellerau, 1930), pp. 29-30 (Bethanien Hospital), 55-57 (German-Jewish Hospital), and 66 (AOK building); Heinrich Schmieden, *Krankenhausbau in neuer Zeit* (Kirchhain, 1930), pp. 107-10 (Bethanien Hospital); Rudolf Schmidt, "Das Stresowstift in Hamburg-Volksdorf," *Deutsche Bauzeitung* (February 3, 1932), pp. 105-7.

Distel and Grubitz, Rear bay window, AOK (Allgemeine Ortskrankenkasse; General Health Insurance Fund) building, Burgstrasse and Bethesdastrasse, Hamburg-Hamm, 1925. Photograph 1990.

Distel and Grubitz. Bethanien Hospital addition, Martinistrasse 20, Hamburg-Eppendorf, 1927-28. Photograph 1989.

Distel and Grubitz. Stresowstift home for the elderly, Farmsener Landstrasse 60, Hamburg-Volksdorf, 1927. Photograph 1991.

Dyrssen and Averhoff. Fuhlsbüttel airport, Hamburg, 1927-28 (altered). Photograph 1989.

Karl Schneider. Standard gasoline station, Rothenbaumchaussee and Hansastrasse, Hamburg-Rothenbaum, c.1930-32 (demolished). From *Moderne Bauformen* (1934).

Preussische Staatshochbauverwaltung (Prussian State Building Administration). Seefahrtsschule, Rainvilleterrasse 4, Hamburg-Ottensen, 1931-32. Photograph 1991.

Extant buildings of the twenties and thirties in Hamburg include good examples of structures for transportation, though some have been altered almost beyond recognition. Two painfully obvious instances are Fuhlsbüttel airport and the S-Bahn station Alte Wöhr. Fuhlsbüttel's airport, the work of Friedrich Dyrssen and Peter Averhoff, dates from 1927-28. Behind a postwar addition lies the original curved terminal facade, complete with dramatic curved corner windows at the entrance. Extensions currently under construction, and no doubt future additions, will alter the appearance even further, but at least it has not been demolished, like the famous airport buildings at Travemünde by Fritz Schumacher. The Alte Wöhr S-Bahn station, built in 1939 by an architect named Eitner, stands roughly as it did when constructed, though over the years it has suffered the physical neglect and abuse typically visited upon urban transportation structures. Karl Schneider's overpass of 1930 at the Kellinghusenstrasse overhead railroad station has received better treatment in reality and in publications; its influence may be seen as far way as Glogau (now Głogow, Poland). In connection with buildings related to road and sea transport mention should be made of Schneider's skeletal Standard gasoline station on Rothenbaumchaussee and Hansastrasse, which, however, was long ago replaced by another station, now occupied by Esso. On the other hand, the Seefahrtsschule (Seafarers' School) of 1931-32, though slightly altered, imparts a good overall impression of what it was like originally.

Selected Sources

Architektur in Hamburg seit 1900, site 85 (Kellinghusenstrasse station; cf. "Das neue Bahnhofsgebäude in Glogau," *Deutsche Bauzeitung* [October 30, 1935], pp. 874-79); *Hamburg und seine Bauten,* pp. 256 (Alte Wöhr station) and 267-69 (Fuhlsbüttel airport); Hipp, *Hamburg,* p. 461; "Neuere Hamburger Bauten: Flugbahnhof in Hamburg-Fuhlsbüttel," *Moderne Bauformen* (1932), pp. 63-65; "Flughafen Hamburg," *Der Baumeister* (1930), pp. 366-69; "Standard-Tankstelle an der Rothenbaum-Chaussee bei Hamburg," *Moderne Bauformen* (1934), pp. 194-95; "Die Seeflughalle des Hanseatischen Flughafens bei Travemünde," *Wasmuths Monatshefte für Baukunst und Städtebau* (1928), pp. 523-25.

As with buildings in the commercial sector, industrial structures in Hamburg have had their fair share of good designers. Buildings by modernists as different as Karl Schneider and Fritz Höger still exist. Prime examples are Höger's famous 1927 Neuerburg cigarette factory at Walddörfer Strasse 103 in Wandsbek, its brick detailing akin to a medieval mason's masterwork, and the greatly altered Röntgen factory of 1929-30 by Schneider, which stands at Röntgenstrasse 22-26 in the midst of a much changed industrial complex near the airport. Two further industrial buildings relate to Hamburg's food products and the agricultural basis of the north German economy. The striking Voss Margarine works, or at least the entry pavilion, was restored in 1989 as part of a large complex of insurance company buildings. It houses exhibition space for the local Architektenkammer (architects' association) as well as the Hamburgisches Architekturarchiv. Hamburg's reputation for beer is reflected in its cityscape. The Bavaria and St. Pauli brewery is prominently situated above the old harbor and boasts a dramatic brick and masonry addition by Elingius and Schramm from 1936, complete with picture windows to view the large fermentation vats. Finally, the harbor contains some spectacular *Kühlhäuser* (cold storage warehouses) from this period, such as Fritz Schumacher's Herings-Kühlhaus of 1928 on Am Hübenerkai and Otto Hoyer's slightly altered, somewhat expressionist Kühlhaus Ross of 1926, which could hold some 144,000 eggs!

Grell and Pruter. Voss Margarine factory (now Hamburgisches Architekturarchiv), Bramfelder Strasse 140, Hamburg-Barmbek, 1925-26. Photograph 1990.

Elingius and Schramm. Addition to Bavaria and St. Pauli brewery, Taubenstrasse and Nochstrasse, Hamburg, 1936-38. From *Moderne Bauformen* (1940).

Selected Sources

Architektur in Hamburg seit 1900, sites 47 (Voss works) and 56 (Kühlhaus Ross); "Einige Bauten mit Stahlskelett," *Deutsche Bauzeitung* (June 7, 1930), p. 366 (Kühlhaus Ross); *Hamburg und seine Bauten,* pp. 187 (St. Pauli Brewery) and 205 (Kühlhaus Ross); Hipp, *Hamburg,* pp. 445 (Röntgen factory) and 469 (Neuerburg factory); Stommer, *Hochhaus,* pp. 196-97 (Kühlhaus Ross); "Karl Schneider: Röntgenröhrenfabrik," *Moderne Bauformen* (1932), pp. 491-95; "Verwaltungsgebäude und Brauerei in Hamburg," *Moderne Bauformen* (1940), pp. 117-21; "Zigarettenfabrik Haus Neuerburg, Hamburg-Wandsbek," *Deutsche Bauzeitung* (April 18, 1928), pp. 273-77.

Hamburg's war memorials have been extensively published in various histories and guides. Two from the 1930s in the city center evince quite different approaches. In a 1930 competition architect Klaus Hoffmann, with sculptor Ernst Barlach, won the commission to erect a war memorial slab on the water near the Rathaus (city hall) marketplace. Its design, with concentric steps leading into the water of the Klein-Alster and an incised relief by Barlach, is compelling in its abstract simplicity. Equally powerful, yet representational and eclectically modernist in character, is sculptor Richard Kuöhl's 1934-36 memorial to the dead of the 76th Infantry Regiment. Kuöhl was one of Hamburg's most important architectural sculptors, his works ornamenting such major buildings of the twenties as Fritz Schumacher's Finanzbehörde and Fritz Höger's Chilehaus (see pp. 116, 120). He encircled his horizontal memorial block with a frieze of marching soldiers that forms part of an abstract pattern. Both monuments include post-World War II commemorations to the fallen.

Selected Sources
Architektur in Hamburg seit 1900, sites 86 and 96;
Ein Kriegsdenkmal in Hamburg (Hamburg, 1979).

Richard Kuöhl. Memorial to the 76th Infantry Regiment, Am Dammtor, Hamburg, 1934-36. Photograph 1990.

Klaus Hoffmann with Ernst Barlach. War memorial near the Rathaus marketplace, Hamburg, 1930-31. Photograph 1989.

top left: Sckopp and Vortmann. DAG-Haus, Karl-Muck-Platz, Hamburg, 1921-22, 1929-30. Photograph 1989.

top right: Rudolf Brüning. Shellhaus (now BATIG-Haus), Alsterufer 4-5, Hamburg, 1929-31. Photograph 1990.

Elingius and Schramm. Hamburg-Mannheimer Versicherung building, Alsterufer 1-3, Hamburg, 1934-35. Photograph 1991.

Hamburg had its share of modernist masonry office buildings in the twenties and thirties, though relatively few in comparison with their brick expressionist brethren. One, the Volksfürsorge (public welfare) building of 1930-31 by Hermann Distel, still stands at An der Alster 57, but has been completely resurfaced. Two others, the Shellhaus by Düsseldorf architect Rudolf Brüning and the brick and masonry DAG-Haus by Sckopp and Vortmann, are also extant, and in a form that is closer to their original appearance. Both incorporate relief sculptures in their bold, simple massing. Boldly massed office buildings continued to be constructed in Hamburg during the Third Reich, but with abstract classical patterns incised as decoration. Two particularly striking examples

are by Elingius and Schramm. Erich Elingius and Gottfried Schramm formed their partnership in 1924, as successor to Frejtag and Elingius; the firm still exists today, as Schramm, von Bassewitz and Hupertz. Elingius and Schramm also built houses, hospitals, clubs, and factories, works that reveal the firm to have been adept at designing in a variety of styles. During World War II they worked with Konstanty Gutschow on plans to rebuild Hamburg. After the war the successor firm participated in the reconstruction of the city, and continued to design new houses, apartment blocks, office buildings, and even subway stations there during the fifties, sixties, and seventies.

Selected Sources

Architektur in Hamburg seit 1900, sites 80 (DAG-Haus) and 93 (Hamburg-Mannheimer Versicherung); Hipp, *Hamburg*, pp. 261 (Volksfürsorge building) and 369 (Shellhaus); Jürgen Elingius and Christiane Leiska, *Erich Elingius: Ein Architekt in Hamburg* (Hamburg, 1989); Schramm, von Bassewitz and Hupertz, *Häuser aus einem Hause* (Hamburg, 1985); "Das Haus der Volksfürsorge in Hamburg," *Deutsche Bauzeitung* (February 24, 1932), pp. 165-67; "Hochhaus des Deutschnationalen Handlungsgehilfen-Verbandes in Hamburg," *Deutsche Bauzeitung* (September 16, 1931), pp. 447-52; "Neues Bürohaus in Hamburg," *Der Baumeister* (1936), pp. 235-39; "Neue Grossbauten in Hamburg," *Der Baumeister* (1936), pp. 1-7; "Das Shellhaus in Hamburg," *Monatshefte für Baukunst und Städtebau* (1932), pp. 399-401; "Das Standardhaus in Hamburg," *Moderne Bauformen* (1938), pp. 580-84.

Elingius and Schramm. Standardhaus (now HWWA Institut für Wirtschaftsforschung), Neuer Jungfernstieg 21, Hamburg, 1937. Photograph 1989.

left: Rudolf Klophaus, Alfred Puls and Emil Richter, Wilhelm Behrens, Hans Ludwig, and others. Sanierungsgebiet, Rademachergang, Hamburg-Neustadt, 1934-36. Photograph 1989.

Rudolf Klophaus. Altstädter Hof, Alstädter Strasse 11-13, Hamburg-Altstadt, 1936-37. Photograph 1989.

Altstädter Hof, Olympic Games relief by Richard Kuöhl.

Hamburg still possesses numerous examples of housing and homes constructed during the Third Reich. The most famous are the projects of the urban renewal Sanierungsgebiet and the Altstädter Hof, both from the mid-thirties.

Carl Winand. Legienstrasse housing estate, Im Ried, Vierbergen, and Riedstieg, Hamburg-Horn-Geest, 1937-38. Photographs 1989.

Herbert Sprotte with Peter Neve. Apartment house, Krochmannstrasse and Ohlsdorfer Strasse, Hamburg-Winterhude, 1938. Photograph 1989.

Willy Eggers. Single-family houses, Blankenstieg, Alsterdorf Garden City, Hamburg, 1937. Photograph 1989.

Elingius and Schramm. Two-family houses, Fontenayallee, Hamburg-Rotherbaum, 1934-35. Photograph 1990.

Willy Eggers. House, Borgweg 17, Hamburg-Winterhude, 1936 (added to and altered, especially windows). Photographs 1989.

Both incorporate clearly historicist forms and compare tellingly with the less reserved, but more simply designed expressionist and modernist predecessors built throughout Fritz Schumacher's and Gustav Oelsner's housing districts. Other apartment buildings are less well known and rather less overtly historicist, combining some modern features, such as large windows or stuccoed planes, with traditional roof forms. Individual homes of this period range from developments of cottages and single-family houses in the Alsterdorf district to two-family homes by Elingius and Schramm. All these are brick houses not dissimilar to ones built in Britain and the United States in the late thirties and early forties.

Selected Sources

Architektur in Hamburg seit 1900, sites 94 and 98; *Hamburg und seine Bauten,* pp. 24-25; "Hamburger Einfamilienhäuser," *Moderne Bauformen* (1942), pp. 55-60; Schramm, von Bassewitz and Hupertz, *Häuser aus einem Hause,* pp. 62-63; Harms and Schubert, *Wohnen in Hamburg,* pp. 82-84 and 253-55; "Elingius und Schramm, Hamburg: Zweifamilienhäuser am Fontenay," *Moderne Bauformen* (1937), p. 142; "Herbert Sprotte: Miethäuser in Hamburg," *Moderne Bauformen* (1940), pp. 177-87; "Willy Eggers, Hamburg: Mehrfamilienhaus mit Druckerei," *Moderne Bauformen* (1942), pp. 61-62; "Volks-wohnungen in Hamburg-Horn-Geest," *Moderne Bauformen* (1940), pp. 415-20.

Shortly after the outbreak of war in 1939, a series of circular air raid bunkers appeared near various transportation nodes in Hamburg to offer shelter to inhabitants in transit. Built with historicist details to blend into the city fabric in the manner of water towers, these were an ingenious local solution to the problem of protection from air raids. They are constructed entirely of reinforced concrete, but decorated with brick and masonry as contextual additions to the cityscape. These so-called "System Zombeck" bunkers of 1939-40 have a spiral floor or ramp around a central core. Their shape was probably influenced by bomb-deflecting shelters used by the French in World War I. According to official statistics, each shelter could accommodate some six hundred people, but they often held several times that number. These historicist responses to an urban defense problem had counterparts in other German cities, such as Cologne and Hanover, where bunkers also fitted into the urban context in a historicist way. Lower, functionalist, rectilinear designs were developed by Konstanty Gutschow and his architects from 1940 to 1942 for camouflage within housing complexes and residential areas, and a number of these bunkers survive too. Like their round predecessors, they often have walls ranging from about three to ten feet in thickness. The square bunkers were designed to shelter roughly the same number of people as the "Zombeck" type, but, with increasing risk of serious air attacks — not foreseen at the beginning of the war — came a more comprehensive solution to air raid shelters. These were often designed by Friedrich Tamms, a close associate of Albert Speer who had been trained as a modernist and was to have a highly successful career as city planner and architect in Düsseldorf after the war. From 1942 to 1944 he used his engineering skills to build enormous concrete, castlelike shelters in cities throughout the Third Reich, from Vienna and Berlin to Hamburg. These had walls some six to ten feet thick and were often built in city parks. Each could shelter tens of thousands of people, as well as accommodate searchlights,

opposite:
top left: Air raid bunker, near Baumwall and the harbor, Hamburg, 1939-40. Photograph 1991.

top right: Air raid bunker, northeast corner of Dobbelersweg and Döhnerstrasse, Hamburg-Hamm, c.1941-42. Photograph 1989.

Friedrich Tamms. Bunker, Heiligengeistfeld, Hamburg-St. Pauli, 1942-43. Photograph 1989.

anti-aircraft guns, and radar. Despite the seeming indestructibility of all these types of shelter, a number of people suffocated in them during the fire storm produced by the "Operation Gomorrah" bombing of Hamburg on July 27/28, 1943, which killed some forty thousand people. The fire storm was centered in the east and northeast of the city and, together with the bombing, destroyed large sections of the housing districts there, which included the famous twenties Karstadt store by Philipp Schaefer, where six hundred people alone lost their lives. Examples of all three types of bomb shelter survive in Hamburg — a constant reminder of the horrors of life there half a century ago.

Selected Sources

Architektur in Hamburg seit 1900, sites 100 and 101; *Hamburg und seine Bauten,* pp.135-36; Durth, *Deutsche Architekten,* passim for Tamms; Hans Brunswig, *Feuersturm über Hamburg* (Stuttgart, 1987), pp.153-54, 185, 235, and 252-58; Hans Erich Nossack, with photographs by Erich Anders, *Der Untergang: Hamburg 1943* (Hamburg, 1981); Keith Mallory and Arvid Ottar, *The Architecture of War* (New York, 1973), pp. 238-47.

A few of Hamburg's ecclesiastical buildings of the twenties have appeared in popular guides. They include the expressionist Bugenhagen Church of 1917-29 by Emil Heinrich Carl Heynen, with sculpture by Richard Kuöhl and others; the former modernist masonry synagogue of 1930 on Oberstrasse by Felix Ascher and Robert Friedmann; and Fritz Schumacher's crematorium of 1930-33 in Ohlsdorf Cemetery.

Bomhoff and Schöne. Bismarck Memorial Church, Börsener Strasse between Schulweg and Bürgerstrasse, Aumühle, 1930. Photograph 1991.

Bensel, Kamps and Amsinck. St. Paulus Augustinus, Dürerstrasse, Hamburg-Gross Flottbek, 1930. Photographs 1991.

Clemens Holzmeister. Maria Grün Church, Elbchausee and Schenefelder Landstrasse, Hamburg-Blankenese, 1930. Photograph 1991.

Bensel, Kamps and Amsinck. Protestant Church, between Haidrath and Kirchberg, Wohltorf, 1929 (rebuilt 1950). Photograph 1991.

Most ecclesiastical structures in Hamburg and its outlying areas, however, have faded into obscurity, even though a number have survived to act as a reminder that modern design was not confined to housing projects or office buildings. Some are relatively conservative, such as the round Bismarck Memorial Church in Aumühle, while others, in their use of some angular modernist forms, appear more avant-garde. Two examples of the latter type were built in 1930: the churches of Maria Grün by Viennese architect Clemens Holzmeister and St. Paulus Augustinus by Bensel, Kamps and Amsinck. Both have been slightly altered. The firm of Carl Bensel, Gerhard Kamps and Heinrich Amsinck also designed, in 1929, the

church in the eastern suburb of Wohltorf, which was partly destroyed by fire in 1950. The current structure, rebuilt by church specialist Gerhard Langmaack, retains much of the original exterior, though the cap atop its tower is a post-1950 addition.

Selected Sources

Architektur in Hamburg seit 1900, sites 64, 87, and 91; *Hamburg und seine Bauten*, p. 71; *Die Bugenhagenkirche in Barmbek* (Hamburg, 1991); "Ein Architekt besucht Hamburg," pp. 572 (Wohltorf church) and 573 (Wohltorf church, Bismarck Memorial Church); *Architektur in Schleswig-Holstein*, p. 101 (Bismarck Memorial Church); "Neue kleinere Katholische Kirchen von Clemens Holzmeister," *Der Baumeister* (1931), p. 205.

Karl Schneider. Bauer House, Duvenstedter Trift-
weg on the Alster, Hamburg-Wohldorf, 1925-28
(slightly altered). Photographs 1991.

Karl Schneider. Müller-Drenkberg House, Breden-
bekstrasse 29, Hamburg-Ohlstedt, 1929. Photograph 1991.

Martin Elsaesser. Reemtsma Villa, Parkstrasse 51,
Hamburg-Othmarschen, 1930-32. From *Moderne
Bauformen* (1933).

In Hamburg, Karl Schneider's suburban villas,
commissioned by well-to-do clients, come first
to mind when we think of elegant expressions
of modernism comparable to the private
homes designed by such famous modernists as
Ludwig Mies van der Rohe or Walter Gropius.
The two villas to have been published most
consistently are the Michaelsen House of
1923-25 at Grotiusweg 79 in Blankenese
(today a puppet museum), somewhat traditionally roofed yet modernist in design, and the
more radical Römer House of 1927-28 at
Ernst-August-Strasse 37 in Othmarschen (now
demolished). But there are other, equally
important modernist homes by Schneider in
the area that survive barely noticed by architectural historians. Two such are the almost
Wrightian Bauer House in a wooded area on
the Alster in Wohldorf and the stark, brick
Müller-Drenkberg House in Ohlstedt, both from
the late twenties. Although these are beautiful
examples of his work, other architects produced comparably striking modernist homes in
the environs of Hamburg.

Schneider protégé Hellmut Lubowski designed a curvilinear modernist home on the
Elbe in Blankenese in c.1929-30 (now
demolished). Gottfried Schramm built a sleek,

144   The North: Hamburg and Hanover

opposite page:
Gottfried Schramm of Elingius and Schramm. Summer house, Mittelweg 6, Reinbek, 1927-28 (altered). Contemporary photographs by Ernst Scheel.

Johann Michael Bossard. Bossard House (right) and Temple of Art (left), Bossardweg, Jesteburg, 1926-27. Photograph 1991.

this page:
Bensel, Kamps and Amsinck. Polo Club, Jenisch-strasse and Polostrasse, Hamburg-Klein Flottbek, c. 1930. Photograph 1991.

Elingius and Schramm. Falkenstein Golf Club, In de Bargen, Hamburg-Blankenese, 1930 (altered). Photograph 1991.

three-story summer house for himself in Rein-bek in 1927 which, though still standing, has been heavily altered and added to in the post-war period. Frankfurt-based Martin Elsaesser designed what was probably Hamburg's most spectacular modernist estate: the Reemtsma Villa of 1930-32 in Othmarschen, recycled into an office complex by Godber Nissen in 1953. And what must be one of the most eccentric modern (though not modernist) homes is the Bossard Home and Temple of Art in Jesteburg of 1926-27. The artist Johann Michael Bossard bought a large farmhouse and turned it into something resembling a set from the film *The Cabinet of Dr. Caligari*, complete with painted and sculpted expressionist rooms. He built his Temple of Art next to the farmhouse, incorporating mechanistic and "primitive" imagery throughout. The site will eventually be made into a museum. It serves to remind us that, although a number of so-called International Style villas were built in the Ham-

burg area, an alternative, personal approach to modern living could be as strong in expression.

The leading architects who designed these mostly modern, large suburban homes also were often responsible for recreational facilities built for the affluent local population. Two extant buildings of this type, published together in *Moderne Bauformen* in 1932, are the Falkenstein Golf Club in Blankenese by Elingius and Schramm (1930) and the Polo Club in Klein Flottbek of about the same date by Bensel, Kamps and Amsinck. The Golf Club, though its interior, especially, has been altered, in some ways recalls those works by Frank Lloyd Wright that relate contextually to the landscape. This, and the same architects' summer house in Reinbek, are more than merely competent exercises in modernism, by designers who are more readily associated with conservative, almost historicist works of the thirties (see pp. 135, 136, 139).

Selected Sources
Architektur in Hamburg seit 1900, sites 44 (Michaelsen House) and 88 (Reemtsma Villa); *Karl Schneider,* ed. Koch and Pook, pp. 118-53 (Michaelsen, Römer, Bauer, and Müller-Drenkberg houses); "Amburgo," *Abitare* (July-August 1991), pp. 178-79 (Michaelsen House) and 206-7 (Bossard Home and Temple of Art); "Bensel, Kamps und Amsinck: Poloklubhaus Klein-Flottbek," *Moderne Bauformen* (1932), p. 506; "Elingius und Schramm, Hamburg: Golfklubhaus in Altona-Rissen," *Moderne Bauformen* (1932), p. 504; "Haus Bauer in Wohldorf bei Hamburg," *Der Baumeister* (1931), pp. 382-85; "Haus Müller-Drenkberg," *Moderne Bauformen* (1929), p. 179; "House K in O, Berlin [sic; recte, Hamburg], Germany," *American Architect* (September 1933), pp. 25-32; "Ein Landsitz in Norddeutschland," *Moderne Bauformen* (1933), pp. 1-23; "Haus Römer in Othmarschen . . .," *Moderne Bauformen* (1928), p. 370; Barbara Miller Lane, *Architecture and Politics in Germany 1918-1945* (Cambridge, Mass., 1968; 2nd ed., 1985), pp. 30-32; "Hellmut Lubowski, Hamburg: Wohnhaus einer Dame in Blankenese," *Moderne Bauformen* (1931), p. 557; "Wochenendhaus in Reinbek," *Moderne Bauformen* (1932), pp. 82-85.

The Düsseldorf architect Emil Fahrenkamp, highly regarded for his conservative modernist buildings at locations as far apart as the Ruhrgebiet and Berlin, also designed two private homes in the far north of Germany. One is fairly well known, the Wenhold Villa of 1927 in Bremen. This house, built for savings bank director Hermann Wenhold, juxtaposes historicist details within the brick construction common to the region on the lower floor with bold, white stucco, modernist massing above. Fahrenkamp also built the Kruspig House in Hamburg, which has been overlooked in almost every architectural history and survey of the area. This modernist brick block, constructed in 1931 for the director of Shell in Germany, is sited in Hamburg's villa district on a hill overlooking the Aussen-Alster and not far from the company's local offices, the Shellhaus (see p. 135). (Fahrenkamp, it will be remembered, designed the contemporary Shellhaus in Berlin, perhaps his most famous work; Fig. 2, p . 22.) The Kruspig House, which now serves as offices for the publishers Hoffmann and Campe, was renovated by architect Friedhelm Grundmann in 1990.

Emil Fahrenkamp. Wenhold Villa, Unter den Eichen, Bremen, 1927. Photograph 1991.

Selected Sources
Hipp, *Hamburg,* p. 381; *Architektur in Bremen und Bremerhaven,* site 80; "Haus Dr. Kruspig in Hamburg," *Moderne Bauformen* (1931), pp. 597-602 (cf. *Der Baumeister* [1932], p. 17); "Haus Wenhold in Bremen," *Moderne Bauformen* (1929), p. 5.

Emil Fahrenkamp. Kruspig House, Harvestehuder Weg 45, Hamburg, 1931. Photograph 1991.

Oberpostdirektion, Bremen. Utbremen post office, Utbremer Strasse near St.-Magnus-Strasse, Bremen-Westend, 1929-31. Photograph 1991.

bottom: Hermann and Eberhard Gildemeister. Nordwollehaus, Contrescarpe, Richtweg, Röve-kamp, and Schillerstrasse, Bremen, 1928-30. Photograph 1989.

The most famous twenties buildings in Bremen are those of Böttcherstrasse, with their individu-alistic, expressionist, and highly picturesque decorated walls, spaces, and towers, many of them designed by sculptor Bernhard Hoetger. It is a spectacular experience to explore these spaces, one similar to that provided by the Bossard House and Temple of Art (see p. 144). Significantly, both sites were designed by artists, rather than architects: as a result of their daily dealings with the practi-calities of building, architects tend to be less extreme in their approach. Bremen's other ex-pressionist buildings exhibit a more familiar range of styles: no-nonsense simplicity, as in the post office of 1929-31; more historicist, as with the 1927 Glocke next to the cathedral; modernist masonry, as in the 1928-30 Nord-wollehaus; or *moderne,* as with the 1935-37

Borgward automobile works. The last two buildings are examples of particularly impor-tant modernist work in Bremen that has been overshadowed by the artistic *horror vacui* of Böttcherstrasse.

Bremen native Eberhard Gildemeister de-signed the Nordwollehaus (later Haus des Reiches). He studied in Darmstadt from 1919 to 1924 before working with Lothar Gürtler in Osnabrück and Rudolf Jacobs in Bremen in 1926-27. It was the Nordwollehaus, a large-scale courtyard office building, the competi-tion for which he won, that launched Gilde-meister's career as an independent architect. The building combines stylized classical ele-ments, such as engaged sculptures and certain

features of the facade decorations, with modernist massing, particularly in the clock tower, and curvilinear modernist forms for the staircase and corners of the court. Subse-quently, Gildemeister received numerous com-missions in the area for historicist homes. The only large building that he designed was the Hafenhaus of 1939-40, which was to combine offices and warehouse space with some living quarters — a thirteen-story historicist sky-scraper that was never built. His postwar work included traditional homes and both historicist and modernist churches.

Rudolf Lodders, a native of Altona, studied at the Höhere Schule für Baukunst (Advanced School for Architecture) in Hamburg from 1921

to 1924. In 1924-25 he worked for Karl Schneider and, from 1925 and 1927, with Gustav Oelsner. After another short stay with Schneider in 1927, he went to Frankfurt to collaborate with Ernst May and Martin Elsaesser, before moving to Berlin in 1929 to spend that and the following year working with Martin Wagner. In 1931 he set up his own practice in Altona. Considering the architects with whom he collaborated, it comes as no surprise that his orientation was toward radical Modern Movement expressions. In 1932-33 he designed the Ilo Motorworks offices at Pinneberg, northwest of Hamburg, and this led to his most important prewar commissions — various buildings for the Borgward-Goliath factory in Bremen. The famous 1935-37 Borgward building on Hastedter Osterdeich has survived intact, but the related factory complex for Hansa-Lloyd-Goliath southeast of Seebaldsbrücker Heerstrasse and Brüggeweg from the mid-thirties was heavily bombed during the war. Later operated by Daimler-Benz, the site has seen numerous alterations and additions down to the present day. Lodder's wartime service involved continued design of industrial buildings. After the war, he participated in the rebuilding of these Bremen factories and designed numerous industrial and residential structures for other clients.

Selected Sources

Architektur in Bremen und Bremerhaven, sites 4.1 (Glocke), 5 (Böttcherstrasse), 25 (Nordwollehaus), 54 (Goliath-Werke), and 118 (post office); *Eberhard Gildemeister: Ein bremischer Architekt,* exhibition catalogue (Bremen, 1973); *Rudolf Lodders,* ed. Olaf Bartels (Hamburg, 1989). Contemporary references include: "Bauten für die Industrie," *Moderne Bauformen* (1938), pp. 585-86; "Das neue Postgebäude in Bremen," *Deutsche Bauzeitung* (March 15, 1933), pp. 207-8; "Das Nordwollehaus in Bremen," *Wasmuths Monatshefte für Baukunst und Städtebau (1932), pp. 577-81;* "Neue Industriebauten: Ein Kraftwagenwerk von Rudolf Lodders," *Monatshefte für Baukunst* (1938), pp. 313-26, and "Eine neuzeitliche Kraftwagen-Fabrik in Bremen," *Der Baumeister* (1938), pp. 128-34 (cf. "Truck, Tank Factories Smashed," *Impact* [November 1944], p. 7).

Rudolf Lodders. Former Borgward-Goliath-Werke, Hastedter Osterdeich and Malerstrasse, Bremen, 1933-35 (rebuilt 1948). Photograph 1991.

City Architectural Department for Housing. Westfalensiedlung, Ruhrstrasse and Wupperstrasse,
Bremen, 1927. Photograph 1991.

Gerd Offenberg. Former "Asocial Citizens'
Housing Colony," Warturmer Platz near Senator-
Apelt-Strasse, Bremen-Woltmershausen, 1935-37.
Photograph 1991.

Despite some starkly modernist projects, similar to twenties blocks in Hamburg, at Friedrich-
Ebert-Strasse 179-217 (1930-31) and at other
sites, housing in Bremen was generally more
traditional in roofing and decoration. Eclectically modern buildings of the type designed
by Heinz Stoffregen are the norm here. This is
because Bremen had a particularly effective
"Heimatschutz" lobby, a movement aimed at
protecting traditional design and life-style
values. In 1928 some activists, Stoffregen
among them, even formed an anti-modernist
association called "Block." A typical example
of Bremen's traditionally styled housing is the
Westfalensiedlung of 1927. This low-density
Garden City project relates to Bremen's nineteenth-century row house tradition and to comparable undertakings in England and Holland.
But looks can be deceiving, as with the estate
for "asocial citizens" developed by the Nazis
in 1935. This seemingly benign colony of traditional row houses around a village green was

policed from a control booth in the entrance
gatehouse and office building. Though it functioned as a sort of urban concentration camp,
its planning and overall concept derive from
Dutch and American prototypes of the
nineteenth and twentieth centuries, with the
"controlled living" colony of 1923 in The
Hague serving as model. The Bremen colony
was converted to its present housing function
after the war.

Selected Sources

Architektur in Bremen und Bremerhaven, sites 53
(Westfalensiedlung) and 108 (Friedrich-Ebert-Strasse);
Nils Aschenbeck, *Heinz Stoffregen 1879-1929:
Architektur zwischen Tradition und Avantgarde*
(Braunschweig and Wiesbaden, 1990); Wolfgang
Voigt, "Wohnhaft: Die Siedlung als panoptisches
Gefängnis," *Arch +* (1984), pp. 82-89; idem, *Das
Bremer Haus*, pp. 106 (Westfalensiedlung), 143
("asocial citizens" housing), and pp. 9 and 64
(conservatism of design in Bremen).

Fritz Höger. Cemetery Chapel, Hermann-Allmers-Weg, Delmenhorst, 1926-28. Photographs 1989.

bottom right: Dominikus Böhm. Herz Jesu Church, Kornstrasse and Stenumer Strasse, Bremen-Huckelriede, 1935-38. Photograph 1991.

Churches from the interwar years in Bremen, its suburbs, and nearby towns have barely rated a mention in the literature on the architecture of this region. There are at least two by well respected designers from the era under study. The first is the diminutive cemetery chapel of 1926-28 in Delmenhorst by Fritz Höger. This little gem still stands in the form in which it was constructed, only now it is covered in ivy. The second is the massive neo-Romanesque Herz Jesu Church of 1935 on Bremen's Kornstrasse by Dominikus Böhm. Though essentially historicist in inspiration, it contains modernist elements in its main entry door and in the adjacent parish house, as well as displaying an unornamented massing of the facade and tower that one would associate with a more modern building. The interior and the entrance were remodeled in 1963.

Selected Sources

Architektur in Bremen und Bremerhaven, site 109 (Herz Jesu Church); "Die Friedhofskapelle in Delmenhorst," *Deutsche Bauzeitung* (November 30, 1929), pp. 817-19; August Hoff and Josef Habbell, *Dominikus Böhm* (Regensburg, 1943), pp.173-75; August Hoff, Herbert Much, and Raimund Thoma, *Dominikus Böhm* (Munich and Zurich, 1953), pp. 338-40.

Flesche and Kölling. Apartment building, Sieg-friedstrasse, centering on Burgundplatz, Braun-schweig, 1926-27. Photograph 1989.

top right: Karl Mühlenpfordt. AOK building, Am Fallersleber Tor 3-4, Braunschweig, 1929. Photograph 1989.

bottom right: Emil Herzig. Kant-Hochschule, Konstantin-Uhde-Strasse 16, Braunschweig, 1934-37. Photograph 1989.

The industrial city of Braunschweig contains several buildings from the twenties and thirties that embody differing notions of modernism. Although radical modernist buildings could be found in the 1929-30 housing complex August-Bebel-Hof by Hamburg architect Friedrich Ostermeyer (which was rebuilt to a new scheme after World War II), architecture in Braunschweig was generally more conserva-tive in approach. In the twenties, modernist masonry buildings, such as the Allgemeine Ortskrankenkasse (AOK; General Health Insurance Fund) building by Karl Mühlen-pfordt, or brick housing complexes, such as the little-known Siegfriedstrasse apartments by Hermann Flesche and Johannes Kölling, were the rule. The latter — clean, brick modernist masses topped by hipped roofs — still exist as designed, except that their natural brick facades have been painted over and all their windows changed. Perhaps the most widely published and appreciated building in Braun-schweig is the brick skyscraper of eight stories constructed between 1934 and 1937 to designs by Emil Herzig. Originally built as a teachers' college, with planetarium dome at the top, it is today part of the local poly-technic, the Kant-Hochschule. Its exterior would seem to prefigure the quasi-historicist modern buildings constructed during the fifties in Rostock and other eastern German cities.

Selected Sources

Hartwig Beseler and Niels Gutschow, *Kriegsschick-sale deutscher Architektur*, 2 vols. (Neumünster, 1988), vol. 1, p. 228 (August-Bebel-Hof); Ulrich H. Mey and Christian Streibel, *Braunschweig: Architekturführer* (Braunschweig, 1989), sites 18 (August-Bebel-Hof), 137 (AOK building), and 188 (Kant-Hochschule); Stommer, *Hochhaus*, p. 222 (Kant-Hochschule); "Neu-bauten in Braunschweig," *Wasmuths Monatshefte für Baukunst und Städtebau* (1931), pp. 106-8 (Siegfried-strasse apartments).

Gustav August Münzer. Marine-Ehrenmal, Prof.-Münzer-Ring, Strandstrasse, and Birkenweg, Kiel-Laboe, 1927-36. Photograph 1989.

Two almost contemporaneous buildings close to each other on the outskirts of Kiel offer two very different approaches to modern design. The first is the Marine-Ehrenmal (naval memorial) of 1927 on Kieler Förde in Laboe by Gustav August Münzer. Its sweeping brick- and stone-covered concrete tower soars to a height of more than 278 feet. The image projected by this expressionistic tower, which can be ascended for spectacular views over the sea, is a cross between a ship's prow and a lighthouse. At its base lies a circular court of honor, beneath which is a concrete and brick domed room that commemorates the 35,000 and 120,000 members of the German navy who died in World War I and II, respectively. At the outer edge of the court of honor is an exhibition hall. The tower itself was complete by 1929, but the rest of the complex, including the underground space, was built over the following years, the whole being officially dedicated on May 30, 1936. Just south of this monument, and in striking contrast to it, stands one of the most modernistic of summer houses. This tiny structure was built in 1931 by Rudolf Schroeder for his own use, and it received favorable coverage in periodicals of the thirties. Schroeder, it should be noted, was a student of Paul Schmitthenner in Stuttgart and subsequently worked with Willy Hahn on the design of public buildings in Kiel, notably the modernist Arbeitsamt (employment office) of 1928-29. The Schroeder house and the Marine-Ehrenmal represent the extreme poles of modernist architecture to be found in northern Germany.

Selected Sources

Architektur in Schleswig-Holstein 1900-1980, pp. 84, 89, and 104; sites originally published in: "Das Arbeitsamt in Kiel," *Wasmuths Monatshefte für Baukunst und Städtebau* (1931), pp. 25-30 (cf. *Deutsche Bauzeitung* [March 11, 1931], pp.130-33); "Das Marine-Ehrenmal," ibid., p. 78; "Wohnen und Wochenende in Einem," *Der Baumeister* (1933), p. 324; and *Moderne Bauformen* (1937), p. 406.

Rudolf Schroeder. The architect's summer house, Strandweg 48 near Mühlenwiesen, Kiel-Heikendorf, 1931. Photographs 1991.

Willy Hahn and Rudolf Schroeder. Arbeitsamt building, Wilhelmplatz, Kiel, 1928-29. Photograph 1991.

top left: Adelbert Kelm. Apartment building, Niebuhrstrasse, Fichtestrasse, Hardenbergstrasse, Schillstrasse, and Kleiststrasse, Kiel, 1925-30. Photograph 1991.

center left: Ernst Stoffers. Sartori & Berger warehouses, Wall 49-51, Kiel, 1925. Photograph 1989.

above: Friedrich Wilhelm Virck. Holstentorhalle, Holstentorplatz, Lübeck, 1925. Photographs 1990.

bottom: Schweinfurth and Siebert. Baugruppe Marli, Marlistrasse, Gneisenaustrasse, Goebenstrasse, Hovelnstrasse, and Kleiststrasse, Lübeck-Marli, c.1929. Photograph c.1990.

top left: Hans Pieper. Gatehouse of the Seegrenz slaughterhouse, Warendorp Platz, Lübeck-St. Lorenz, 1927-29. Photograph 1990.

bottom left: Klophaus, Schoch and zu Putlitz. Public baths, Sandstrasse and Sydowstrasse, Niendorf, 1927 (altered). Photograph 1991.

right: Paul Schaeffer-Heyrothsberge. Apartment block, Bothwellstrasse and Stoschstrasse, Kiel-Gaarden Ost, c.1935-38 (altered). Photograph 1989.

Architecture of the twenties and thirties in Kiel and Lübeck is generally quite conservative, drawing, in an almost historicist way, on the brick structures and stepped gables of earlier eras in the history of the region. Such references can be quite literal, as in Adelbert Kelm's 1925 housing in Kiel, the mixture of quasi-Victorian and expressionist details in the Baugruppe Marli of the late twenties in Lübeck, and the famous, simply massed Sartori & Berger warehouses of 1925 in the harbor of Kiel; but they can also involve an almost Pop Art-like distortion of scale, as in the Holstentorhalle, Lübeck. A blend of historical and modernist forms in one and the same complex is best seen in the previously unpublished slaughterhouses of 1927 by Hans Pieper in Lübeck. The main building (now engulfed by a later addition) draws upon the traditions of setback gable ends, all the setback forms being placed longitudinally along the side of the structure, while most of the other buildings are straightforward designs in brick or concrete, with few historical associations. Among the few structures to have escaped alteration or demolition are the concrete overhead pathway used by the cattle and the curvilinear brick gatehouses flanking the entrance to the compound.

Between these extremes lie the restrained brick modernism of Lübeck's Stadtbibliothek (city library) of 1926-27, the somewhat greater expressionism of the Klingenberg department store of 1928-30, also in that city, and the reserved expressionism of the heretofore unpublished baths in Niendorf. Built in 1927 by Hamburg architects Klophaus, Schoch and zu Putlitz, the latter have been altered through street-level changes and additions to the front facade, but the restrained approach to expressionist design is still clearly visible in, say, the reverse setback, concentric brickwork of the main tower, whose sides corbel out toward the top. It is surprising to note that, after the Nazis' accession to power in 1933, brick architecture in this region did not revert to the kind of local historicism embodied in Kelm's apartment buildings. Instead, forms of generic historicist design tempered by modernist massing continued to appear, as in the 1935-38 Bothwellstrasse apartment blocks in Kiel by Paul Schaeffer-Heyrothsberge, one of Magdeburg's leading modernists in the twenties (see p. 236). Today, the buildings are without their sculpture, and their corbeled, arched cornices bear a differently tiled and profiled roof, sans dormers.

Selected Sources

Architektur in Schleswig-Holstein 1900-1980, pp. 63 (Sartori & Berger warehouses), 70 (apartments by Kelm), 71 (Holstentorhalle), 75 (Stadtbibliothek), and 93 (Klingenberg department store); "Baugruppe Marli in Lübeck," *Deutsche Bauzeitung* (June 17, 1931), pp. 298-300; "Der Seegrenz-Schlachthof in Lübeck," *Deutsche Bauzeitung* (August 12, 1931), pp. 385-89; "Seewasser-Warmbad in Niendorf an der Ostsee," *Deutsche Bauzeitung* (March 24, 1928), pp. 209-11; "Arbeiten von Paul Schaeffer-Heyrothsberge," *Der Baumeister* (1941), pp. 78-79.

Adolf Thesmacher. Provinzialbank (later Haus der Gewerkschaften), Alter Markt 7, Stralsund, 1930. Photograph 1991.

Alfred Stieler, with reliefs by Adolf Wamper. Marine-Lazarett (now Krankenhaus am Sund), Grosse Parower Strasse 47-53, Stralsund-Knieper Vorstadt, 1938. Photographs 1991.

The ports of Stralsund and Rostock on the Baltic Sea had their share of Modern Movement buildings, although architecture there was usually expressionist or hybridized in nature. Generally, Rostock's modernist buildings did not figure in mainstream architectural publications of the time and, moreover, the city was heavily bombed in World War II. The air raids laid waste to the area's most important modernist complex, Herbert Rimpl's Heinkel aircraft company works in Rostock. The winning entry in a 1927 competition, Rimpl's design would lead him to receive commissions from that company for bigger and better factories elsewhere (see Fig. 3, p. 11, and p. 36).

For present purposes, a visit to Stralsund is of greater interest, since it emerged relatively undamaged from the war. Two buildings published in the twenties and thirties still exist almost as constructed. One is the 1930 Provinzialbank on the town square by Adolf Thesmacher of Stettin (now Szczecin, Poland). Akin to some Prairie School banks by Louis Sullivan, Frank Lloyd Wright, and their followers from the early years of the century, this brick and masonry jewel is a fine example of a restrained expressionist building executed with a contextual nod to the small commercial buildings that had been constructed around it in the same materials on the square. Equally well preserved is the former Marine-Lazarett (naval hospital) of 1938 by Alfred Stieler of Berlin.

With the exception of the eagle and swastika relief in the center of the entrance gate (for which the symbol of the city of Stralsund has been substituted), the architecture and sculptural elements have been subjected to only minor alterations. The curvilinear forms and large windows — most of them belonging to the rooms of tuberculosis patients located on the concave facade and corner facing the park — are obvious survivals from Modern Movement buildings and represent a most elegant solution to a specific architectural problem.

Selected Sources

Hans-Otto Möller, Helmut Behrendt, Klaus Marsiske, Ekkehard Franke, Matthias Stahl, and Gerd Baier, *Architekturführer DDR: Bezirk Rostock* (Berlin, 1978), esp. pp. 108 (Provinzialbank) and 116 (Marine-Lazarett); "Das Marine-Lazarett in Stralsund," *Der Baumeister* (1940), pp. 69-92 and pls. 29-36; "Die Provinzialbank in Stralsund," *Deutsche Bauzeitung* (December 3, 1930), pp. 657-61; "Industriebauten von Prof. Dr. Ing. Herbert Rimpl," *Der Baumeister* (1953), pp. 169-83. See *Impact* (September 1943), p. 14, and (November 1944), pp. 2-3, for reports on the bombing of the Heinkel and Focke Wulf factories in Rostock. The Focke-Wulf plant was on the site of the current Warnowwerft shipyard, while the Heinkel factory was situated in the south, at the Gross Klein site now occupied by postwar housing.

Karl Elkart. Stadtbibliothek, Hildesheimer Strasse between Aegidiendamm and Maschstrasse, Hanover, 1929-31. Photograph 1989.

Stadtbibliothek. View on Maschstrasse, with Städtische Bühnen (1928). Photograph 1989.

Karl Elkart was the Hanover equivalent of Fritz Schumacher in Hamburg or Gustav Oelsner in Altona. At the Technische Hochschule (polytechnic) in Stuttgart he was a student of Theodor Fischer, an architect-teacher who trained many of Germany's great architects of the twenties (see p. 166). After graduating in 1907, Elkart worked in Hamburg and Bochum before taking a position in 1918 as City Architect in Spandau. This was the beginning of a long career in public service in Brandenburg and Berlin, where he assisted with the planning and coordination of housing developments and projects relating to Potsdamer Platz and Leipziger Platz, Tempelhof airport, and the Messe (trade fair) grounds. In 1925 he left Berlin to become Senator for Building and City Architect of Hanover. In this position, he designed a number of the city's public buildings, from the famous Stadtbibliothek (city library) near the city center to neighborhood schools and waterworks outside Hanover, as well as the city's main park, on the Maschsee. His planning activities ranged from coordinating the various housing projects in the city to siting the airport of 1938 (now demolished) within a landscaped area outside the city. During World War II, he also planned a new city center for Hanover as part of the program, supervised by Albert Speer, to redesign many German cities. Widely published in various journals and in *Neues Bauen in Hannover* (1929), Elkart's work was the subject of a favorable review in a 1940 issue of *Monatshefte für Baukunst und Städtebau*. Because of his age (he retired in 1946) he did not participate in the rebuilding and replanning of Hanover after the war. As happened with Schumacher's work in Hamburg, which postwar architects associated with the "old" Germany, Elkart's architecture was pushed aside in an effort to build a new Germany from the ashes of "Stunde Null" (zero hour). It is interesting to note, however, that the modernist design

implemented in postwar Hanover was the work of Rudolf Hillebrecht, who had been deputy director of Konstanty Gutschow's office in Hamburg during the war.

Selected Sources

Gaststätten, ed. Herbert Hoffmann (Stuttgart, 1939), p. 46; *Neues Bauen in Hannover* (Hanover, 1929); "Stadtbaurat Professor Karl Elkart 60 Jahre," *Monatshefte für Baukunst und Städtebau* (1940), pp. 225-28; Stommer, *Hochhaus,* pp. 225-26; "Das Wasserwerk Berkhof der Stadt Hannover," *Deutsche Bauzeitung* (March 25, 1931), pp. 149-52; "Flughafen Hannover," *Deutsche Bauzeitung* (November 13, 1935), pp. 918-21; "Neubauten der Volksbücherei in Hannover," *Deutsche Bauzeitung* (June 3, 1931), pp. 262-66; Wolfgang Ness, Ilse Rüttgerodt-Riechmann, Gerd Weiss, and Marianne Zehnpfennig, *Baudenkmale in Niedersachsen,* Part 1, *Stadt Hannover* (Braunschweig and Wiesbaden, 1983), pp. 106, 116, and 132-34.

top left: Karl Elkart. Berkhof waterworks, south of Berkhof on the road to Elze outside Hanover, 1929-30. Photograph 1990.

top right: Karl Elkart. Anna-Siemsen School, Im Moore 38, Hanover, 1930. Photograph 1990.

Karl Elkart. Am Maschsee park, Hanover, 1934-36. The Pylon, Nord Ufer; Pavilion, Nord Ufer; and Freibad (public bath) with dressing cabins, south side of the Maschsee, designed by Barlinghaus. Photographs 1990.

Hanover's high-rises are well known, and of four extant from the twenties, two are by Fritz Höger. First and foremost is the *Anzeiger* Hochhaus of 1927-28, the centrally planned, dramatically domed, and angularly detailed offices of the eponymous newspaper. It is one of Höger's masterpieces, almost as famous as his Chilehaus in Hamburg (see p.116), and evokes the image of the "Stadtkrone" (city crown) popularized in the 1919 book of that title by expressionist architect Bruno Taut. Stommer, however, notes its Islamic overtones and its relationship to Wilhelm Kreis's Rheinhalle of 1926 in Düsseldorf (see p.93). Additional comparison can be made with Paul Bonatz's Stadthalle of 1914 on Corvinusplatz in Hanover, a domed prototype that was closer geographically. Höger's dome, however, housed a planetarium. Höger also designed the Hochhaus Günther, a distinctive apartment house complex of 1927 that is

Fritz Höger. *Anzeiger* Hochhaus, Goseriede 9, Hanover, 1927-28. Photographs 1989.

below: Fritz Höger. Hochhaus Günther, Am Stephansplatz, Hanover-Südstadt, 1927. Photograph 1989.

The North: Hamburg and Hanover 159

similar to other buildings by him, notably a contemporaneous apartment block on Ohlsdorfer Strasse in Hamburg.

Wilhelm Ziegler topped Höger's design three years later by building a nine-story apartment tower as a grand entrance to a large housing block in Geibelplatz park. The composition that Ziegler used for the tower is related, visually, to a water tower and apartments built in 1926-27 in Bremerhaven. Often published, but underrated, is the 1930 Capitolhaus by Friedrich Hartjenstein. This office building includes brick detailing similar to, though not as elaborate as, Höger's. It is more hybrid than the latter's work because its corner turret emulates more dramatically round-cornered buildings designed by masonry modernists and others at the time, such as Erich Mendelsohn and Emil Fahrenkamp. Furthermore, attached to this ten-story tower is a three-story rectilinear building whose neo-Gothic arches on the ground floor make it look even more an eclectic child of historicist, modernist, and expressionist parentage.

Thus, we can see a variety of design approaches in these four tall buildings, even though it is tempting to place them all in the single category of regional brick architecture influenced by expressionism. Although not a skyscraper, Hans Poelzig's 1923 office building for a textile factory conforms more closely to the image of Hanover as a city of brick expressionist architecture in the Hamburg mold. Its appearance is very different from that of other buildings by Poelzig in Berlin or Frankfurt (see p. 65).

Selected Sources

"Das Hochhaus des Hannoverschen Anzeigers in Hannover," *Deutsche Bauzeitung* (August 8, 1928), pp. 537-41; Stommer, *Hochhaus*, pp. 56-57, 208-11, 242, and 248-52; *Neues Bauen in Hannover*, pp. 28 (Hochhaus Günther) and 37 (*Anzeiger* Hochhaus).

Wilhelm Ziegler. Apartment high-rise, Geibelplatz 5, Hanover-Südstadt, 1930. Photograph 1990.

bottom left: Friedrich Hartjenstein. Capitolhaus, Ihmebrücke, Hanover-Linden, 1930. Photograph 1990.

Hans Poelzig. Former Mayer Brothers textile factory, Benecke-Allee, Hanover-Vinnhorst, 1923-24. Photograph 1990.

The Siebrecht brothers were among the most influential architects in Hanover in the twenties and thirties. Karl Siebrecht studied at the Technische Hochschule (polytechnic) in Hanover and at those in Berlin-Charlottenburg and Munich. With his younger brother Albert, he formed an architectural firm in about 1910. The Siebrecht brothers were responsible for major constructions in Hanover, beginning in 1910-12 with their first major commission, the Bahlsen cookie factory. *Neues Bauen in Hannover* (1929) featured many of their twenties buildings, most of which have received little attention since. For instance, the offices of the *Hannoverscher Kurier* newspaper still exist as a background building on Georgstrasse in the city center, its brick construction stuccoed over and its entrance lighting fixtures removed. The brothers also designed a number of brick and stucco apartment blocks, many published in *Neues Bauen in Hannover* and still extant. Even at its most expressionist, as in the Im Kreuzkampe apartments, their work was always somewhat historicist in orientation, although they continued to build hybridized

Karl and Albert Siebrecht. *Hannoverscher Kurier* office building, Georgstrasse 52, Hanover, c.1925 (altered). Photograph 1989.

Karl and Albert Siebrecht and Friedrich Wilhelm Schick. Apartment block, Grillparzerstrasse and Im Kreuzkampe, Hanover, 1929. Photograph 1989.

Karl and Albert Siebrecht. Addition to the Bahlsen cookie factory, Lister Strasse near Borkstrasse, Hanover-List, c.1938. Photograph 1989.

top right and bottom: Karl and Albert Siebrecht. Apartment block, Am Listholze, Hanover, c.1927-28. Photographs 1989.

modernist extensions for their biggest client — the Bahlsen company — that were published during World War II. The addition on Lister Strasse appears today as it did when constructed, incorporating ceramic reliefs by Georg Herting at the entrance.

Selected Sources
[Obituary Karl Siebrecht], *Der Baumeister* (1952), p. 269; "Arbeiten der Architekten Brüder Siebrecht, Hannover," *Moderne Bauformen* (1943), pp. 161-68 (includes Bahlsen addition); "Neue Wohnhausbauten in Hannover," *Deutsche Bauzeitung* (November 5, 1930), pp. 616-19; *Neues Bauen in Hannover,* pp. 13 (Am Listholze) and 18-19 (Im Kreuzkampe apartments).

top left: Kröger, Jürgens and Menche. Apartment block, De-Haen-Platz 3, Hanover-List, 1928-29. Photograph 1990.

top right: Koelliker, Springer and Fricke. Single-family house, Kleefeld Garden City, Senator-Bauer-Strasse, Hanover-Kleefeld, 1927-28. Photograph 1989.

Stille and Herlitzius. Apartment block, Böhmer-strasse and Sallstrasse at Karl-Peters-Platz, Hanover-Südstadt, 1928. Photograph 1989.

bottom left: Friedrich Wilhelm Schick with Karl Elkart. Apartment buildings, Brehmstrasse, Hanover-Bult, 1924-25. Photograph 1989.

bottom right: Wilhelm Mues. Apartment block, Ebellstrasse, near Berckhusenstrasse, Hanover-Kleefeld, c.1927-28. Photograph 1989.

The best known apartment complex in Hanover is that on De-Haen-Platz, its re-strained expressionist, boxlike forms accen-tuated, on one of the buildings, by an angled corner turret. This development and most of the other housing projects published in *Neues Bauen in Hannover* (1929) still survive more or less as designed. Karl Elkart reported in that book that approximately 13,500 housing units, financed by a combination of public and private funds, were constructed from 1926 to 1929. Aside from the De-Haen-Platz units, housing in Hanover ranged from little expres-sionist row houses in Kleefeld Garden City, to more overtly historicist examples on Böhmer-strasse, Brehmstrasse, and Ebellstrasse, to the hybrids of modernist, expressionist, and tradi-tional elements on Redenstrasse, Spilcker-strasse, Spielhagenstrasse, and Auf dem Dorn. Perhaps the most interesting apartment complex of all is that which incorporates the church of

top left: Rudolf Schroeder. Apartment block, Spilckerstrasse, near Berckhusenstrasse, Hanover-Kleefeld, c.1927-28. Photograph 1989.

top center: Koelliker and Springer. Apartment block, Spielhagenstrasse and Tiestestrasse, Hanover-Südstadt, c.1928-29. Photograph 1989.

top right: Rudolf Schröder. Apartment block, Auf dem Dorn 27, Hanover-Nordstadt, c.1928-29. Photograph 1990.

Eduard Endler, Church of St. Heinrich, Sallstrasse and Geibelstrasse, Hanover-Südstadt, 1929. Photograph 1989.

St. Heinrich in its design. The church serves as an urban landmark that peeks above the roofs of the twenties housing that dominates Hanover-Südstadt.

Selected Sources

Neues Bauen in Hannover, pp.11 (Ebellstrasse and Spilkestrasse), 20-21 (Kleefeld Garden City), 22 (De-Haen-Platz), 24 (Spielhagenstrasse), 26 (Redenstrasse), 32 (Auf dem Dorn), and 33 (Sallstrasse); "Die Katholische St. Heinrichskirche in Hannover," *Deutsche Bauzeitung* (August 6, 1930), pp. 505-6; "Gartenstadt Hannover-Kleefeld," *Deutsche Bauzeitung* (September 16, 1931), pp. 453-58.

Franz Erich Kassbaum and Willi Palaschewski. Technische Universität (polytechnic), Bismarck-strasse 2, Hanover-Südstadt, 1929-35. Photograph 1989.

left: Henry van de Velde and Georg Seewald. Heinemannsche Foundation home, Brabeck-strasse 86, Hanover-Bemerode, 1930-31. Photograph 1989.

Karl Grabenhorst and Franz Erich Kassbaum. Gymnasium of the Tierärztliche Hochschule (Veterinary College), Robert-Koch-Platz 10, Hanover-Bult, 1930. Photograph 1989.

Other institutional buildings exist in Hanover besides those designed by Karl Elkart. Two prominent ones are by Franz Erich Kassbaum, whose clean, modernist designs contrast with the more traditional or expressionist twenties work that determined the appearance of the city at that time. The Belgian architect Henry van de Velde designed one of his late works in Hanover, a home for the Heinemannsche Foundation; its restrained brick design was executed at the same time as the buildings by Kassbaum. Considering the bias in architec-tural publications toward Modern Movement functionalism, and particularly toward the work of celebrity architects such as Van de Velde, it comes as no surprise to see these buildings featured time and again at the expense of the more historicist or eclectic modern architecture to be found throughout the city.

Selected Source
Bauen in Deutschland, pp.173, 176, and 180.

Stuttgart, Munich, and Modernist Masonry Architecture

John Zukowsky

Both Stuttgart and Munich had strong regional schools of architecture in the first four decades of the twentieth century. They centered around the figures of Paul Bonatz in Stuttgart and Theodor Fischer in Munich, respectively, so a brief review of their interconnected lives will help to explain the nature of, and relationship between, modernist architecture in these two cities.

Schweinfurt-born Theodor Fischer was a student of Friedrich von Thiersch at the Technische Hochschule (polytechnic) in Munich. From 1885 to 1888 he was a member of the office of Paul Wallot, and is likely to have assisted Wallot on his famous Reichstag building in Berlin. After working in Dresden and subsequently traveling throughout Germany, Fischer returned to Munich in 1893 to work for Gabriel von Seidl. He came into his own in 1901, when he was appointed to teaching positions in Stuttgart and Munich. Fischer is best known for the major buildings, sometimes Jugendstil, but often downright historicist in manner, that he designed in and around Stuttgart and Munich from the early 1900s through the late 1920s. Perhaps the most famous of these is the 1906-10 Garnisonkirche on Frauenstrasse in Ulm. Toward the end of his life, during the Third Reich, his work was confined to a few small projects, along with an autobahn bridge and a memorial. Even in the twenties he designed relatively few buildings; the least historicist of them is the Ledigenheim für Männer (Home for Single Men) of 1925-27 on Munich's Bergmannstrasse. Still more important than his buildings was Fischer's activity as a teacher. He trained a variety of modernist architects, such as Martin Elsaesser, Hugo Häring, Ernst May, and Lois Welzenbacher, and employed students with differing approaches to modern design, such as Bruno Taut and Bonatz. It is likely that Fischer's impact on the diversity of mainstream modernism in Germany and, indeed, on the essence of German modernism was far greater than that of the much-vaunted teachers at the Bauhaus.

Paul Bonatz was born near Metz and educated in Berlin and Munich. He entered Fischer's office at the beginning of the century to work with him on Munich commissions, and a few years later he began assisting his teacher with courses at the Technische Hochschule in Stuttgart. It was in Stuttgart, in 1910, that Bonatz formed a partnership with a student friend, Eugen Scholer. They received a number of important commissions, including the Stadthalle of 1910-14 in Hanover and the massive Hauptbahnhof (main railroad station) in Stuttgart, which, although the competition for it had been held in 1911, was not built until 1914-28. Bonatz worked on major buildings throughout the twenties (see pp. 188-89). In 1908 he had followed in the footsteps of his mentor Fischer by taking up a post at the Technische Hochschule in Stuttgart, where he continued to teach until 1943. The work of Bonatz's students received coverage in the 1931 book *Paul Bonatz und seine Schüler*, edited by Bonatz's assistant Gerhard Graubner. Although most of these pupils did not achieve a degree of fame comparable to that enjoyed by many followers of Fischer, as lesser exponents of Bonatz's modernist masonry style they spread that style both within Germany and abroad. Together with the conservative architects Paul

Schmitthenner and Heinz Wetzel, Bonatz designed the traditional, wood-framed housing of the Kochenhof estate of 1933 in Stuttgart — the Nazis' much-touted answer to the avant-garde modernism of the Weissenhof Siedlung of 1927. Among his other works were historicist as well as functionalist bridges for the autobahn in the thirties, such modernist sports facilities as the Willy Sachs Stadium of 1936 in Schweinfurt (pp. 180-81), and the skeletal wooden flag towers and adjacent stadium for the Fifteenth German Gymnastic Festival held on the Neckar River in the Canstatt district of Stuttgart in 1933 (Fig. 1). During the Third Reich, Bonatz also collaborated with Albert Speer's office on buildings in Berlin and designed a new skeletal, domed main railroad station for Munich, which remained unexecuted. Yet, following several misunderstandings with officials about modernism's role in public buildings, he finally left Germany for Turkey in 1943. After the war, he worked in both countries until his death in 1956.

These two leaders — Fischer and Bonatz — set the tone of the architectural environment in Munich and Stuttgart, respectively. Their followers and other like souls propagated hybridized, highly eclectic modernist masonry architecture throughout Bavaria and Baden-Württemberg. Most of these architects lived and worked in either Stuttgart or Munich. Alfred Daiber, Richard Döcker, Eisenlohr and Pfennig, and Adolf Schneck were among those from Stuttgart; Hans Döllgast, Otto Kurz, and Robert Vorhoelzer were their Munich counterparts. Each had his own approach to modernist design, the one tending to be more conservative, the other more avant-garde. But they, and their less well known colleagues in both cities, shared an emphasis on plastic expressions of volume and surface, in contrast to the revealed structures or the stark, boxlike massings of simple planes that are associated with radical modernism. This distinguishes the work of a number of these mainstream modernists from the industrially oriented modernism of the architects who contributed to the Weissenhof

Fig. 1   Paul Bonatz. Flag tower on the Festival Meadow, Fifteenth German Gymnastic Festival, Stuttgart, 1933 (demolished). From *Moderne Bauformen* (1933).

Fig. 2   Richard Gebhardt. Englisch department store, Königstrasse, Stuttgart, c. 1930 (demolished). From *Moderne Bauformen* (1931).

Fig. 3   Eisenlohr and Pfennig. Breuninger department store, Marktstrasse and Adenauerstrasse, Stuttgart, 1931 (substantially altered). From *Moderne Bauformen* (1931-32).

Fig. 4   Erich Mendelsohn. Schocken department store, Eberhardstrasse 28, Stuttgart, 1926-28 (demolished). From *Glas in der Architektur der Gegenwart* (Stuttgart, 1929).

Siedlung under the direction of Ludwig Mies van der Rohe (see pp. 171-72).

The conservative character of mainstream modernism in both Stuttgart and Munich during the twenties and early thirties facilitated the transition to even more conservative design after the implementation of National Socialism — especially in Munich, the city that Hitler termed the "Hauptstadt der Bewegung" (Capital of the [Nazi] Movement). In the mid- and late thirties major office buildings, governmental structures, and cultural and transportation facilities were built in both Munich and Nuremberg, the Bavarian city some ninety miles north of Munich (see pp. 212-13). Although these have received extensive coverage elsewhere, we include discussion of them in the pages that follow because their juxtaposition with public structures, particularly post offices and kiosks, that had been erected in the course of building campaigns of the twenties and early thirties in Bavaria is especially revealing. Robert Vorhoelzer oversaw the construction of many of these post offices, and they often include mainstream modernist designs that continued to be built and publicly approved after the change in government in 1933.

Because Munich and Nuremberg were closely associated with the Nazis — and their cityscapes bore the imprint of that association — both cities suffered particularly heavy

bomb damage in World War II, perhaps even more than Stuttgart, Regensburg, or Augsburg, where industrial facilities were the principal targets. Yet in the latter cities, too, architectural losses were considerable. In Stuttgart, for example, although many of the homes and villas in the hilly districts around the city center still survive, along with some downtown buildings, a number of major and minor masterpieces were destroyed — and not just during the war (see Figs. 2-4). Many structures, especially department stores, survived the war only to be altered or demolished. In view of this, it is, perhaps, surprising that some buildings from both the twenties and the thirties were preserved and renovated in Munich and Nuremberg. These and other examples of eclectic modernist masonry design are discussed in the pages that follow.

Sources in Brief

The more famous buildings in Stuttgart and Munich are dealt with in good architectural guidebooks. Martin Wörner and Gilbert Lupfer, *Stuttgart: Ein Architekturführer* (Berlin, 1991) is the most recent. Two for Munich are Gerd Fischer, *Architektur in München seit 1900: Ein Wegweiser* (Braunschweig and Wiesbaden, 1990) and *Bauten und Plätze in München: Ein Architekturführer*, ed. Oswald Hederer, 3rd ed. (Munich, 1985). The former, however, often ignores buildings that are more historicist in nature. For Fischer and Bonatz, see Winfried Nerdinger, *Theodor Fischer: Architekt und Städtebauer 1862-1938* (Berlin and Munich, 1988), *Paul Bonatz: Leben und Bauten* (Stuttgart, 1950), and *Paul Bonatz: Arbeiten aus den Jahren 1907 bis 1937*, ed. Friedrich Tamms (Stuttgart, 1937). Other useful books include *Süddeutsche Bautradition im 20. Jahrhundert*, ed. Winfried Nerdinger (Munich, 1985), and Wend Fischer, *Die andere Tradition* (Munich, 1981).

The work of two Stuttgart architects of the period under study, Hugo Schlösser and Eduard Krüger, has scarcely been published at all since the time when they were active. Furthermore, data on Krüger is virtually nonexistent, perhaps because he had a prominent local career under the Nazis.

Schlösser, born in 1874 in Ratingen, near Düsseldorf, died in Stuttgart in 1967 at the age of ninety-four. After studying in Stuttgart, Munich, and Düsseldorf, Schlösser opened his own office in Stuttgart in 1906. Two years later he associated with an architect named Johann Weirether, with whom he designed various apartment buildings, factories, schools, and hospitals. At the same time, he developed a specialty in ecclesiastical design. Schlösser is best remembered for two buildings that date from the beginning and end of his career respectively: the Villa Reitzenstein at Richard-Wagner-Strasse 15 of 1910-13 and the Eberhardskirche at Königstrasse 7 of 1953-55. Yet twenties and thirties eclectic modernist buildings by him survive. Wörner and Lupfer have published one such, the brick Georgskirche of 1929-30 (Schlösser replaced its flat roof with a pitched one when he reconstructed the church in 1948). Another, about which little is known, is the 1935 extension to the Schachenmayr-Mann factory in Salach, southeast of Stuttgart.

Eduard Krüger was a student of Heinz Wetzel at the Technische Hochschule (polytechnic) in Stuttgart. Wetzel, along with Paul Schmitthenner and Paul Bonatz, was the intellectual leader of the Stuttgart School. Krüger seems to have first made his mark on Stuttgart with a student fraternity house of 1927-28. Situated on a hill in one of the city's mostly residential areas, this clean modernist structure reflects the influence of the radical homes then being erected in the Weissenhof Siedlung (see pp. 171-72). Now known as "Wingolf," with its window patterns somewhat changed and its rooftop terrace roofed over, the building still serves a function similar to its original one. Krüger appears next in publications as one of the architects who designed homes in the 1933 "Deutsches Holz" (German Wood) exhibition in Am Kochenhof (the one published was at Stitzenburgstrasse 16, now the corner of Otto-Reiniger-Strasse and Kalckreuthweg). He also executed more significant commissions.

One of these was for a wood-framed Gedächtnishaus (memorial lodge) atop the Schliffkopf mountain, which, at about 3,450 feet above sea level, overlooked the Black Forest between Rastatt and Freudenstadt. The Schwäbische Schneelaufbund (Association of Swabian Skiers) built this in 1931-32 as a functional memorial to their dead comrades. The structure, its stark, sweeping, clean lines related to the dramatic landscape, served as one of Hitler's command posts in 1939. In 1973 it became a hotel; alterations included an addition housing a swimming pool that used an underground bunker as its foundation.

left: Eduard Krüger. Schwabenhalle, Stuttgart-Canstatt, 1937-39 (demolished). From *Moderne Bauformen* (1940).

Eduard Krüger. Kreissparkasse (now Stadtkasse), Herrenstrasse and Paradiesstrasse, Wangen im Allgäu, 1937. Photograph 1990.

The entire complex was destroyed by fire in 1991. Krüger's next large building was the glass and stucco pump room at the spa of Bad Mergentheim near Würzburg from 1934-35. The structure and spaces still exist essentially as designed. In its detailing and in certain design features, notably some of the elevations, it is related to the 1933-34 spa at Wildbad in the Black Forest, which still stands. Krüger received yet another major commission with the Schwabenhalle, built from 1937 to 1939 near Bonatz's stadium in Stuttgart-Canstatt. This simple wooden shed structure, measuring about 525 by 209 feet, had a staggering capacity of 22,000 people and was obviously intended for public rallies. Nonetheless, with a height of less than twenty feet, its profile in the landscape was notably low. The entrance elevation bore a skeletal wood-framed structure painted rust red and gold and adorned with a stylized eagle and swastika. Krüger's career flourished throughout the Third Reich, his buildings ranging from the hybridized modernist to the classical and even including a medieval-style bank of 1937 in Wangen im Allgäu that is said to be a copy of a fifteenth-century structure shown in old prints of the site. After the war, however, his career faded, possibly because of his association with the Nazi power structure. A short notice in a 1955 issue of *Der Baumeister* (p. 396) states simply that he had accepted a post teaching architecture in Indonesia.

Selected Sources

For Schlösser, see Wörner and Lupfer, *Stuttgart*, sites 4, 150, and 187; "St. Georgskirche in Stuttgart," *Moderne Bauformen* (1935), pp. 192-93; Hartwig Beseler and Niels Gutschow, *Kriegsschicksale Deutscher Architektur*, 2 vols. (Neumünster, 1988), vol. 1, p. 1250; "Ein Spinnereineubau für Schachenmayr, Mann + Cie in Salach," *Moderne Bauformen* (1935), pp. 509-16; [Obituary], *Stuttgarter Zeitung*, June 22, 1967. For Krüger, see "Ein Verbindungshaus in Stuttgart," *Der Baumeister* (1931), pp. 42-43; *Wasmuths Monatshefte für Baukunst und Städtebau* (1931), pp. 221-23; "Das Gedächtnishaus am Schliffkopf im Schwarzwald," *Moderne Bauformen* (1933), pp. 283-302; A. Gut, "Wandelhalle und Brunnenhäuser in Bad Mergentheim," *Moderne Bauformen* (1936), pp. 661-80; Paul Bonatz, "Volksschule und Stadthalle in Künzelsau — Festhalle Ingelfingen — Schwabenhalle in Stuttgart," *Moderne Bauformen* (1940), pp. 201-28; "Kreissparkasse Wangen im Allgäu," *Moderne Bauformen* (1943), pp. 125-31; "Die neue Trink- und Wandelhalle in Wildbad im Württ. Schwarzwald," *Der Baumeister* (May 1935), pp. 149-55.

Of all the housing developments carried out during the Weimar Republic, the Weissenhof Siedlung of 1927 is the most famous. Organized by Ludwig Mies van der Rohe and Hugo Häring, it included work by Germany's best-known avant-garde architects and by such foreigners as J. J. P. Oud from Holland and Le Corbusier from France. Its apartment blocks, town houses, and single-family homes have been discussed thoroughly in recent books by Karin Kirsch and by Richard Pommer and Christian Otto. Although the Weissenhof Siedlung may not have been the successful prototype for industrialized housing that it was intended to be, its surviving buildings have been recently restored and they testify to the striking nature and importance of these modernist dwellings. Writers often compare this estate with the more conservative building exhibition "Deutsches Holz" (German Wood) of 1933, which consisted of model homes and small apartment buildings constructed in Am Kochenhof by a variety of Stuttgart School architects led by Paul Bonatz, Paul Schmitthenner, and Heinz Wetzel. The Kochenhof estate was ultimately developed as an explicitly nationalist answer to what was perceived as the soulless, internationalized modernism of the Weissenhof Siedlung. Yet by concentrating on these two contrary housing projects, it is easy to ignore the wealth of mainstream

Ludwig Mies van der Rohe. Apartment building in the Weissenhof Siedlung, Am Weissenhof, Pankokweg, and Brückenweg, Stuttgart, 1927. Photograph 1989.

Aerial view of the Weissenhof Siedlung, Stuttgart. Photograph September 21, 1927, by Strähle Luftbild.

Le Corbusier and Pierre Jeanneret. House in the Weissenhof Siedlung, Rathenaustrasse and Friedrich-Ebert-Strasse, Stuttgart, 1927. Photograph 1985.

Hans Scharoun. House in the Weissenhof Siedlung, Rathenaustrasse and Hölzelweg, Stuttgart, 1927. Photograph 1985.

modern housing constructed throughout Stuttgart in the twenties and thirties. The following sections on apartment buildings and single-family homes will help redress the balance.

Selected Sources

Wörner and Lupfer, *Stuttgart*, sites 175 and 180-85; Karin Kirsch, *Die Weissenhofsiedlung* (Stuttgart, 1987), trans. as *The Weissenhof Siedlung* (New York, 1989); Richard Pommer and Christian Otto, *Weissenhof 1927 and the Modern Movement in Architecture* (Chicago, 1991); Hans Volkart, "Ausstellung 'Deutsches Holz' Stuttgart 1933," *Der Baumeister* (1933), pp. 387-89; "Die Holzsiedlung am Kochenhof bei Stuttgart," *Moderne Bauformen* (1933), pp. 567-95.

Only two of the architects who contributed to the Weissenhof Siedlung came from Stuttgart: Richard Döcker and Adolf Schneck. We shall speak later of Schneck (see pp. 178-79, 182). Döcker was born in 1894 in Weilheim-Teck, a small community in Württemberg, and he studied in a variety of schools before enrolling at the Technische Hochschule (polytechnic) in Stuttgart in 1912. After service in World War I, he returned to that school to graduate and to undertake occasional work for Paul Bonatz. In 1923 he became a member of the avant-garde group *Der Ring*, and that association launched him on a prolific career with international modernist connections. He spent the years of Nazi rule in isolation, separated from friends, such as Erich Mendelsohn, who had left Germany shortly after Hitler's rise to power. During World War II, from 1941 to 1944, he worked in the reconstruction office in Saarbrücken, near the Franco-German border. In 1946 he returned to Stuttgart to help with the rebuilding of the city, teaching and practicing architecture there until his retirement in 1958. He died in 1968. Döcker is well known to architectural historians for a variety of building

Richard Döcker. Apartment buildings, Im Wallmer estate, Fiechtnerstrasse, Sattelstrasse, and Wallmerstrasse, Stuttgart-Untertürkheim, 1929-30. Photograph 1989.

Richard Döcker, Ernst Wagner, and others. Apartment buildings, Schönbühl estate, Klingenstrasse, Ostendstrasse, and Schönbühlstrasse, Stuttgart, 1929-30. Photograph 1989.

Peter Feile and Walter Loos. Double house and setback house type A, Lerchenhain estate, Steubenstrasse and Richard-Wagner-Strasse, Würzburg, 1928-30. Photographs 1990.

types, the most prominent being hospitals (see p. 95) and multi-family housing blocks. His housing projects from the twenties evince an increasing move away from his somewhat expressionist beginnings.

An example of this simple style in the work of other architects is the apartment complex on Taubenheimstrasse and Kissinger Strasse. A similar approach is apparent in the additions of c. 1930 by Bloch and Guggenheimer to the Eiernest estate. Sadly, these architects' work on Karl-Kloss-Strasse and Raabestrasse has been altered beyond recognition. The call of the extreme modernism represented by the Weissenhof Siedlung could be heard far and wide, even in the conservative, Baroque

environment of Würzburg, where Peter Feile and Walter Loos designed avant-garde single and double houses in the Lerchenhain estate from 1928 to 1930.

The accession to power of the Nazis in 1933 influenced taste in housing, but not substantially. For instance, the apartment house from 1934 on Alexanderstrasse — a boulevard still lined with large nineteenth-century villas — combines conservative elements on the street facade with *moderne* balconies and bay windows overlooking the hilly landscape behind. And the double house by Paul Schmohl at Hauptmannsreute 17 from c. 1933-35 has horizontal and vertical strip windows akin to those in work of the twenties and thirties by,

S. Stantscheff. Four-family apartment house, Alexanderstrasse 8b, Stuttgart-Mitte, 1934 (windows altered). From *Moderne Bauformen* (1936) and photograph 1991.

bottom left: Paul Schmohl. Two-family house, Hauptmannsreute 17, Stuttgart-Nord (near Kräherwald), 1933-35. Photograph 1991.

bottom right: Ernst Wagner. Houses on Am Vogelhang, corner of Gähkopf and Ehrenhalde, Stuttgart-Nord, 1932-34. From *Moderne Bauformen* (1935).

top and center: Ernst Wagner and Werner Commichau. Multi-family houses, Schottstrasse 5-7, Stuttgart-Nord (near Kräherwald), 1935. Photographs 1990.

Hans Eitel. House, Vogelsang estate, Botnangerstrasse and Stirnbrandstrasse, Stuttgart-West, 1934-39. Photograph 1989.

say, Frank Lloyd Wright and his followers. Finally, there are multi-family houses from the mid-thirties designed by Ernst Wagner that continued to employ modernist design elements, despite the pitched roofs deemed essential to residential buildings at the time. Wagner was one of Stuttgart's modernist architects who had worked with Döcker on the Schönbühl estate and who had been a candidate to design a house in the Weissenhof Siedlung until Mies van der Rohe rejected him in favor of Adolf Schneck. Wagner's homes of the thirties often display modernist, simpleplaned facades within picturesque groupings of housing blocks. These groups or clusters of large and small units tend to de-monumenta-

lize the multi-family houses, making them appear as variously sized single-family homes. This contrasts with the more conservative, row house arrangement of Hans Eitel's Vogelsang estate of 1934-39.

Selected Sources

Wörner and Lupfer, *Stuttgart*, sites 93, 139, and 249; Friederike Mehlau-Wiebking, *Richard Döcker: Ein Architekt im Aufbruch zur Moderne* (Braunschweig and Wiesbaden, 1989); *Richard Döcker 1894-1968*, exhibition catalogue, Stuttgart, BDA-Architekturgalerie (Stuttgart, 1982); *Neuzeitliche Miethäuser und Siedlungen*, ed. Leo Adler (Berlin, 1931), esp. p. 179 (Taubenheimstrasse estate); "Ein Architekt besucht Stuttgart," *Moderne Bauformen* (1936), p. 4 (Hauptmannsreute double house by Schmohl); "Neue Wohnbauten in Stuttgart der Architekten O. Bloch + E. Guggenheimer, Stuttgart," *Moderne Bauformen* (1931), pp. 7-15; "Ernst Wagner, Stuttgart: Wohnhausgruppe," *Moderne Bauformen* (1935), pp. 22-27, and *Moderne Bauformen* (1936), pp. 498-99 (Schottstrasse apartments); "S. Stantscheff, Stuttgart: Vierfamilienhaus," *Moderne Bauformen* (1936), pp. 281-83. For Würzburg, see "Die Siedlung Lerchenhain in Würzburg," *Der Baumeister* (1931), pp. 466-67, and "Rationelle Terrassenhaustypen/Einfamilienhäuser," *Die Form* (1933), pp. 13-18.

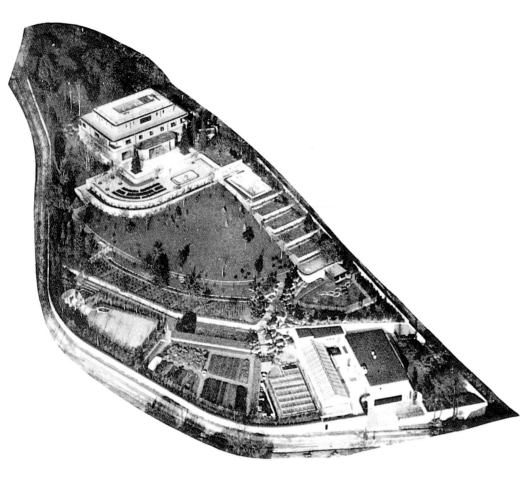

opposite page:
top: Fritz August Breuhaus de Groot. Am Tatzel-wurm estate, Stuttgart 1929 (demolished). From *F. A. Breuhaus*, Neue Werkkunst (Berlin, Leipzig, and Vienna, 1929).

bottom: Richard Döcker. Vetter House, Birken-waldstrasse 169, Stuttgart-Nord, 1927-28. Photograph 1990.

this page:
Alfred Daiber. Fuchs House, Gänswaldweg 9, Stuttgart, c. 1930. Photograph 1990.

Gustav Daucher. House, Grüneisenstrasse 7, Stuttgart, c. 1933. Photograph 1990.

The most spectacular modernist villa built in Stuttgart has not survived. It was not part of the Weissenhof Siedlung, as one might expect, but a curvilinear, *moderne* structure on Am Tatzelwurm, in the Lumpenwulf estate, designed by Fritz August Breuhaus de Groot in 1929. The house was destroyed in World War II and apartment blocks from the seventies and eighties now occupy the site. Yet many important single-family homes from the twenties still stand in the hilly landscape to the north, west, and southeast of the city center. The best known are those by Richard Döcker, whose

Paul Schmohl and Georg Staehelin. Hahn House,
Gustav-Siegle-Strasse 30, Stuttgart-West, 1929.
Photographs 1990.

work has been widely published. His Klipper
and Vetter houses of 1927-28 are striking
examples of clean modernist design. Other
architects, among them Alfred Daiber, Gustav
Daucher, and Paul Schmohl, peppered the
nearby lots with like-styled homes. Of these,
the Hahn House of 1929 by Schmohl is Stuttgart's hidden treasure.

Schmohl, architect of Stuttgart's famed Hindenburgbau (see p. 188), and Georg Staehelin
designed the Hahn House as a mixture of
modern and slightly more traditional elements.
Travertine exterior walls on the ground floor
contrast with the stucco surfaces of the upper
floor and the tiling of the hipped roof. The
dining room had a window which, as with

one in Mies van der Rohe's Tugendhat House
in Brno, Czechoslovakia (now Czech
Republic), could be electrically lowered into
the travertine base. It no longer functions.
Slightly damaged in the war, the house was
subsequently confiscated and repaired by the
U. S. Army, which used it as officers' quarters
until 1959. Then Mrs. Hahn, the ex-wife of the
original owner, occupied the premises again
until her death in 1961. Renovated, it served
as the Spanish Consulate until 1969. Later,
more extensive remodeling took place, leaving
the house with new windows and roof
dormers. Descendants of the original owner
live there today. Its situation in the middle of a
large double lot atop one of Stuttgart's hills

offers spectacular views of the city and the
surrounding countryside.

The story of the Hahn House is doubtless
representative of the fate of many residential
structures, whose combination of traditional
and modern tastes was continually altered
over time. Homes affected in this way range
from large ones by Denis Boniver to more traditional cottage-like designs by Eugen Zinsmeister. Other structures erected in the Stuttgart
hills during the thirties, including the Höhengast-
stätte restaurant in Geroksruhe by the Eckert
brothers and the remodeling of the Charlottenhaus Frauenklinik (gynecological clinic) by
Schneck and Wacker, adopted the imagery of
this local residential architecture.

top left: Eugen Zinsmeister. "H" House, Gustav-Siegle-Strasse 27, Stuttgart-West, 1932. Photograph 1990.

top right: Denis Boniver. "F" House, Richard-Wagner-Strasse 79, Stuttgart, c. 1935-37. Photograph 1989.

Adolf Schneck with Eugen Wacker. Charlottenhaus Frauenklinik, Gerokstrasse 31, Stuttgart, before 1935. Photograph 1989.

Selected Sources

Wörner and Lupfer, *Stuttgart*, sites 151 and 168 (Vetter House, for which see also *Moderne Bauformen* [1929], p. 217); "Adolf Schneck, Mitarbeiter Eugen Wacker: Entbindungsheim, Schwesternhaus und Arzthaus," *Moderne Bauformen* (1935), pp. 397-416; "Denis Boniver: Wohnhäuser in und um Stuttgart," *Moderne Bauformen* (1937), pp. 194-202; *Gaststätten*, ed. Herbert Hoffmann (Stuttgart, 1939), p. 13; "Eugen Zinsmeister, Stuttgart: Wohnhaus H an der Gustav-Siegle-Str.," *Moderne Bauformen* (1934), pp. 494-95; "Gustav Daucher, Stuttgart: Mehrfamilienhaus in Stuttgart," *Moderne Bauformen* (1935), p. 436; "Haus Dr. Fuchs — Stuttgart,"*Der Baumeister* (1931), p. 251; "Paul Schmohl + Georg Staehelin, Stuttgart: Zwei Wohnhäuser in Stuttgart," *Moderne Bauformen* (1931), pp. 61-65.

Most guidebooks and architectural histories cite the Stadtbad Heslach of 1927 as representative of sports facilities in the Stuttgart region. Although its arched swimming pool is a significant example of its type, it has overshadowed a number of other sports facilities in the city and region that are really just as important. Virtually unknown is the swimming pool in Reutlingen of c. 1930 (recently renovated and altered), and the sports facilities designed by Paul Bonatz have also largely been ignored. His swimming pool of 1928-29 in the Stuttgart district of Untertürkheim, for instance, has not been published since it was built. Its long lines and brick construction place it among the hard core of modernist buildings, fit to rank with the work of Ludwig Mies van der Rohe and others. A comparable functionalism informs Bonatz's Willy Sachs Stadium and sports park in Schweinfurt from 1936. The brick and concrete tribune has skeletal glass walls and markedly modern spiral staircases. In keeping with the contextualism promoted by the Nazis in the

Gustav Schaupp. Swimming pool (now Hallenbad), Albstrasse between Innere Kelterstrasse and Äussere Kelterstrasse, Reutlingen, c. 1930. Photograph 1990.

Bonatz and Scholer. Swimming pool, Inselstrasse, Stuttgart-Untertürkheim, c. 1928-29. Photograph 1989.

Paul Bonatz, with Kurt Dübbers and Franz Dölker. Willy Sachs Stadium, Niederwerrner Strasse near Kasernenweg, Schweinfurt, 1936. Photographs 1989.

mid-thirties, however, the adjacent restaurant and entry gates are stylized images of houses. The restaurant interior and furnishings still look as they did in publications of the thirties. Indeed, the entire site seems to be preserved in its original state, even down to the park furniture. The park's location at the north-western edge of the city probably spared it the extensive destruction wrought by American air raids on the city center and on the industrial

district that contained the city's ball bearing factories. Bonatz likely owed the receipt of the commission for the stadium less to his experience in working on such facilities than to his architectural connections with the Sachs family: in the early thirties he had designed the headquarters of the Fichtel and Sachs company on Ernst-Sachs-Strasse.

Selected Sources

Wörner and Lupfer, *Stuttgart*, site 112 (Stadtbad Heslach), and "Stadtbad Stuttgart-Hesloch [sic]," *Der Baumeister* (1931), p. 53; "Inselbad Untertürkheim," *Der Baumeister* (1929), p. 324; *Paul Bonatz, und seine Schüler*, p. 22; "Schwimmbad in Reutlingen," *Der Baumeister* (1931), pp. 76-78; "Willy-Sachs-Stadion Schweinfurt," *Moderne Bauformen* (1937), pp. 507-24; *Gussglas* (Düsseldorf, 1938), p. 128. For aerial reconnaissance photographs showing the wartime damage done to Schweinfurt's industrial center and the unscathed stadium, see "Bombing Through Smoke," *Impact* (September 1944), p. 34.

Alfred Schmidt. Kinderheilstätte (now Fachklinik Burgelitz), on the outskirts of Wangen im Allgäu, 1929 (altered). Photograph 1990.

bottom left: Albert Eitel. Karl Olga Krankenhaus, Werderstrasse, Hackstrasse, and Schwarenbergstrasse, Stuttgart, 1930 (altered). Photograph 1989.

bottom right: Hans Daiber. Chirurgische Universitätsklinik (University Hospital for Surgery), Calwerstrasse 7, Tübingen, 1930-35. Photograph 1991.

Richard Döcker is usually credited with creating the region's most important hospital, at Waiblingen, north of Stuttgart, in 1927. Unfortunately, this sweepingly terraced building, complete with murals by Willi Baumeister, has been demolished. Yet other large health care facilities survive more or less intact in the city and the surrounding area. These include: Albert Eitel's setback, yet conservatively roofed, Karl Olga Hospital of 1930; the similarly massed Robert Bosch Hospital of 1936-40 by Früh and Mehlin; the American-looking modernist skyscraper hospital of 1930-35 in Tübingen by Hans Daiber; and the greatly altered Kinderheilstätte (children's hospital) of 1929 at Wangen by Stuttgart architect Alfred Schmidt. Of the extant hospitals and sanatoria in the region, none is as dramatically situated or as strikingly designed as Adolf Schneck's Haus auf der Alb of 1928-30. Originally a spa hotel for workers in business and industry, this building is currently being renovated as the region's center for political and civil service conferences. Its architect's career flourished from the twenties (see pp. 178-79) through the fifties, and even included the design of hybridized modernist interiors for the Wehrmacht during the Third Reich. Schneck also wrote books on furnishings before and after the war, such as *Schrank, Tisch und Bett* (Cupboard, Table, and Bed; Stuttgart, 1932) and *Das Polstermöbel* (Upholstered Furniture; Stuttgart, 1951). His versatility in conservative and modernist

J. Früh and Heinz Mehlin. Robert Bosch Hospital (now Landespolizei Direktion, or State Police Headquarters), Hahnemannstrasse, Stuttgart, c. 1936-40. Photograph 1989.

Adolf Schneck. Haus auf der Alb, Bad Urach, 1929-30. Photograph during restoration, 1991.

design, comparable to that of Fritz August Breuhaus de Groot and Cäsar Pinnau (see pp. 14-15), will come as something of a surprise to those who know him only for his house in the Weissenhof Siedlung.

Selected Sources

Mehlau-Wiebking, *Richard Döcker*, pp. 121-23; *Neuzeitliche Hotels und Krankenhäuser* (Berlin, c. 1930), pp. 352-61 (Waiblingen); "Adolf Schneck 75 Jahre," *Der Baumeister*, (1958), p. 652; "Das Haus auf der Alb bei Urach," *Der Baumeister* (1930), pp. 378-85; "Das Robert-Bosch-Krankenhaus in Stuttgart," *Der Baumeister* (1942), pp. 113-16; "Die Chirurgische Universitätsklinik in Tübingen," *Moderne Bauformen* (1936), pp. 5-25; Rainer Stommer, *Hochhaus: Der Beginn in Deutschland* (Marburg, 1990), pp. 236-38; "Kinderheilstätte in Wangen im Allgäu," *Moderne Bauformen* (1941), pp. 494-501; Heinrich Schmieden, *Krankenhausbau in neuer Zeit* (Kirchhain, 1930), pp. 239-41; "Neubau des Karl-Olga-Krankenhauses in Stuttgart," *Moderne Bauformen* (1930), pp. 225-31; Hubert Ritter, *Der Krankenhausbau der Gegenwart* (Stuttgart, 1932), p. 77; "Officierheim eines Panzerregiments," *Moderne Bauformen* (1940), pp. 259-72.

left: Hans Volkart and Paul Trüdinger. Evangelische Kirche, Amstetter Strasse and Seemoosweg, Stuttgart-Hedelfingen, 1929-30. Photograph 1989.

right: K. Weidle. Neuapostolische Kirche, Brunnstrasse 10, Tübingen, c. 1930-31. Photograph 1990.

Guides to, and histories of, architecture in the Stuttgart region include only a few churches from the period under study. As one would expect of buildings of this type, they tend to be representative in character. An example is the Südkirche on Spitalstrasse in the Pliensauvorstadt district of Esslingen (1925-26) by Frankfurt architect Martin Elsaesser (see pp. 56, 61-63), its setback forms and buttresses, and its position atop a hill, recalling a fortified church from the Middle Ages. Surprisingly, however, there exist churches whose modernism tran-

scends the traditional associations customarily evoked by ecclesiastical structures. These churches never appear in literature on the Modern Movement in Stuttgart, perhaps because they do not fit the stereotype view of this region as the home of the rather conservative Stuttgart School. One such church is the cemetery chapel in Kornwestheim, just north of Stuttgart, from the late twenties. It still stands, at the intersection of Bergstrasse and Aldinger Strasse, but is difficult to photograph. Two further modernist churches have survived virtually as built. The first is the Evangelische Kirche (Protestant church) in Stuttgart-Hedelfingen, with a capacity of nine hundred, which was begun on September 29, 1929, and completed on October 26, 1930. The other is the Neuapostolische Kirche in Tübingen, with a capacity of seven hundred. Although the roof, windows, and doors have been replaced, the curved expressionist facade of brick and stucco presents an avant-garde

image appropriate to this evangelical congregation. The complex includes a similarly styled parish house.

Selected Sources

Martin Elsaesser: Bauten und Entwürfe aus den Jahren 1924-1932, vol. 2 (Berlin, 1933), pp. 207-12; Falk Jaeger, *Bauen in Deutschland* (Stuttgart, 1985), p. 121; "Die neue Friedhofskapelle in Stuttgart-Kornwestheim," *Der Baumeister* (1933), p. 249 and pls. 74-77; "Evangelische Kirche in Hedelfingen," *Der Baumeister* (1931), pp. 18-21; "Neuapostolische Kirche in Tübingen," *Deutsche Bauzeitung* (April 1, 1933), p. 287, and *Der Baumeister* (1932), p. 197.

Stuttgart's school buildings of the late twenties and thirties include interesting examples of modernism by architects who are not necessarily associated with the Modern Movement. The Evangelische Töchterinstitut (Protestant girls' school) near Stadtbad Heslach, designed by E. Weippert, has been somewhat altered since construction in the twenties. It projects an image of industrial efficiency on its Arminstrasse facade, with the clock on its stair tower hinting at its institutional function. Little information on Weippert is available, though the firm of Aldinger, Dürr and Weippert is known to have executed the conservative homes of 1932-35 and 1937-40 in the Wolfbusch estate. The Sammelschule by Paul Schmitthenner is equally functional, even industrial, in appearance. This applies particularly to its courtyard facade, which contrasts with the more formal, bilateral symmetry of the Suevenstrasse front. Considering the arch-conservative nature of Schmitthenner's other buildings, the school ranks as something of an exception in his oeuvre.

Gerhard Graubner, Paul Bonatz's assistant at the Technische Hochschule (polytechnic), has been overshadowed by his mentor. Graubner's name rarely appears in connection with constructed buildings, but at least one is extant, though considerably altered. This is the Handels- und Berufsschule addition of 1935, which Graubner appended to a school that he had designed in the late twenties. The addition, now with new windows, still functions as part of the Höhere Handelsschule und Kaufmannsschule (advanced business school). By contrast with the work of

E. Weippert. Evangelisches Töchterinstitut (now Mörike-Gymnasium), Arminstrasse, Stuttgart-Süd, 1929-30. Photograph 1989.

Gerhard Graubner. Addition to the Handels- und Berufsschule, Rotebühlstrasse and Hasenbergstrasse, Stuttgart, 1935 (altered). Photograph 1990.

top and center: Paul Schmitthenner. Sammel-schule (now Hohenstein-und-Robert-Bosch-Schule), Suevenstrasse and Hohenstrasse 25, Stuttgart-Zuffenhausen, 1929. Photographs 1989.

Helmut Weber. Turnhalle of the Stöckach-Schule, Werrastrasse 138, Stuttgart-Ost, c. 1936-37. From *Moderne Bauformen* (1937).

an older Stuttgart School modernist such as Graubner, Helmut Weber's now forgotten Turn-halle (gymnasium) for the Stöckach-Schule from the later thirties combines a traditional roof line and flat-arched entrance with the large windows necessary for a building of this type. This small structure launched Weber on a career that would blossom in the postwar period with, among other commissions, work on Stuttgart's Messe (trade fair) grounds and on the city's university buildings.

Selected Sources

Wörner and Lupfer, *Stuttgart*, sites 208 (Schmitthen-ner), 132, 176, 296 (Weber), and 202 (Weippert); Julius Vischer, *Der neue Schulbau* (Stuttgart, 1931), p. 55 (Weippert); *Der Baumeister* (1933), pp. 62-65 (Schmitthenner); "Die Städtische Handels- und Berufs-schule, Stuttgart," *Monatshefte für Baukunst und Städtebau* (1938), p. 312 (see also Vischer, *Der neue Schulbau*, p. 90); "Turnhalle für eine Schule," *Moderne Bauformen* (1937), pp. 257-61.

left: Ernst Otto Osswald. *Tagblatt*-Turmhaus, Eberhardstrasse 61, Stuttgart, 1924-28. Photograph 1990.

right: Bonatz and Scholer. Rathaus and water tower, Kornwestheim, 1933-35. Photograph 1989.

Stuttgart's two most famous skyscrapers deserve mention here even though they have been extensively published elsewhere. The first is the *Tagblatt*-Turmhaus of 1924-28 by Ernst Otto Osswald. The design for this eighteen-story newspaper headquarters, which is two hundred feet high, was the winner of a controversial competition that included entries by Paul Bonatz, Heinz Wetzel, Adolf Schneck, and Hugo Keuerleber. It reveals some influence from the 1922 Chicago Tribune Tower competition, Walter Gropius's entry to that

competition being a likely source of the projecting balconies. Although some have likened the *Tagblatt*-Turmhaus to American skyscrapers, its design and massing bear little relationship to the predominately Art Deco and historicist work then being done in the United States. On the contrary, the overall appearance and some individual forms prefigure the famous Philadelphia Savings Fund Society Building of 1932 by Howe and Lescaze. The *Tagblatt*-Turmhaus was probably the first building in Germany to employ light-toned poured concrete and, aside from the jarringly new windows, no substantial alterations have been made to it.

One of the last high-rises to be erected in this region before the war was Bonatz's water tower of 1933-35, designed as part of the town hall complex in Kornwestheim, north of Stuttgart. Constructed of reinforced concrete and brick infill, it is 157 feet high and tapers slightly toward the top. Its stark, industrial look corresponds to its function. Among the few

discernible alterations to have been made to the structure is the clock placement. Next to the tower is the Rathaus (town hall), which Bonatz designed with Scholer in a more contextual style, as befits the building's civic function.

Selected Sources

Wörner and Lupfer, *Stuttgart*, site 70 (*Tagblatt*-Turmhaus) and pp. 198-99 (water tower); Stommer, *Hochhaus*, pp. 148-49 and 213-16; "Das Tagblatt-Turmhaus in Stuttgart," *Deutsche Bauzeitung* (January 1, 1929), pp. 13-18.

Albert Schleber. Hahn and Kolb building, König-strasse 14, Stuttgart, 1925-27 (Haus der Technischen Werke on the right). Photograph 1990.

Paul Schmohl, Georg Staehelin, Albert Eitel and Richard Bielenberg. Hindenburgbau, Arnulf-Klett-Platz, Stuttgart, 1926-28. The Zeppelinbau is on the right. Photograph 1990.

The Stuttgart School's approach to masonry modernism is best seen in buildings for commerce and industry. In addition to the *Tagblatt-Turmhaus* (see p. 187), a number of large masonry commercial structures from this period still survive. They range from the massive central post office of 1928, complete with appropriate sculptural decoration, to the cubic, setback Hahn and Kolb building of 1925-27 by Albert Schleber, from the *moderne* Mittnachtbau of 1926-28 by Ludwig Eisenlohr and Oscar Pfennig to the severe inheritor of the twenties traditions embodied in these buildings, the 1936 Haus der Technischen Werke. The most famous of the commercial buildings in the city, however, are two structures on the same street: the offices, stores, and theater complex of the Hindenburgbau of 1926-28 by Paul Schmohl, Georg Staehelin, Albert Eitel and Richard Bielenberg and, across the street, the bank, hotel, and offices of the Zeppelinbau of 1929-31 by Bonatz and Scholer (with additions of 1956-59 by Karl Ellsässer after Bonatz's original plans).

The latter building became famous because of the 1928 competition from which it emerged. The competition, for a multi-use structure on this site, drew entries from Adolf Abel, Bonatz and Scholer, Richard Döcker, Alfred Fischer, Carl Krayl, Schleicher and Gutschow, Adolf Schneck, Wetzel and Schuhmacher, and Mies van der Rohe. Mies's proposed glass building subsequently achieved renown as a precursor

Bonatz and Scholer. Zeppelinbau (now Hotel Graf Zeppelin), Lautenschlagerstrasse and Arnulf-Klett-Platz, Stuttgart, 1929-31. Photograph 1990.

Schleicher and Gutschow. Model of premiated entry for the Zeppelinbau competition, 1928.

of his postwar American work. The premiated design was that of Schleicher and Gutschow from Hamburg (see pp. 113-14), but it was not constructed: apparently, the political clout of Bonatz and Scholer, architects of the main railroad station just across the boulevard, was too great. It was thus their design that was built, existing today as the Hotel Graf Zeppelin.

Two further modernist masonry structures have been overlooked by architectural historians and guide writers. One is the Allgemeine

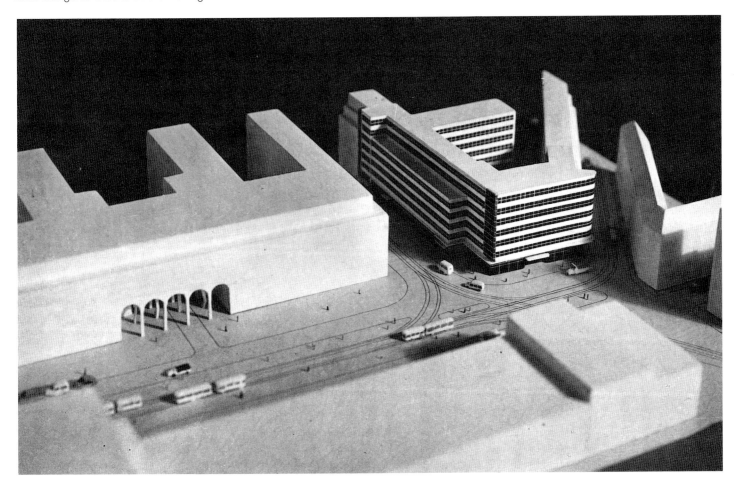

Alfred Daiber. Allgemeine Ortskrankenkasse building, Falkerstrasse and Breitscheidstrasse, Stuttgart, c. 1929-32. From *Moderne Bauformen* (1933) and photograph 1989.

Albert Hauschildt. D. H. V. Haus (now Deutsche Angestellten-Gewerkschaft building), Jägerstrasse 24, Stuttgart, c. 1930-32. Photograph 1989.

Ortskrankenkasse (General Health Insurance Fund) building by Alfred Daiber. This consists of two separate buildings, one for offices and laboratories, one for medical treatment. The former is the larger of the two and still exists, though its fenestration, in particular, has been altered. The second forgotten structure is the small D. H. V. Haus, with its four-story masonry facade designed by Albert Hauschildt. Its windows, too, have been changed, and the walled-in garden at the building's front now serves as garages and parking space. Both buildings demonstrate that masonry modernism in Stuttgart could be modern in the generally accepted sense of the term, with unornamented cubic massing pierced by numerous windows.

Selected Sources

Wörner and Lupfer, *Stuttgart*, sites 2, 3, 13, and 37-39; Stommer, *Hochhaus*, pp. 108-9 and 186-87; *Mies Reconsidered*, ed. John Zukowsky (Chicago, 1986), pp. 114-16 and 168-71; "D. H. V. Haus in Stuttgart," *Der Baumeister* (1933), p. 9 and pls. 1-5; "Die Ortskrankenkasse Stuttgart," *Moderne Bauformen* (1933), pp. 166-83.

Thomas Wechs. Schuberthof, Rosenaustrasse, Schlettererstrasse, and Johann-Rösle-Strasse, Augsburg, 1927-28. Photograph 1989.

Thomas Wechs. Lessinghof, Rosenaustrasse and Schlettererstrasse, Augsburg, 1930-31. Photograph 1989.

In discussions of modernism in Germany the city of Augsburg never rates a mention. Yet a student of Theodor Fischer made his mark there: Thomas Wechs. Wechs is best known for being one of the designers of Munich's World War I memorial (see p. 202), but his contributions to architecture in Augsburg were more substantial, climaxing in a number of Catholic churches erected in the fifties and sixties. In the prewar period he had designed two important large housing blocks near the main railroad station: the Schuberthof of 1927-28 and the Lessinghof of 1930-31. They remind one of the large blocks done by Bruno Taut and others in Berlin, though Wechs's are rather more restrained in style. The Schuberthof provided 186 units of two to four rooms in one- and two-bedroom apartments, while the Lessinghof offered four types of flat,

Architectural Offices of the GAGFAH — Gemeinnützige A. G. für Angestellten-Heimstätten. Apartment houses, Holzbachstrasse and Rosenaustrasse, Augsburg, 1928. Photographs 1990.

center left: Clemens Böhm. Post-Siedlung, Speyerer Strasse, Stainingerstrasse, and Birkenfeldstrasse, Augsburg, 1930-31 (altered). Photograph 1989.

center right: Reichsbahndirektion Augsburg. S-Bahn station, Augsburg-Oberhausen, before 1935. Photograph 1990.

City Architect Freyberger. Apartment houses, Karl-Wahl-Siedlung (now Volkssiedlung), Haunstetter Strasse, Lehninger Strasse, and Waldrand, Augsburg-Haunstetten, c. 1936. Photograph 1989.

from two to five rooms, that accommodated some 68 families. Modernist housing by other architects from the same period survives nearby. Examples are the 1928 triple-courtyard housing at Rosenaustrasse and Holbachstrasse and the now greatly altered Post-Siedlung of 1930-31 by Clemens Böhm slightly to the northwest, across the Wertach River. Simply designed and almost modernist in some details and elevations, several buildings from the Nazi era also exist in Augsburg. They include the barrack-like two-family homes and slightly more modern apartment blocks of the Karl-Wahl-Siedlung from the mid-thirties, and the contemporary streamlined masonry S-Bahn station at Oberhausen.

Selected Sources

Robert Vorhoelzer: Ein Architektenleben, ed. Florian Aicher and Uwe Drepper (Munich, 1990), pp. 185 (Schuberthof, Lessinghof) and 170 (Post-Siedlung); *Neuzeitliche Miethäuser und Siedlungen*, pp. 98-99; "Augsburg-Oberhausen," *Deutsche Bauzeitung* (December 25, 1935), p. 1044; "Der Schuberthof," *Die Form* (1931), pp. 225-28; "Die Karl-Wahl-Siedlung in Augsburg," *Der Baumeister* (1937), pp. 37-47; "Die neue Post-Siedlung in Augsburg," *Wasmuths Monatshefte für Baukunst und Städtebau* (1932), pp. 1-5; "Lessinghof," *Moderne Bauformen* (1932), pp. 188-90 (part of an article on new apartment buildings, pp. 182-95).

Carl August Bembé. The architect's summer home. Riederau am Ammersee, near Diessen, 1929 (later additions). Photograph soon after construction.

Carl August Bembé. Kramer House, Seeweg, Diessen, 1930-31. Photographs 1990.

Hans Holzbauer. The architect's house, Tallweg, Holzhausen (Utting), 1932. Photograph 1990.

The area around the Ammersee south of Munich is known as a repository of beautiful Baroque churches, but it is also a favorite place for summer holidays, and holiday homes are a major architectural presence in the region. Summer homes of modern design were popularized in publications of the interwar years, in magazines, such as *Die Form* (1932), and in promotional booklets, such as *Wochenende* (1935). Architects from Munich built a number of summer homes here. Some of the most interesting were by Carl August Bembé (see p. 16), who combined an overall modernist approach with vernacular wood-frame details. His own home and the Kramer House are examples from the early thirties that survive. Although Bembé's own residence has been altered and added to, the Kramer House is almost as it was in the thirties, except that its

original barn-red color (still in evidence on the garage) has been painted over. Another architect, Hans Holzbauer, also built his own home in this area, at a site called, appropriately enough, Holzhausen. Holzbauer was a student of German Bestelmeyer (see p. 197) in Munich. After working with Peter Behrens in Berlin, he returned to Munich to open his own practice, which concentrated on eclectic, almost historicist, buildings that related to the region's townscapes. Despite this somewhat conservative approach, Holzbauer's own home was very modern in appearance. Its horizontal siding and strip windows are akin to those in some eclectic modern homes built in America at that time.

Selected Sources
For summer houses in general, see *Die Form* (1932), pp. 183-88, and *Wochenende: Entwürfe von Architekt W. v. Breunig, München, Köln* (Munich, 1935). For a survey of American homes similar to those of Bembé and Holzbauer, see James and Kathleen Morrow Ford, *The Modern House in America* (New York, 1940; repr. 1989), pp. 24-27. For Holzbauer and Bembé, see "Bauten von Hans Holzbauer," *Monatshefte für Baukunst und Städtebau* (1940), pp. 29-36; [Obituary for Carl August Bembé], *Der Baumeister* (1955), p. 115; "Wohnhaus am Ammersee: Architekt Hans Holzbauer," *Moderne Bauformen* (1940), pp. 139-42; "Wohnhäuser und Ferienhäuser auf dem Lande," *Moderne Bauformen* (1935), pp. 277-88 (see *Moderne Bauformen* [1933], p. 641, and *Der Baumeister* [1933], pp. 170-71 for Bembé's own home). For a more conservative, Japanese-influenced home by Bembé, see "Ein Ferienhaus am Ammersee," *Der Baumeister* (1940), pp. 117-25.

194   The South: Stuttgart and Munich

opposite page:
top: Robert Vorhoelzer, Franz Holzhammer, and Walther Schmidt. Paketzustellamt, Arnulfstrasse 62, Munich, 1926-27 (recent renovation as cafeteria and library for postal employees by Franz Stauda). Photographs 1989.

center left: Robert Vorhoelzer, Walther Schmidt and others. Arnulfstrasse housing estate, Arnulfstrasse, Richelstrasse, Schäringerstrasse, and Burghausener Strasse, Munich, 1928-29. Photograph 1988.

center right: Robert Vorhoelzer, Walther Schmidt and Hans Schnetzer. Post office and apartments, Tegernseer Landstrasse 57, Munich, 1929-30. Photograph 1989.

bottom: Robert Vorhoelzer and Walther Schmidt. Post office and apartments, Fraunhoferstrasse 22a, Munich, 1930-31. Photographs 1988 and 1991.

this page:
Robert Vorhoelzer and Hans Schnetzer. Post office and apartments, Am Harras 2, Munich, 1930-33. Photographs 1988.

One of Munich's answers to the depression of the early 1930s was a massive campaign to build post office facilities. A public building program for such structures already existed, with important post offices having been erected just west of the main railroad station and in neighborhoods throughout the city; but it was not until the nation was embroiled in the financial difficulties of the Great Depression that the Bavarian postal authorities created innovative multi-use complexes that combined retail and residential functions. Robert Vorhoelzer was the man most closely associated with this development.

Vorhoelzer trained at the Technische Hochschule (polytechnic) in Munich and worked in civil service positions related to architecture in that city and in Augsburg before military service in World War I interrupted his career. At the cessation of hostilities he returned to Munich. In 1920 he became Oberpostbaurat (Chief Architect of the Postal Service), a position that enabled him to control a wide-ranging design program for new post offices throughout Bavaria. His own designs, and

Franz Holzhammer and Walther Schmidt. Post office and apartments, Goetheplatz 1, Munich, 1931-33 (interiors completely altered by Herwig Palacky, 1988-89). Photograph 1989.

bottom left: Georg Werner, Lars Landschreiber and Wilhelm Wichtendahl. Post office, Dachauer Strasse and Maisacher Strasse, Fürstenfeldbruck, 1930.

bottom right: Franz Holzhammer and Hanna Löv. Post office, Bahnhofstrasse 36, Herrsching, 1933. Photograph 1992.

those of projects designed by others, can still be seen today throughout Munich, in such nearby towns as Herrsching and Fürstenfeldbruck, and even as far away as Coburg (this last, however, has been extensively modified and partly demolished in recent years). Numerous journals of the day recorded his achievement. His role in bringing modernism to Bavaria doubtless led to his participation in the 1931 Berlin Building Exposition. Many of the better known post offices of this time in Bavaria were his own work, but Franz Holzhammer, Walther Schmidt, and Georg Werner also contributed designs. All are clean-lined examples of modern stucco and masonry design, and some even continued to be con-

structed, published, and praised well into the Third Reich.

In the thirties Vorhoelzer taught at his alma mater and, following in the footsteps of Bruno Taut, in Istanbul in 1939-40. Vorhoelzer returned to Munich in 1941 and, after serving in the war, participated in the postwar reconstruction of the city. His post offices of the twenties and thirties have brought him well-deserved fame: of Munich's modernist buildings, they are the ones that have been most thoroughly studied, ever since the time of their construction. Their simple-planed masonry forms compare favorably with Paul Bonatz's similarly designed contributions to Stuttgart's urban environment.

left: German Bestelmeyer. Luftgaukommando building (now Bayerisches Staatsministerium für Wirtschaft und Verkehr), Prinzregentenstrasse 28, Munich, 1937-39. Photograph 1987.

right: German Bestelmeyer. Library and former Convention Hall, Deutsches Museum, Museumsinsel and Ludwigsbrücke, Munich, 1928-35. Photograph 1989.

Selected Sources

Bauten und Plätze in München, sites 221 and 285; Fischer, *Architektur in München*, sites 25 and 37-41; *Neuere Postbauten in Bayern*, 3 vols. (Munich, 1925, 1928, and 1934); *Robert Vorhoelzer: Ein Architektenleben*. Selected articles on post office buildings: Justus Bier, "Neue Münchener Postbauten," *Die Form* (1930), pp. 469-86; "Das neue Postdienstgebäude in Coburg," *Deutsche Bauzeitung* (March 15, 1933), pp. 209-13; "Der neue Grosssender München," *Die Form* (1933), pp. 151-55; "Die Post-Versuchssiedlung an der Arnulfstrasse in München," *Der Baumeister* (1930), pp. 113-15; "Ein neues Postamt in München," *Die Form* (1932), pp. 51-54 (Fraunhoferstrasse); "Treppen: Postdienstgebäude am Harras," *Moderne Bauformen* (1944), p. 91; "R. Vorhoelzer: Wohnblock und Postamt," *Moderne Bauformen* (1934), pp. 1-17 (Am Harras); "Zweigstelle am Harras," *Der Baumeister* (1936), p. 413.

By contrast with Vorhoelzer's pragmatically designed post offices, public buildings erected in Munich during the Third Reich served both a practical and an overtly propagandistic purpose. The latter was particularly evident because Munich was the so-called "Hauptstadt der Bewegung" (Capital of the [Nazi] Movement), and therefore earmarked for special architectural treatment. The work of Paul Ludwig Troost is well known in this regard; less familiar is that of Oswald Bieber (see p. 205) and German Bestelmeyer. Bestelmeyer, especially, was highly praised during the Third Reich, and influential afterward as well through the students he had taught at Munich's Technische Hochschule (polytechnic). He himself had studied there under Friedrich von Thiersch and Gabriel von Seidl. Subsequently, Bestelmeyer worked in Regensburg and various other cities, including Berlin, before returning to his alma mater to teach in 1922. His work of the twenties is considered to be rather conservative, but it includes one of Germany's early skyscrapers (see p. 235) as well as a number of institutional buildings, such as hospitals and churches (see p. 212). In view of his conservative design background, it should come as no surprise that Bestelmeyer's Luftgaukommando (air force) building in Munich of 1937-39 appears as a contextual urban palace opposite the equally palatial Bavarian National Museum of 1894-99 by von Seidl, one of his mentors. Somewhat less ornate, with a few

unexpected bows to conservative modernism, is Bestelmeyer's Library and Convention Hall of 1928-35 at the Deutsches Museum in Munich. The modern overtones of its simple facades may well reflect the building's function, since the Deutsches Museum is devoted to the history of science and technology. Bestelmeyer's addition survived wartime bombing, but has suffered renovations since. At his death in 1942, German specialist journals eulogized his contributions to the country's architecture.

Selected Sources

Bauten und Plätze in München, sites 123, 211, and 212 (Troost), 106, 124, 125, 158, and 230 (Bestelmeyer); Heinz Thiersch, *German Bestelmeyer* (Munich, 1961) (for a contemporary survey of Bestelmeyer's work, see *Der Baumeister* [1942], pp. 222-24; *Der Baumeister* (1940), pp. 49-60 and pls. 17-24 (Haus des Deutschen Rechts by Bieber), pp. 66-67 and pl. 25 (Luftgaukommando building); "Saalbau und Bibliotheksbau des Deutschen Museums in München," *Moderne Bauformen* (1937), pp. 173-78.

Architects from outside Munich also designed some of the city's public buildings. One such was Ludwig Ruff of Nuremberg, whose original design for the Nordbad, published in *Moderne Bauformen* in 1930, was a modernist masonry structure. It appears not to have been constructed. The Nordbad, eventually built between 1936 and 1941 on a site several streets further north from that originally envisaged, was the work of City Architects Karl Meitinger (see pp. 202-3) and Zametzer — a drastically different design for these public baths that reflects the more conservative style of architecture favored in the Third Reich. Nordbad, destroyed during the war, was rebuilt from 1949 to 1951 in essentially the same form. It has been recently renovated. A more familiar landmark — at least until recently — is the airport in the suburb of Riem by Berlin architect Ernst Sagebiel, who also designed the airport in Stuttgart in the 1930s. Stuttgart, Munich, and Berlin all had existing airports in the twenties. Stuttgart's, built from 1928 to 1931 to designs by Bregler and Barthle, was just northwest of Böblingen railroad station, some fourteen miles southwest of Stuttgart. Some of its buildings survived until removed during reconstruction work in the eighties. Munich's airport at Oberwiesenfeld, designed by Karl Johann Mossner, opened in 1931. Located on the site of a former military parade ground, its remaining structures had been demolished by 1972, when the Olympiapark was laid out. In the

Meitinger and Zametzer. Nordbad, Schleissheimer Strasse 142, Munich-Nord, 1936-41 (rebuilt 1951). Photograph 1989.

thirties Air Ministry architect Sagebiel designed new airports at Stuttgart and Munich to replace these earlier ones, just as he did in Berlin (see Fig. 16, p. 25). His terminal building of 1936-41 at Stuttgart-Echterdingen has been overwhelmed by subsequent additions, including the 1991 building by Gerkan, Marg and Partners. At Munich-Riem, Sagebiel's building of 1937-39 was a curvilinear complex similar to, but not as large as, the one he built for Berlin's Tempelhof airport. As with Tempelhof and other airports of the era, he designed it on an elongated circular, or egg-shaped, plan without runways, to provide maximum flexibility for takeoffs and landings. Although Munich's terminal suffered substantial bomb damage during the war, it was repaired and added to throughout the postwar period until a new airport still further from the city forced its closure in 1992. The fate of these historic buildings is uncertain, but it is possible that they will be demolished.

Selected Sources

Wörner, *Stuttgart*, site 275; *Bauten und Plätze in München*, site 236 (Nordbad); "Karl Meitinger 80 Jahre," *Der Baumeister* (1962), p. 148; "Ludwig Ruff, Nürnberg: Hallenschwimmbad München-N.," *Moderne Bauformen* (1930), pp. 396-97; "Das neue Bezirks-Hallenbad München-Nord," *Der Baumeister* (1942), pp. 137-57 and pls. 53-64; "Flughafen München," *Deutsche Bauzeitung* (April 8, 1931), pp. 173-81 (also see earlier reports in *Der Baumeister* [1930], pp. 81-96); John Walter Wood, *Airports* (New York, 1940), pp. 215-25; *50 Jahre München Riem*, special issue no. 1 of *Luftfahrt* (1990).

Ernst Sagebiel. Airport, Munich-Riem, after completion in 1939.

Karl Johann Mossner. Office building and terminal of Munich airport, Munich-Oberwiesenfeld, 1931 (demolished).

Georg Hallhuber. Remodeling of the F. X. Hieber bakery, Pestalozzistrasse 21, Munich, c. 1935. From *Der Baumeister* (1936).

In 1936 *Der Baumeister* reported on the remodeling of a bakery that, surprisingly, still exists in altered form on Pestalozzistrasse. The architect's task was to renovate a nineteenth-century classical building. He modernized the facade by removing the historicist window moldings and the rusticated base with its heavily molded shop front, substituting concrete moldings with simple rectilinear profiles. He redesigned the shop itself from an almost square room into a dramatic curvilinear space. Although the bakery still stands today, its facade has been renovated yet again, painted decoration reinstating the lintels removed by the thirties architect. Unfortunately, the Art Deco-like interior has been removed, but the building remains as a curious example of urban archaeology.

Selected Source

"Bäckereiladenumbau F. X. Hieber, München," *Der Baumeister* (1936), pp. 123-25.

Historians of architecture in the Third Reich have concentrated on the Ramersdorf estate of 1933-34 when discussing Nazi housing projects in and around Munich. Although this estate fits generally accepted notions of German housing at the time, apartment buildings erected in Munich in the mid- to late thirties encompass a wide range of styles, from historicist to modernist. Some were published in the 1938 books *München baut auf* and *Das Bauen im neuen Reich*. The latter includes an apartment block by Hanns Atzenback at the corner of Kurfürstenplatz and Hohenzollernstrasse, in the city's Schwabing district. Its facade had a historicist entrance tower capped with an onion dome (later removed). Yet *München baut auf* juxtaposes a view of blocks on Pognerstrasse and Zinnerstrasse, with traditionalist sculpture, with one of the more functional facade of the roughly contemporaneous Auto Henne apartments. The Auto Henne building, though capped with a traditional roof, may have had a more simple, modernist facade because it sat atop a garage, a technical structure. The roof here appears as a contextual salute to the historicist building from the 1910s and 1920s nearby. In addition to these relatively minor buildings, a number of striking, eclectically modern housing projects were designed in the late thirties by Franz Ruf. These usually have simple, straightforward facades with *moderne* porthole windows. Of special interest is the Neuaubing estate of

1939, with more than four hundred units. These single- and double-family houses wind their way along curvilinear streets that lead to a marketplace complete with stylized historicist clock tower. Ruf's postwar career included participation in the design of large housing blocks during the fifties and sixties.

Selected Sources

Gerdy Troost, *Das Bauen im neuen Reich* (Bayreuth, 1938), p. 144; *München baut auf* (Munich, 1938), p. 172; "Die Ludwig-Siebert-Siedlung in Neuaubing bei München," *Der Baumeister* (1939), p. 251; *Franz Ruf: Bauten und Pläne* (Munich, 1950).

opposite:
Auto Henne apartments and garage, Lindenschmitstrasse 35, Munich, c. 1935-37. From *München baut auf* (1938) and photograph 1991.

Franz Ruf. Apartment block, Balanstrasse and Werinherstrasse, Munich-Giesing, 1938. Photograph 1991.

Franz Ruf. Ludwig-Siebert-Siedlung, Ehrenbürgstrasse, Giechstrasse, and Aufsesser Platz, Munich-Neuaubing, 1937-39. Photographs 1990.

top left: Hermann Leitenstorfer and Fritz Beblo. Technisches Rathaus, Blumenstrasse 28b, Munich, 1927-29. Photograph 1986.

top right: Hans Grässel. Altersheim St. Josef, Luise-Kiesselbach-Platz 2, Munich-Mittersendling, 1927. Photograph 1990.

Thomas Wechs and Eberhard Finsterwalder. War Memorial, Hofgarten, Munich, 1924. Photograph 1990.

Karl Meitinger. Office building, Grossmarkthalle, Thalkirchner Strasse and Kochelseestrasse, Munich-Thalkirchen, c. 1927. Photograph 1990.

Fritz Beblo, the head of Munich's Building Department, is best known for being one of the architects of the Technisches Rathaus, the city's early brick skyscraper of 1927-29. But he also prepared an important book in the *Neue Stadtbaukunst* series which surveyed the accomplishments of Munich's architects in the creation of both public and private buildings. Surprisingly enough, most of the structures published in that 1928 volume still exist. A few are well-known public monuments, such as the World War I memorial of 1924, designed by Thomas Wechs and Eberhard Finsterwalder, with sculpture by Bernhard Bleeker and Karl Knappe (some of the latter's reliefs have been removed); others, such as the 1927 Altersheim

Karl Badberger. Bayerisches Landesamt für Mass und Gewicht, Franz-Schrank-Strasse 9, Munich-Nymphenburg, 1930. Photograph 1989.

Richard Schachner and Karl Meitinger. Dermatological Clinic, Thalkirchner Strasse 8, at Waltherstrasse, Munich, 1928. Photograph 1989.

Karl Meitinger. Tram depot offices and apartment block, Seerieder Strasse and Einsteinstrasse, Munich-Steinhausen, c. 1927 (tram garage yard now demolished). Photograph 1990.

(home for the elderly) by Hans Grässel in western Munich, have not rated a mention in subsequent publications. Particular prominence is accorded in the book to the municipal work of Karl Meitinger. This includes designs from the later twenties for the office building at the Grossmarkthalle (market hall) in the Thalkirchen district, for the Städtisches Kinderkrankenhaus (city children's hospital) on Parzivalstrasse in Schwabing, for the apartments and S-Bahn service buildings at Seerieder Strasse in Steinhausen, and for the Dermatological Clinic, done in conjunction with Richard Schachner. Even less well known is his Dantestrasse stadium of 1927, even though it stands near the famous Borstei housing blocks of

opposite: Karl Meitinger. Stadium, Dantestrasse and Baldurstrasse, Munich-Gern, 1927. Photographs 1989.

above: Bernard Borst and Oswald Bieber. Borstei, Dachauer Strasse, Pickelstrasse, and Lampadiusstrasse, Munich-Gern, 1924-29. Photograph 1989.

1924-29 by Bernhard Borst and Oswald Bieber. These works are evidence of the historicist orientation of much of Munich's architecture well into the interwar period, existing side by side with the more avant-garde post offices and other modernist masonry buildings, such as Karl Badberger's 1930 Bayerisches Landesamt für Mass und Gewicht (Bavarian State Department of Weights and Measures).

Selected Sources

Fritz Beblo, *Neue Stadtbaukunst München* (Berlin, Leipzig, and Vienna, 1928), pp. 10-11 (Altersheim), 13 (Dermatological Clinic), 14 (Technisches Rathaus), 23 (Grossmarkthalle office building), 24 (Seerieder Strasse), 26 (Kinderkrankenhaus), 37 (Dantestrasse), 50-52 (War Memorial); Fischer, *Architektur in München*, sites 22, 27, and 28; Stommer, *Hochhaus*, pp. 136, 229-30; *Bauten und Plätze in München*, sites 99, 249, and 262; "Das Bayerische Landesamt," *Deutsche Bauzeitung* (January 27, 1932), pp. 85-86; "Das neue Technische Rathaus in München, " *Deutsche Bauzeitung* (August 4, 1928), pp. 529-34; "Grosssiedlung mit Famielienbad und Sportplatz an der Dachauer-Dantestrasse in München," *Deutsche Bauzeitung* (August 4, 1928), pp. 529-34.

opposite:
top left: Kurz and Herbert. Apartment blocks, Meindlstrasse and Lindenschmitstrasse, near Am Harras, Munich, 1926. Photograph 1990.

top right: Kurz and Herbert. Apartment block, Rosenbuschstrasse and Reitmorstrasse, Munich, c. 1927. Photograph 1989.

bottom left: Kurz and Herbert. Apartment block, Rheinstrasse and Mainzer Strasse, Munich, c. 1927. Photograph 1989.

bottom right: Kurz and Herbert. Apartment blocks, Rheinstrasse and Simmernstrasse, Munich, c. 1926-27. Photograph 1989.

Of the buildings published in Fritz Beblo's 1928 book on Munich architecture, those by Otto Orlando Kurz have been bypassed by most subsequent literature. Kurz was born in Florence and studied at the Technische Hochschulen (polytechnics) in Karlsruhe, Berlin, and Munich. He apprenticed with Gabriel von Seidl and, in 1908, he began private practice in Munich. His works in the twenties combined historicist roofs, sculpture, gables, and Jugendstil-like iron balconies with more modernist-influenced elements, such as glass stairwells and corner windows that project from wall planes. A number of these eclectic apartment blocks appeared in the Beblo book, notably those on Meindlstrasse and Lindenschmitstrasse, on

Kurz and Herbert. Apartment block, Böttingerstrasse, Munich, c. 1930. The tower of St. Sebastian's Church, 1927, is in the background. Photograph 1989.

left: Otto Orlando Kurz. Apartment block, Arnulf-strasse and Steubenplatz, Munich, 1929-30 (balconies rebricked). Photograph 1989.

above: Otto Orlando Kurz. Apartment block, Karl-Theodor-Strasse, near St. Sebastian's Church, Munich, c. 1929-31. Photograph 1989.

Rheinstrasse and Mainzer Strasse, and on Rosenbuschstrasse. Kurz, later of Kurz and Herbert, also designed the Early Christian Revival-style St. Gabriel's Church of 1926 on Schneckenburger Strasse near Prinzregenten-strasse. In addition to these more or less histo-ricist buildings, Kurz's oeuvre includes apart-ment blocks with curvilinear balconies that recall Erich Mendelsohn's work on the WOGA apartments of 1927 in Berlin, although Kurz's structures incorporate relief sculptures. Both Kurz's historicist and modernist buildings were published in the architectural press of the time. His most interesting work is the housing clus-tered around St. Sebastian's Church of 1927, also designed by him.

Selected Sources

Beblo, *Neu Stadtbaukunst München*, pp. 43-45; Fischer, *Architektur in München*, site 36; "Die St. Sebastians-Kirche in München," *Wasmuths Monatshefte für Baukunst und Städtebau* (1930), pp. 501-2; "Ein Architekt besucht München," *Moderne Bauformen* (1937), pp. 117-20 (esp. p. 119); "Mietwohnungsblock in München," *Der Baumeister* (1932), pp. 134-35; *Neuzeitliche Miethäuser und Siedlungen*, ed. Leo Adler (Berlin, 1931), pp. 204-12; *O. O. Kurz und E. Herbert*, Neue Werkkunst (Berlin, Leipzig, and Vienna, 1927).

Hans Döllgast is a well-known Munich architect. After studying at the city's Technische Hochschule (polytechnic) from 1910 to 1914, he served in the army during World War I. After the war he worked for Franz Zell, Richard Riemerschmid, and, finally, Peter Behrens, before starting a practice of his own in 1927. He is best known for his reconstruction jobs after World War II and as a teacher at the Technische Hochschule from 1929 to 1956. His most famous project from the years between the world wars is the extensive housing project of 1930 in the Neuhausen district. He was not the only architect to build modernist housing blocks in Munich: the contributions of Helmut Wolff and Franz Lebrecht, and of Emil Freymuth, were just as important as Döllgast's, yet these architects remain virtually unknown. Their buildings survive today with relatively minor alterations. Freymuth's work was published regularly in the late twenties and thirties, before blossoming in numerous postwar reconstruction schemes. One of his more prominent structures from the latter period is the eight-story office building of 1951 at Ottostrasse 10 which, though published three years later in *Der Baumeister*, has been ignored by historians. Despite his prolific career, biographical data on Freymuth is scant. It is to be hoped

Helmut Wolff and Franz Lebrecht. Apartment block, Cannabichstrasse and Vossstrasse, Munich-Giesing, c. 1927-28 (windows, particularly at roof level, altered). Photograph 1989.

Emil Freymuth. Apartment building, Ettenhueberstrasse and Agnes-Bernauer-Strasse, Munich-Laim, 1924-36. Photograph 1989.

that the present publication will encourage research on him and other lesser lights in the region's interwar architectural history.

Selected Sources
Michael Gaenssler, Friedrich Kurrent, Winfried Nerdinger, and Franz Peter, *Hans Döllgast 1891-1974* (Munich, 1987); Fischer, *Architektur in München*, site 34 (Neuhausen); "Das Ferienheim in Kochel für Arbeiter, Beamte u. Angestellte von Staat u. Gemeinden," *Der Baumeister* (1931), pp. 166-69; "Ein neues Bürohaus in München," *Der Baumeister* (1954), pp. 75-81; Ludwig Seemüller, "Die Beton-Oberflächenbehandlung mit Contex," *Wasmuths Montatshefte für Baukunst and Städtebau* (1929), pp. 401-2 (article on the stucco, now altered, of the apartment buildings at Cannabichstrasse, Voss-strasse, and Pilgersheimer Strasse); "Siedlung 'Frei-land' München, Aidenbachstrasse," *Der Baumeister* (1930), pp. 150-51, pl. 23; "Siedlung in Laim-München," *Der Baumeister* (1930), pp. 148-49; "Genossenschaftlich errichtete Volkswohnungen (München)," *Der Baumeister* (1936), pp. 348-51.

Emil Freymuth. Freiland housing estate, Aiden-bachstrasse and Dönnigesstrasse, Munich-Ober-sendling, c. 1929. Photograph 1989.

Emil Freymuth. Holiday hotel for workers, civil servants, and municipal employees, Kochel, c. 1930. Photograph 1990.

Hermann Herrenberger. Städtisches Krankenhaus, Jakob-Henle-Strasse, Vacherstrasse, Kochstrasse, and Friedrich-Ebert-Strasse, Fürth, 1928.
Photograph 1989.

Albert Bosslet. Laundry building, Barmherzige
Brüder Hospital, Prüfeninger Strasse near Loh-
graben Bridge, Regensburg-Prüfening, c. 1929.
Photograph 1989.

Several cities in Bavaria had interesting examples of hospitals built in the twenties. The Städtisches Krankenhaus (city hospital) at Fürth,
near Nuremberg, is a massive complex with a
main building of some 3,380,000 cubic feet
constructed in brick and reinforced concrete.
The cornerstone ceremony of May 29, 1928,
was held on the centennial of the first hospital
on the site; the building was opened about
two years later. Although some details have
been changed (notably, the sculptures flanking
the entrance have been removed), the building
itself stands much as it did when erected.
Regensburg's Barmherzige Brüder (Hospitalers)
Hospital by Albert Bosslet also retains its modernist massing and some original outbuildings.
Munich architect Bosslet designed further
health care buildings in the region that are

extant, such as the Missionsärztliches Institut of
1925 in Würzburg. Other hospitals have not
fared as well, being more obtrusively marred
by later additions. Passau's Städtisches Krankenhaus of 1927-29, for example, has lost the
beautiful fountain that once graced its drive-
way entry, and an addition has been built
directly on its southeast elevation, blocking the
view of the statues on that facade. One of
Nuremberg's most widely published hospitals,
the Krankenhaus Hallerwiese of 1927 by German Bestelmeyer, does not even seem to have
survived the war; if any part of it was preserved, it doubtless fell victim to the expansion
of the hospital along the Pegnitz River —
a fate typical of many institutional buildings
from this period.

Selected Sources

Schmieden, *Krankenhausbau in neuerer Zeit*, pp. 49-
51 (Krankenhaus Hallerwiese); "Das Krankenhaus
Hallerwiese in Nürnberg," *Wasmuths Monatshefte
für Baukunst und Städtebau* (1929), pp. 313-18;
"Krankenhaus der Barmherzigen Brüder in Regensburg," *Deutsche Bauzeitung* (March 26, 1930),
pp. 193-200, and (March 29, 1930), pp. 201-4; "Das
Missionsärztliche Institut in Würzburg," *Deutsche
Bauzeitung* (April 5, 1930), pp. 217-19; "Das Städtische Krankenhaus in Fürth i. Bayern," *Deutsche
Bauzeitung* (Sept. 2, 1931), pp. 423-29; *Erläuterungs-
bericht: Entwurf für den Neubau des städtischen
Krankenhauses in Fürth i. Bay* (Fürth, 1928); "Das
Städtische Krankenhaus in Passau," *Der Baumeister*
(1931), pp. 371-75.

Nuremberg is known for its medieval and its
Nazi buildings. It would seem that the positive
image of this city as a historic center, and the
negative image of it associated with events
during the Third Reich, have obliterated all
other aspects of its built environment from the
general consciousness. The scale of the Nazi
buildings does indeed render them inescap-
able, even in the mutilated form to which some
of them were reduced by repeated bombings
of the city during the war. Ones to have survived include Albert Speer's famous Zeppelin
Field of 1934-37, the enormous, unfinished
Nazi Party Congress Hall by Ludwig and
Franz Ruff — the latter an architect who had
designed restrained modern buildings in the
twenties, such as the 1928 Erzbischöfliches
Priesterseminar (archiepiscopal seminary) at
Heinrichsdamm 32 in Bamberg — and a number of smaller, unknown structures, such as the
Hermann Göring School of 1940. Now called
the Georg-Simon-Ohm-Fachhochschule, the
latter sits in its suburban landscape on Olden-
burger Strasse and Dresdener Strasse minus
some historicist details, such as the cupola
atop the entrance tower. But these sites prevent
us from realizing that the city had an architectural life of its own in the twenties and thirties,
albeit a somewhat provincial or conservative
one, even when compared with Munich and
Stuttgart. Good examples of conservative
historicist buildings in the city include the
Commerzbank building of 1923 opposite
St. Lorenz's Church in the city center, and the
church of St. Johannis by German Bestelmeyer,
designed in 1916 but not constructed until
1926-28. In addition to these conservative
structures, the city has a housing and post
office complex from 1927-30 on Allersberger
Strasse that, although not as radical as the
comparable ones designed by Robert Vorhoelzer in Munich (see pp. 195-96), is a fine
example of a modernized conservative building that blends in with its historic surroundings.

Wilhelm Erhard. Post office and housing complex, Allersberger Strasse, Nuremberg, 1927-30. The Gustav-Adolf-Kirche (1930; rebuilt 1949) by German Bestelmeyer is in the background. Photograph 1989.

More conservative modernist housing of the late twenties existed in and near Am Herschelplatz, but these blocks have all been extensively altered in the postwar period, while Erich Mendelsohn's Schocken department store of 1926 (now Horten, Aufsessplatz 18) was rebuilt to a different design. In view of the conservative tenor of most architecture in Nuremberg in the twenties and thirties, it is surprising that the one architect who did design radical structures and environments was able to practice there at all. This was Otto Ernst Schweizer, a student of Theodor Fischer in Munich and director of Nuremberg's building program from 1925 onward. He was responsible for skeletal modernist buildings within the 1926-29 Nuremberg stadium and its grounds, all of which have since vanished. Schweizer's functionalist imprint on the cityscape survives, however, in several structures that he designed in 1930-31 for the dairy distribution plant of the Bayerische Milchversorgung. Other, more ephemeral examples of early thirties modernist design, such as the Art Deco, curved waiting room at the tram station Am Plärrer, have unfortunately been destroyed.

Otto Ernst Schweizer. Administration building, Bayerische Milchversorgung, southwest corner of Dürrenhofstrasse and Kressengartenstrasse, Nuremberg, 1930-31. Photograph 1989.

Selected Sources

Beseler and Gutschow, *Kriegsschicksale*, vol. 2, pp. 1434 (Friedenskirche and Gustav-Adolf-Kirche) and 1455 (Schocken store); Jaeger, *Bauen in Deutschland*, pp. 254-55; Justus Bier, "Ein Kaffee & Kaffeehaus im Nürnberger Stadion," *Die Form* (1930), pp. 18-21 (see *Moderne Bauformen* [1932], pp. 510-15, for further illustrations); "Der Milchhof der Bayer. Milchversorgung, Nürnberg," *Moderne Bauformen* (1933), pp. 303-17; "Der Neubau der Commerz- und Privatbank in Nürnberg," *Deutsche Bauzeitung* (September 3, 1927), pp. 385-90; "Friedenskirche zu St. Johannis, Nürnberg," *Wasmuths Monatshefte für Baukunst und Städtebau* (1929), pp. 511-16; "Hermann-Göring-Schule, Nürnberg," *Der Baumeister* (1941), pp. 292-313; "Neubauten der Oberpostdirektion Nürnberg an der Allersberger Strasse," *Der Baumeister* (1933), pp. 185-94; *Wasmuths Monatshefte für Baukunst und Städtebau* (1928), pp. 264-67 (housing near Herschelplatz); "Strassenbahnwartenhalle am Plärrer in Nürnberg," *Der Baumeister* (1933), pp. 11-15; "Architekt Professor Ludwig Ruff, Nürnberg," *Moderne Bauformen* (1929), pp. 137-53; *Erzbischöfliches Priesterseminar Bamberg 1928-1978* (Bamberg, 1978), pp. 15-16, 23-26.

The East: Silesia, Saxony, Thuringia, and Brandenburg

Wojciech Lesnikowski

The regions of Silesia, Saxony, Thuringia, and Brandenburg have produced a rich and diverse culture over the centuries. Their location near large masses of Slav populations to the east and south of their borders stimulated sociocultural and political interactions, particularly with Poland. In 1921, following an agreement reached at the Geneva International Convention, Germany ceded portions of Upper Silesia to Poland, while in 1945, with the defeat of Germany in World War II, the entire region became part of the Polish state. The principal cities of Silesia are Breslau (now Wrocław), Oppeln (Opole), Gleiwitz (Gliwice), Hindenburg (Zabrze), Liegnitz (Legnica), and Gorlitz (Gorlice). For historical reasons, the German names for these cities have been retained here.

The past of Saxony, too, has been turbulent and marked by connections with Poland. It became an important kingdom under Augustus the Strong (1694-1733), who was also king of Poland. During the Napoleonic era Saxony sided with the French; it was punished for this in 1815 at the Congress of Vienna, as a result of which it lost half its territory to Prussia. At the end of World War I, Saxony was a free state, but was incorporated into the Third Reich in 1933. Its major cities include Dresden, a center of art and architecture whose population before World War II was about 640,000; Leipzig, a thriving city of some 713,000 inhabitants with an uninterrupted international trade fair tradition that dates back to the Middle Ages; and Chemnitz, Saxony's main center for the metal and textile industries with an interwar population of approximately 346,000.

After World War II, several Saxon cities, including Halle and Magdeburg, became part of the new region of Saxony-Anhalt. Halle, the site of a renowned university, has long been a center of the chemical industry. A focal point of modernist architecture during the Weimar Republic, Magdeburg is characterized by a mix of very old buildings and vigorous modern developments on its outskirts. As the capital of Anhalt, Dessau, too, was included in the newly created region. The city owes its modern fame primarily to the Bauhaus, which moved there in 1925 into a renowned building by Walter Gropius (Fig. 1). Well known to architectural historians and enthusiasts alike, other major structures by Gropius and his successor as director of the school, Hannes Meyer, are scattered throughout Dessau (see Figs. 2, 3).

The cities of Thuringia were no less remarkable. Weimar, the city that gave its name to the republic of 1918 to 1933 (it was there that the Constitution was drawn up), was a center of the arts, made famous by Johann Wolfgang von Goethe, Friedrich Schiller, and Franz Liszt, as well as by such architects as Henry van de

Velde and Gropius, who founded the Bauhaus there in 1919. Jena became world famous after Carl Zeiss set up his optical manufacturing facilities there in 1846, while Erfurt combines the charms of a medieval city with many handsome nineteenth- and twentieth-century quarters.

Beyond the familiar avant-garde works of Dessau, these three regions, and that of Brandenburg, with its cities Frankfurt an der Oder, Cottbus, and Brandenburg an der Havel, contain a wealth of buildings from the 1920s and 1930s that display a wide variety of approaches to modern design.

Selected Sources

Magdalena Droste, *Bauhaus, 1919-1933* (Cologne, 1990); Siegfried Giedion, *Walter Gropius* (New York, 1992).

Fig. 1 Walter Gropius. Bauhaus building, Bauhaus-Platz, Dessau, 1925-26. Photograph 1986.

Fig. 2 Hannes Meyer. Apartment building, Südstrasse, Dessau-Törten, 1928. Photograph 1992.

Fig. 3 Walter Gropius. Arbeitsamt (employment office) building, August-Bebel-Platz, Dessau, 1927-28. Photograph 1992.

Magdeburg is especially associated with modernist housing. Bruno Taut, City Architect there from 1922 to 1924, experimented with the use of color in public housing by painting the facades of buildings undergoing renovation. His new zoning plan laid the foundations of future housing activities in the city. Johannes Goderitz, who succeeded Taut upon the latter's departure to Berlin, was instrumental in the construction, from 1927 to 1929, of housing estates that contained a total of about two thousand units. Four of these developments deserve particular recognition: that by Carl Krayl in the Neustadt district; the Cracau I and Cracau II estates by Krayl, the latter designed in cooperation with Goderitz; and the "Gross-Siedlung" by the team of Ruhl, Gauger, Zebel and Otto. These estates embody planning principles typical of German modernism, such as large blocks enclosing public greenery, "finger plans" (parallel rows of buildings placed at right-angles to the main streets), and picturesquely curving streets. Despite neglect in the postwar, Communist period, some structures retain traces of the original brown, yellow, red, and blue coloring. The beautifully restored estates by Taut in the Zehlendorf and Britz districts of Berlin suggest how their cousins in Magdeburg must have looked at the time of their construction.

The Neu-Gohlis garden suburb to the north of Leipzig's city center, erected in 1929-30 to designs by the team of Paul Mebes and Paul

Emmerich of Berlin (see Figs. 7-9, p. 23), Johannes Koppe, Max Fricke and A. Muesmann, is similar in character to the Magdeburg estates. In the south of Leipzig, Hubert Ritter, the architect of that city's famous Grossmarkthalle (see p. 241), designed the Rundling estate as part of a larger housing development which, however, was never realized. Consisting of three concentric rings of buildings, with streets radiating outward, the Rundling

brings to mind some ideal Italian Renaissance city. Its central, circular space, designed as a public garden, recalls Taut's Hufeisensiedlung in Berlin (Fig. 4, p. 23). The buildings themselves are typically functionalist, their entrance facades extremely simple and the rear elevations strongly articulated by balconies and loggias. As with the Magdeburg estates and the others in Leipzig, the complex is depressingly gray today.

In Erfurt one finds two great modernist housing estates, both dating from 1930: the Hamburger Block by Otto Jacobsen and the apartment buildings on Eugen-Richter-Strasse by Karl Schneider and Erich Sack. Jacobsen's project is very similar to Krayl's Magdeburg estates. It features a large block, with extensive greenery at its center, that consists of long, thin enclosing slabs punctuated by regularly spaced windows and articulated

opposite page:
Carl Krayl. Apartment building, Curiestrasse, Magdeburg-Neustadt, 1927. Photograph 1990.

Carl Krayl. Apartment building, Cracau I estate, Zuckerbusch, Magdeburg, 1927. Photograph 1990.

this page:
Ruhl, Gauger, Zebel and Otto. Apartment buildings, Gross-Siedlung, Welferlinger Strasse, Magdeburg, 1927. Photograph 1990.

Carl Krayl and Johannes Goderitz. Apartment building, Cracau II estate, Buchnerstrasse, Magdeburg, 1927. Photograph 1990.

corners. The colors have faded, but the walls still bear traces of light green and pale blue. Schneider's estate—another "superblock" with a large courtyard at its center—recently has been restored.

Among the many modernist single-family houses built in eastern Germany during the Weimar Republic, architect Max F. Feistel's own home in Chemnitz is perhaps the most rigorous in its Bauhaus-influenced forms. It features a combination of half-cylindrical and cubic masses, a flat roof, and Bauhaus-style windows and surfaces. Curiously enough, the same architect was responsible for two noticeably more conservative projects in the same town: the Wartburghof housing estate (see p. 229) and the Golfclubhaus in the suburb of Oberrabenstein.

Selected Sources

"Grosswohnbauten bei Paris und Magdeburg," *Moderne Bauformen* (1932), pp. 543-54; "Neue Architektur: Wohnungsbauten in Magdeburg," *Die Form* (1926), pp. 332-37; Ludwig Hilberseimer, "Über die Typisierung des Mietshauses," *Die Form* (1926), pp. 338-90; Joachim Schulz, Wolfgang Müller, and Erwin Schrödl, *Architekturführer DDR: Bezirk Leipzig* (Berlin, 1975), pp. 59 (Rundling) and 77 (Neu-Gohlis); "Siedlung Leipzig-Gohlis," *Deutsche Bauzeitung* (October 8, 1930), pp. 571-72; "Siedlung Rundling, Leipzig," *Wasmuths Monatshefte für Baukunst und Städtebau* (1930), p. 339; Karl-Heinz Hüter, Siegward Schulrabe, Wilfried Dallmann, and Rudolf Ziessler, *Architekturführer DDR: Bezirk Erfurt* (Berlin, 1978), p. 43 (Hamburger Block and Eugen-Richter-Strasse block); Sibylle Lohse, Wolfgang Seidel, Helmut Müller, Volker Benedix, Jochen Helbig, and Gerhard Schlegel, *Architekturführer DDR: Bezirk Karl-Marx-Stadt* (Berlin, 1989), p. 19 (Feistel House); "Das Golfclubhaus Oberrabenstein," *Deutsche Bauzeitung* (August 20, 1930), p. 503.

Paul Mebes, Paul Emmerich, Johannes Koppe, Max Fricke and A. Muesmann. Apartment building, Neu-Gohlis estate, Landsberger Strasse, Leipzig, 1929-30. Photograph 1990.

opposite:
center left: Otto Jacobsen. Hamburger Block, Hamburger Strasse 21-23, Erfurt, 1930. Photograph 1992.

bottom left: Karl Schneider and Erich Sack. Apartment building, Eugen-Richter-Strasse, Dortmunder Strasse, and Bebelstrasse, Erfurt, 1930. Photograph 1992.

Hubert Ritter. Apartment building, Rundling estate, Siegfriedplatz and Nibelungenring, Leipzig-Lössnig, 1929-30. Photograph 1990.

Max F. Feistel. The architect's house, Kesselgarten 3, Chemnitz, 1928. Photograph 1992.

Three famous department stores by Erich Mendelsohn still exist in Silesia and Saxony: the 1922 Weichmann store in Gleiwitz, the Petersdorf store of 1927 in Breslau, and the Schocken store (later Warenhaus Centrum) of 1929 in Chemnitz. With its continuous horizontal lines and bold moldings, the Weichmann store, which is relatively well preserved, bears witness to Mendelsohn's early interest in the architecture of Frank Lloyd Wright. The other two stores display the elegant, dynamic curves and transparent elevations that were imitated by so many architects. The tension that originally existed between Mendelsohn's sleek Schocken store and its nineteenth-century urban context has been lost due to bombing in World War II. Today, it is surrounded by monotonous postwar buildings. In addition, the original windows have been replaced by gold-toned, reflecting glass panels that make this elegant building seem rather flat and cheap-looking. By contrast, the Petersdorf store, with its dynamic projecting corner, benefits from the tight urban fabric around it, which was restored after World War II.

The influence of Mendelsohn's dynamic volumes is evident in the Poliklinik administrative offices of 1928 by Heinrich Herrling on the edge of the Old Town in Erfurt. Heavier than Mendelsohn's designs, it is nonetheless an effective urban and architectural composition. Wilhelm Ulrich's Joske department store of 1929 in Weissenfels, near Halle, which is

Karl Fezer. Merkurhaus, Markgrafenstrasse 2, Leipzig, 1937. Photograph 1990.

Hermann Dernburg. Former Wertheim department store, Plac Kościuszki, Breslau (Wrocław), 1928. Photograph 1990.

currently being restored, has an elegant, curving glass curtain wall very much in the spirit of Mendelsohn, while the Merkurhaus store in Leipzig, built in 1937 by architect Karl Fezer, is a surprisingly late example of modernism in Germany. Its curving volume must have been modeled on Mendelsohn too, though its limestone and shellstone elevations are infinitely more solid and heavy than his. Hermann Dernburg's Wertheim department store of 1928 in Breslau also belongs in the category of buildings influenced by Mendelsohn, with its rounded corners, horizontal ribbon windows, setback top floor, and overall simplicity of design. The square on which it is located was rebuilt in the style of Social Realism after World War II, placing the store in a completely different urban context.

Selected Sources

Bruno Zevi, *Erich Mendelsohn* (New York, 1985); *Architekturführer DDR: Bezirk Karl-Marx-Stadt*, p. 32 (Schocken store); Werner Hegemann, "Erich Mendelsohns Kaufhaus Schocken, Chemnitz," *Wasmuths Monatshefte für Baukunst und Städtebau* (1930), p. 345; *Architekturführer DDR: Bezirk Erfurt*, p. 21 (Poliklinik); "Geschäftshaus Joske in Weissenfels," *Deutsche Bauzeitung* (August 6, 1930), p. 474; *Architekturführer DDR: Bezirk Leipzig*, p. 30 (Merkurhaus); "Das Warenhaus Wertheim," *Deutsche Bauzeitung* (July 2, 1930), pp. 409-16.

Hannes Meyer. ADGB school, road to Wandlitz, Bernau, 1927. Photograph 1992.

Adolf Petersen. Former Pädagogische Akademie, Friedrich-Ebert-Strasse 51-52, Frankfurt an der Oder, 1930 (reconstructed 1974-75 with additions). Photograph 1992.

Perhaps the best known modernist school erected between the wars in the eastern part of Germany is that designed by Hannes Meyer in 1930 for the ADGB (Allgemeiner Deutscher Gewerkschaftsbund; Federation of German Labor Unions). Located on the periphery of the small town of Bernau, northeast of Berlin, it now forms part of a trade school campus. Other, less well known buildings betray the influence of Bauhaus precepts. One such is the remarkably interesting Pädagogische Akademie (teachers training college) of 1930 in Frankfurt an der Oder by Adolf Petersen. In excellent condition, this smooth, white, modernist icon challenges its conservative

Salzmann. Hospital, near Route 173 to Dresden, Freiberg, 1928-29. Photograph 1992.

Martin Knauthe. AOK administration building, Robert-Franz-Ring, Halle, 1929. Photograph 1992.

surroundings with its dynamic, assymetrical composition. The two buildings added to the hospital in Freiberg in Saxony in 1928-29 by City Architect Salzmann demonstrate the high standard of hospital design in the Weimar Republic. Long lines of balconies, liberal use of glass, industrial detailing, and pure colors (now faded) constitute a fine example of the functionalist aesthetic. More streamlined in appearance is the administration building of

another medical facility, the AOK (Allgemeine Ortskrankenkasse; General Health Insurance Fund), located on Halle's Robert-Franz-Ring and designed by Martin Knauthe. In 1927 the same architect had produced an apartment building that, with its two elements, one painted black, placed at right-angles to each other in a powerfully dynamic composition, is a fine example of functionalist volumetric articulation.

Fred Otto was the designer of three interesting projects in Chemnitz. The large Stadtbad (municipal baths) complex of 1928-35 (renovated during the GDR years) unites simple, distinctive volumes and elevations with an unusual wooden framework on one side of the entrance court. Otto's new building of 1930 on the grounds of the Nervenheilanstalt (hospital for nervous disorders), although strongly symmetrical, is functionalist in its simply articulated,

plain volumes and elevations. Unfortunately, alterations have robbed the structure of much of its original crisp appearance. The third of these buildings is the multistory Sparkasse (savings bank), which is reminiscent of modern Italian neoclassical architecture in its bold compositional symmetry and the pronounced rhythm of its window arrangements. Such overall symmetry characterized many buildings that were otherwise functionalist in style.

Examples are the Chemnitzer Hof hotel of 1925 by Heinrich Straumer and the Huth department store of 1930 by Wilhelm Ulrich in Halle. The latter is currently being renovated.

Hubert Ritter used the courtyard plan for two projects in Leipzig that demonstrate his mastery of this design approach, one that lay in between radical and conservative modernism. Only half completed, the original plan for the symmetrical campus of the Max Klinger School has a solid, static, traditional appearance. The architecture itself, however, consists of simple, smooth, cubic volumes, horizontal bands of windows, and flat roofs — all characteristic features of functionalist design. The Dermatologische Klinik is a similar hybrid of modernist elements and Beaux-Arts planning.

The Versöhnungskirche (Church of Reconciliation) of 1929 in Leipzig-Gohlis by Hans-Heinrich Grotjahn is another fine example of hybridized design. The simple volume of the church and its towers, with their plain exterior surfaces, lend the building a modern appearance, while the large, symmetrically placed cross on the front elevation constitutes the kind of explicit symbolism that modernist architecture preferred to eschew.

In Dresden, Paul Wolf designed three buildings that similarly combine symmetrical plans with modernist characteristics: the Haus der

Jugend (youth center), the Städtisches Volksbad (municipal public baths), and the Volksschule (elementary school) in the Reick district. These are simple, plain, and symmetrical in composition with flat roofs and fenestration arranged in long horizontal strips. Economy of means and functional soundness are the precepts underlying such buildings, which are modest, contextually oriented structures rather than bold landmarks.

Selected Sources
Peter Güttler, Joachim Schulz, Ingrid Bartmann-Kompa, Klaus-Dieter Schulz, Karl Kohlschütter, and Arnold Jacoby, *Berlin-Brandenburg: Ein Architekturführer* (Berlin, 1990), p. 301 (ADGB school); Ingrid Halbach, Matthias Rambow, Horst Büttner, and Peter Rätzel, *Architekturführer DDR: Bezirk Frankfurt (Oder)* (Berlin, 1987), p. 51 (Pädagogische Akademie); Heinrich Schmieden, *Krankenhausbau in neuer Zeit* (Kirchhain, 1930), pp. 101-06; "Ausgeführte Musterbeispiele für Bezirkskrankenhäuser," *Der Baumeister* (1931), pp. 360-64 (Freiberg); Josef Munz-

opposite page:
Fred Otto. Extension to the Nervenheilanstalt, Dresdner Strasse, north of Waldschlösschen-strasse, Chemnitz, 1930. From *Wasmuths Monatshefte für Baukunst und Städtebau* (1931).

bottom left: Fred Otto. Sparkasse building, Falkeplatz, Chemnitz, 1929. Photograph 1992.

bottom right: Heinrich Straumer. Chemnitzer Hof hotel, Schillerplatz, Chemnitz, 1929 (reconstructed 1976-80). Photograph 1992.

this page:
Wilhelm Ulrich. Huth department store (later Kinderkaufhaus), Am Markt, Halle, 1929. From *Deutsche Bauzeitung* (August 6, 1930).

Hans-Heinrich Grotjahn, Versöhnungskirche, Jonny-Schehr-Strasse 16, Leipzig-Gohlis. Photograph 1990.

berg, Gerhard Richter, and Peter Findeisen, *Architekturführer DDR: Bezirk Halle* (Berlin, 1976), pp. 23 (Huth department store), 31 (AOK building), and 44 (Knauthe apartment building); Hubert Ritter, *Der Krankenhausbau der Gegenwart* (Stuttgart, 1932), pp. 49, 92-93 (Dermatologische Klinik); Julius Vischer, *Der neue Schulbau im In- und Ausland: Grundlagen, Technik, Gestaltung* (Stuttgart, 1931), pp. 52 (Max Klinger School) and 65 (Volksschule); *Architekturführer DDR: Bezirk Karl-Marx-Stadt*, p. 20 (Stadtbad); "Erweiterungsbau der Nervenheilanstalt der Stadt Chemnitz," *Wasmuths Monatshefte für*

Baukunst und Städtebau (1931), pp. 177-81; "Das neue Sparkassengebäude der Stadt Chemnitz," *Wasmuths Monatshefte für Baukunst und Städtebau* (1930), pp. 524-25; "Hotel Chemnitzer Hof," *Deutsche Bauzeitung* (March 4, 1931), pp. 113-19; "Bauten von Architekt BDA Dipl.-Ing. Wilhelm Ulrich in Halle a. d. S.," *Deutsche Bauzeitung* (August 6, 1930), p. 473; *Architekturführer DDR: Bezirk Leipzig*, p. 78 (Versöhnungskirche); "Städtisches Volksbad Dresden-Neustadt-Nordwest," *Der Baumeister* (1931), pp. 72-73.

Hubert Ritter. Max Klinger School (now Pädagogische Hochschule Clara Zetkin), Karl-Heine-Strasse 22b, Leipzig, 1930. From Vischer, *Der neue Schulbau* (1931).

Paul Wolf. Volksschule, Morgenleite, Dresden-Reick, 1930. Photograph 1992.

Several housing estates built during the Weimar Republic, among them the Wartburghof by Max F. Feistel and the Wissmannhof by Curt am Ende in Chemnitz, also possess a hybrid character. The Wartburghof features a series of gable roofs on the courtyard side and two half-turrets framing the main entrance to the courtyard; they give the estate a romantic, almost historicist feel. The Wissmannhof, designed as a modernist "superblock," is nonetheless picturesque in its volumes and detailing. Again, the apartment buildings by Wilhelm Freise on the symmetrically designed Lutherplatz in Halle have traditional pitched roofs and arcades, but plain, simple, functionalist elevations. Similar combinations of old and new characterize the 1929 blocks, erected on a trapezoidal plan, in Brandenburg an der Havel by Werner Schenck, which a 1931 issue of *Wasmuths Monatshefte für Baukunst*

Max F. Feistel. Apartment building, Wartburghof estate, Fürstenstrasse, Chemnitz, 1928. Photograph 1992.

Curt am Ende. Apartment building, Wissmannhof estate, Otto-Schütze-Strasse, Yorckstrasse, Münchner Strasse, and Fürstenstrasse, Chemnitz, 1927-28. Photograph 1992.

Wilhelm Freise. Apartment building, Lutherplatz, Halle, 1929. Photograph 1992.

Werner Schenck. Apartment building, Wilhelmsdorfer Strasse, Brandenburg an der Havel, 1929. Photograph 1992.

und Städtebau even compared to Adolf Loos's famous building on Michaeler Platz in Vienna, and the Paulinenhof estate of 1922 in Frankfurt an der Oder.

The same hybridization can be found in public buildings of the period. An excellent example is Johannes Goderitz's imposing Stadthalle (city auditorium) of 1929 in the Kulturpark on the Elbe River at Magdeburg. Despite its functionalist massing, it registers as an almost expressionist building, somber and heavy, with brick walls and a rather conservative tower. Carl Krayl, Goderitz's collaborator on the Cracau II housing estate in Magdeburg (see p. 217), co-designed another brick structure in that city with Maximilian Worm, the AOK (Allgemeine Ortskrankenkasse; General Health Insurance Fund) building of 1928. This, too, projects an expressionistic image, particularly in the powerful rhythm of the piers

Martin Kiessling. Row houses, Paulinenhof estate, Kiesslingplatz and G. F. Händel-Strasse, Frankfurt an der Oder, 1922-23. Photograph 1992.

Johannes Goderitz. Stadthalle, Kulturpark, Magdeburg, 1929. Photograph 1990.

on its front elevation. Inside, the ground floor was organized around a light court, and the structural system provided the interior with strong articulation.

One brick building outshines all others in the four regions under discussion in terms of dramatic power. This is the Catholic church of St. Josef, built in 1930 in the city of Hindenburg to designs by Dominikus Böhm, the renowned church architect from Cologne. The extraordinary geometrical severity of its volumes, which include an attached bell tower, combines with simple brick walls to create an unforgettable impression. The powerful front elevation, consisting of four stories of arcades flanked by two blank walls, gives onto a narthex that serves as a gathering place for the congregation. The dramatic interior space, lit only by small, circular windows, is framed by a series of brick piers and arches and

Maximilian Worm and Carl Krayl. AOK building, Lüneburger Strasse, Magdeburg, 1928. From *Wasmuths Monatshefte für Baukunst und Städtebau* (1928).

opposite:
Dominikus Böhm. St. Josef Catholic Church, Hindenburg (Zabrze), 1930. From *Moderne Bauformen* (1935).

bottom left: Ernst Neufert. Abbeanum, Lessingstrasse, Jena, 1930. Photograph 1992.

bottom right: Friedrich Wagner-Poltrock. Industrieschule (later Berufsschule), Annenstrasse at Park der Opfer des Faschismus, Chemnitz, 1926. Photograph 1992.

terminates in a semicircular apse. St. Josef's belongs among the finest examples of modern European church architecture and anticipates Louis Kahn's expressionistic projects of the 1960s and 1970s, such as the government buildings in Dacca, Bangladesh.

An example of relatively pure functionalist brick architecture is Berlin architect Ernst Neufert's Abbeanum of 1930 in Jena. Located on a sloping site, this mathematics college comprises a long, simple administration building and a classroom wing with an irregularly shaped auditorium pavilion attached to it. The elevation of the classroom wing has modernist ribbon windows, and a flat roof caps the whole. The Abbeanum might almost be described as a prototype of the buildings designed by Ludwig Mies van der Rohe in the forties for the Armour (now Illinois) Institute of Technology in Chicago.

Rather eclectic examples of brick buildings are Friedrich Wagner-Poltrock's Industrieschule (industrial training school) in Chemnitz and the August Bebel School by Josef Gesing in Frankfurt an der Oder. Both buildings date from 1926 and, despite their modern, functionalist

plans, have facades couched in a picturesque, Gothic-derived style.

Josef Gesing. August Bebel School, August-Bebel-Strasse, Frankfurt an der Oder, 1926. Photograph 1992.

Selected Sources

Albert Gut, *Der Wohnungsbau in Deutschland nach dem Weltkrieg* (Munich, 1928), p. 422 (Wartburghof); *Architekturführer DDR: Bezirk Karl-Marx-Stadt*, p. 35 (Wissmannhof); *Architekturführer DDR: Bezirk Halle*, p. 48 (Lutherplatz); "Wohnungsbau in Brandenburg an der Havel," *Wasmuths Monatshefte für Baukunst und Städtebau* (1931), pp. 59-64; *Architekturführer DDR: Bezirk Frankfurt (Oder)*, pp. 51 (Paulinenhof) and 52 (August Bebel School); "Die Stadthalle in Magdeburg," *Deutsche Bauzeitung* (February 9, 1929), pp. 121-27; "Neubau der Allgemeinen Ortskrankenkasse in Magdeburg," *Wasmuths Monatshefte für Baukunst und Städtebau* (1928), pp. 103-7; "Sankt Josef in Hindenburg," *Moderne Bauformen* (1935), pp. 169-77; "Das Abbeanum in Jena," *Wasmuths Monatshefte für Baukunst und Städtebau* (1931), pp. 516-20; "Die neue Industrieschule in Chemnitz," *Deutsche Bauzeitung* (November 2, 1929), pp. 755-59; Eugen Kurt Fischer (intro.), *F. Wagner-Poltrock, Neue Werkkunst* (Berlin, Leipzig, and Vienna, 1927), pp. 4-13 (Industrieschule).

German Bestelmeyer. Kroch office building, Goethestrasse 2, Leipzig, 1927-28. Photograph 1990.

The designs of tall office and industrial buildings in the four regions under review also range from modernist to more eclectic. Among the former is "Magdeburg's first high-rise," the twelve-story Faber-Verlag building of 1931 by Paul Schaeffer-Heyrothsberge. The structure, which recently has been renovated, lacks an elegant outline but features a bold staircase enclosed in glass and a distinctive, expressive top floor.

Rather more conservative is the Zeiss office tower in Jena, built in 1936 as part of that company's sprawling industrial complex. Its static image results from the austere rhythm of its strongly outlined windows and from the plain geometry of its volume. Lacking distinctive articulation at either the top or the bottom, the building appears somewhat monotonous.

The twelve-story Kroch office high-rise in Leipzig, designed by Munich architect German Bestelmeyer in 1928, and Lothar Neumann's Postscheckamt (Postal Cheque Office)

of 1931 in Breslau represent more eclectic approaches to modernist design. The Leipzig structure has an ornamental top, featuring a clock and large-scale figurative sculptures, while the Breslau building was evidently inspired by Gothic and Art Nouveau sources (its eleven-story corner structure was one of the two high-rises erected in the city at this time; see pp. 248-49). The traditional materials — stone and brick — used to clad their steel skeletons give both buildings a heavy appearance; they lack the transparency characteristic of other modernist designs, including ones in masonry.

Selected Sources

"Magdeburgs erstes Hochhaus," *Deutsche Bauzeitung* (April 16, 1931), pp. 185-89; "Hochhaus in Magdeburg," *Moderne Bauformen* (1931), pp. 360-64; Rainer Stommer, *Hochhaus: Der Beginn in Deutschland* (Marburg, 1990), p. 170 (Zeiss high-rise); *Architekturführer DDR: Bezirk Leipzig*, p. 37 (Kroch office building); Fritz Behrendt, "Das neue Breslau," *Deutsche Bauzeitung* (August 21, 1929), p. 577; "Das Postscheckamt in Breslau," *Deutsche Bauzeitung* (January 28, 1931), pp. 61-66.

Unknown architect. Zeiss high-rise, Carl-Zeiss-Platz, Jena, 1936. Photograph 1992.

Lothar Neumann. Postscheckamt, Ulica Bernhardynska, Breslau (Wrocław), 1930. From *Deutsche Bauzeitung* (January 28, 1931).

Paul Wolf. Houses, Langer Weg, Dresden-Prohlis, 1922. Photograph 1992.

Leopold Fischer. Houses, Kirchstrasse, Dessau-Ziebigk, 1929. From *Wasmuths Monatshefte für Baukunst und Städtebau* (1929).

Dresden's workers' suburb of Prohlis, built in 1922 by City Architect Paul Wolf, was modeled on Hellerau and featured small, simple, cubic cottages with tall, pitched roofs and small front and back yards. A similar village-like atmosphere characterized Leopold Fischer's 1928 estate in the Ziebigk suburb of Dessau and the rural colony of 1920 at Obernigk (now Oborniki) near Breslau by landscape architect Max Schemmel.

Selected Sources
Stadtbaurat Paul Wolf: Dresdener Arbeiten (Berlin, Leipzig, and Vienna, 1927), p. 29; "Siedlungen von Adolf Loos und Leopold Fischer," *Wasmuths Monatshefte für Baukunst und Städtebau* (1929), pp. 70-76; "Reichsheimstättensiedlung in Obernigk," *Der Baumeister* (1932), pp. 56-61.

Alongside urban apartment buildings, public housing in Germany between the wars was marked by a proliferation of rustic, village-like estates, a type pioneered at Hellerau on the outskirts of Dresden. Begun in 1906, Hellerau was modeled on the British concept of the Garden City as developed by Ebenezer Howard and Raymond Unwin. Hellerau was the fruit of pioneering efforts by the Dresdener Werkstätten für Handwerkskunst (Dresden Arts and Crafts Workshops), an organization founded in 1898 by Karl Schmidt in the spirit of the English Arts and Crafts movement which paved the way for the Deutscher Werkbund and, ultimately, the Bauhaus. One of the architects who participated in the creation of Hellerau was Heinrich Tessenow, who would go on to design houses intented for prefabrication. His simple, plain homes greatly influenced the design of estates all over Germany.

A fine example of industrial building in the Third Reich is the 1938-39 modernist renovation of the Total-Werke Foerstner & Co. factory in Apolda, Thuringia, by Egon Eiermann. This is remarkable for its roof, which, in accordance with that concern for hygiene and physical well-being characteristic of modernist architecture, is treated as an open deck providing employees with a space for exercise and social gatherings.

Industrial plants erected at this time include such modernist jewels as the 1934 design and manufacturing facilities of the Junkerswerke in Dessau by Werner Issel. Although this aircraft factory was almost completely destroyed during World War II, its design and administrative facilities still exist. Constructed in brick, both buildings have large windows and detached, glazed staircases, which contribute to their dynamic, modernist appearance. Photo-

Werner Issel. Junkerswerke, Junkersstrasse, Dessau, 1934. From *Monatshefte für Baukunst und Städtebau* (1939) and photograph 1992.

graphs show that the production sheds and hangars were very handsome examples of industrial aesthetics.

Some earlier manufacturing facilities, such as the elegant production shed of the Buchungsmaschinenwerk (bookkeeping machine factory) of 1928 in Chemnitz by Willi Schönefeld, had to reconcile their industrial purpose and character with the requirements of their urban context. Schönefeld created excellent visual rapport between the complex volume of his building and the public square in front of it, enhancing the compositional relationships between the two by means of an expressive tower. This desire to go beyond purely utilitarian appearances is also apparent in Johannes Goderitz's 1926 *Kohlenbunker* (coal storage unit) in Magdeburg, with its elegant, cantilevered top curving round the structure. The long brick facade of Fritz Höger's 1929 Konsumzentrale (consumers' center) in Leipzig-Plagwitz, rather expressionistic in character, constitutes a further demonstration of humane, contextually conscious industrial architecture.

Finally, the building type of the market hall produced one spectacular structure, Hubert Ritter's mighty Grossmarkthalle of 1927-30 in Leipzig. Only two of the three domes originally proposed were built, but they are among the largest in Europe. The building is in very poor condition today.

Egon Eiermann. Total-Werke Foerstner & Co., Auenstrasse 5, Apolda, 1938-39. From *Moderne Bauformen* (1939).

left: Willi Schönefeld. Production shed, Buchungsmaschinenwerk, Altchemnitzer Strasse 41, Chemnitz, 1928. Photograph 1992.

right: Fritz Höger. Konsumzentrale, Industriestrasse 86-95, Leipzig-Plagwitz, 1929-32. Photograph 1992.

Johannes Goderitz. *Kohlenbunker*, Lüneburger
Strasse, Magdeburg, 1926-27. Photograph 1990.

Selected Sources
"Erweiterung und Umbau der Total-Werke Foerstner
& Co.," *Moderne Bauformen* (1939), pp. 561-67;
Architekturführer DDR: Bezirk Erfurt, p. 73 (Total-
Werke); "Bauten der Junkerswerke," *Monatshefte für
Baukunst und Städtebau* (1939), pp. 73-89; *Architek-
turführer DDR: Bezirk Karl-Marx-Stadt*, p. 40
(Buchungsmaschinenwerk); "Neubauten der Stadt
Magdeburg," *Die Form* (1926-27), p. 123; "Neubau
des Konsumvereins Leipzig-Plagwitz," *Deutsche Bau-
zeitung* (February 11, 1931), pp. 94-95; *Architektur-
führer DDR: Bezirk Leipzig*, p. 69 (Konsumzentrale);
"Markthallen in Reims and Leipzig," *Wasmuths
Monatshefte für Baukunst und Städtebau* (1930),
p. 105.

Hubert Ritter. Grossmarkthalle, Zwickauer Strasse
40, Leipzig, 1927-30. From *Wasmuths Monatshefte für Baukunst und Städtebau* (1930).

Helmut Lüdecke. Single-family house, "International Hygiene Exhibition," Dresden, 1930. From *Der Baumeister* (1932).

Wilhelm Kreis. Deutsches Hygiene-Museum, Blüher Strasse, Blüher Park, Dresden-Mitte, 1927-30. Photograph 1990.

Among events associated with the history of modern architecture in Germany the Dresden "International Hygiene Exhibition" of 1930 occupies an important place. For the second time this century, following the construction of the Garden City of Hellerau, Dresden became a crucial place for modern architectural themes and concerns to be brought to public attention. The exhibition was linked to the pioneering work of Karl August Lingner, which had focused on teaching modern hygienic principles to broad sections of German society. It was Lingner who had organized the first hygiene exhibition in Dresden in 1911, which led to the founding of the Deutsches Hygiene-Museum in that city.

The 1930 exhibition was directed by well-known Dresden architect Paul Wolf, who, on 470 acres of land, planned, designed, and coordinated the construction of various exhibition pavilions and their surroundings. The site, which corresponded in part to that of the 1911 exhibition, was located in the Alt-

stadt area, immediately south of the city center, and consisted of a vast public park that included the zoo and the botanical garden. A few buildings remaining from the earlier exhibition were adapted to new purposes, among which were exhibits devoted to various German regions and major cities. These were designed by Hans Hartmann, A. Graziani, and Rudolf Duttmann of Berlin, and Alfons Schneegans, Drescher, and Max Herfurth of Dresden. The exhibition grounds were organized around several thematic centers that were connected with one another by a 1¼-mile-long minitrain, which still exists. The exhibits treated such themes as "The Healthy City," "Hygienic Clothing," "Combatting Vermin," and "Women in Family and Career." There was also an exhibit titled "The Hospital," in which the latest medical instruments were exhibited and modern notions of patient care explained.

One of the most interesting exhibits consisted of a series of prototypical hygienic houses. Among them was a small, elegantly restrained, cubic structure by architect Helmut Lüdecke of Hellerau with the name "Südbelichtung" (Lit from the South). Lüdecke's earlier houses in Dresden, such as the Haus eines Geistesarbeiters (House of an Intellectual Worker) and various *Kleinhäuser* (small

houses) had been described by Bruno Taut in his well-known tract *Ein Wohnhaus* as exemplary cases of economic and functional residential design. Other houses in the exhibition itself included one for an occupant suffering from a lung disease, one for a war invalid, designed by architect Wrede, and one for a large family, the work of Hans Richter of Dresden. The exhibit of the Reichsforschungsgesellschaft für Wirtschaftlichkeit in Bau- und Wohnungswesen (Imperial Research Association for Economy in Building and Housing), designed by Lubbert and Kammler of Berlin, included a series of model modern apartments and furnishings.

The chief building of the exhibition was the hygiene museum of 1927-30, designed by Wilhelm Kreis of Dresden in a "stripped," monumental neoclassical style. A large-scale plaza, Lingnerplatz, was laid out in front of it. Kreis would later become one of the more important Nazi architects with his proposals for war memorials to be built in countries conquered by the Germans. In addition to the museum, a large sports stadium designed by Paul Wolf for 3,500 spectators (which still exists) was incorporated in the exhibition. Kreis was responsible for the Platz der Nationen (Square of the Nations), in which were displayed exhibits by nineteen foreign countries, including a handsome pavilion for the Soviet Union, an international restaurant, an open-air theater, the Halle des Völkerbundes

(League of Nations Hall), a reception hall, police and fire departments, and an elegant, surprisingly modernistic 36-foot-high tower. Other exhibition structures were the metal and glass pavilion of the Munich Hofbräu brewery, the exhibit of the paint manufacturing industry, the Halle der Leibesübungen (Physical Exercise Hall) by Hans Richter, the Sporthalle and swimming baths by Paul Wolf, and the Chlorodont-Turm by Lossow and Kühne.

The imaginative use of lights and colors was a particularly important factor in the night-time appearance of this vast exhibition. Several fountains contributed to its fantastic nocturnal image, of which surviving photographs give some idea. Since only a few structures from the exhibition are extant, it is now difficult to recapture the enormous social and architectural significance that it possessed at the time. It was, in effect, a world's fair for hygiene.

Selected Sources

"Das Hygiene-Museum in Dresden," *Deutsche Bauzeitung* (September 3, 1930), pp. 517-20; Paul Wolf, "Die Internationale Hygiene-Ausstellung in Dresden," *Deutsche Bauzeitung* (July 16, 1930), pp. 433-44; "Einfamilien (Reihen) Haus," *Der Baumeister* (1932), pp. 238-39; Bruno Taut, *Ein Wohnhaus* (Stuttgart, 1927), p. 114; "Ein Architekt besucht Dresden," *Moderne Bauformen* (1937), pp. 1-4.

Otto Bartning. Frankfurter Musikheim (now Kleist-Theater), Gerhart-Hauptmann-Strasse 3-4, Frankfurt an der Oder, 1929. Photograph 1992.

German modernist architecture brought forth several great mavericks, who, although they participated in the development of functionalism, evolved highly individual creative ideas and methods. Hans Scharoun and Otto Bartning are well-known instances (see Fig. 11, p. 24, and pp. 80-81, 244). Less familiar examples of their work, such as Scharoun's Schmincke House of 1931 in the small Saxon town of Löbau, can be found in the regions under discussion. Bartning, in fact, designed two of his most interesting buildings in Brandenburg: the Frankfurt Musikheim (today the Kleist-Theater) of 1929 in Frankfurt an der Oder and the Kinderkrankenhaus (children's hospital) in Neuruppin near Berlin. Both structures were conceived as complex and often contradictory collages of irregularly defined volumes and shapes. Their rich textural effects have a regionalist flavor.

Selected Sources

Christoph J. Burkle, *Hans Scharoun und die Moderne* (Frankfurt am Main, 1986); "Das Frankfurter Musikheim," *Wasmuths Monatshefte für Baukunst und Städtebau* (1929), pp. 502-5; *Architekturführer DDR: Bezirk Frankfurt (Oder)*, p. 51 (Frankfurter Musikheim).

Behrendt and Knipping. Airport, Breslau, 1928 (demolished). From *Der Baumeister* (1933).

Hans Scharoun. Wohnheim für Ledige und Jungverheiratete, Werkbund exhibition, Breslau (Wrocław) 1929. Photograph 1992.

Moritz Hadda. Single-family house (right), Werkbund exhibition, Breslau (Wrocław) 1929. From *Der Baumeister* (1929).

Fortunately, many of Breslau's modernist buildings escaped destruction in the intensive bombardment of the city during the final days of World War II. City Architect Max Berg built one of the boldest reinforced concrete structures of its time: the Jahrhunderthalle (Centenary Hall) of 1912-13, whose cupola is among the largest in the world. He also designed the Messehof (exhibition hall) and the hydroelectric power station, both dating from 1925. Other early modernist sites in the city included a reinforced concrete department store of 1911 by Hans Poelzig (which survived the war) and the new airport of 1928 (which did not).

The most famous architectural event in the history of modern Breslau was the 1929 exhibition of the Deutscher Werkbund. Titled "Wohnung und Werkraum" (Living and Working Space), it followed on Stuttgart's Weissenhof exhibition of 1927 (see pp. 171-72) and demonstrated the high architectural ambitions of the Silesian city. The exhibition grounds were located to the east of the city center, in what is now the Szczytniki park, in the vicinity of Berg's Jahrhunderthalle and the Zimpel estate (see p. 247). The exhibition itself was planned as a picturesque village consisting of irregularly placed, experimental single-family homes, town houses, apartment buildings, and a kindergarten. Only local architects were allowed to take part; nine individuals and one team did so. Architectural standards were generally as high as at Weissenhof. Indeed, it might be argued that they were higher, since the number of interesting types of building was greater and the overall result therefore more varied.

The most acclaimed structure was Hans Scharoun's Wohnheim für Ledige und Jungverheiratete (Apartment Building for Unmarried Persons and Young Married Couples). Expressively designed in the spirit of an ocean liner, with a roof recalling a modern ship deck, it featured split-level apartments for the single tenants. A communal kitchen on the ground floor served all these apartments, in the manner of such Russian Constructivist buildings as the Narkomfin blocks of 1928-29 by Moisei Yakevlevich Ginsburg in Moscow. Each apart-

Adolf Rading. High-rise apartment building, Werkbund exhibition, Breslau (Wrocław) 1929. From *Der Baumeister* (1929).

Heinrich Lauterbach. Single-family house, Werkbund exhibition, Breslau (Wrocław) 1929. From *Der Baumeister* (1929).

ment had its own balcony. The building has survived in fairly good condition, despite having been used as a brothel for members of the SS during the war. Adolf Rading's apartment high-rise was similar to Scharoun's building in that its top floor—which has been considerably altered—included reminiscences of maritime design. Above the ground floor, the high-rise consists of two separate blocks with four apartments on each floor, linked by a narrow, glazed stairwell. Today, it houses a student dormitory. In their Laubenganghaus (arcaded apartment building), which was serviced by an open gallery and a kindergarten, the team of Paul Heim and Adolf Kempter explored single loaded slab construction of the kind pioneered by Hannes Meyer in Dessau. In designing the kindergarten, the same architects implemented modern notions of hygiene in an attempt to stress the connection between high-quality housing and child care. Skylights admit light to the central space of this simple, symmetrical structure.

The two interconnected, single-family houses by Moritz Hadda and Heinrich Lauterbach, with their simple, elegant curves, roof terraces,

and horizontal windows, are particularly fine
examples of Bauhaus-influenced villa design.
Unfortunately, they are now in poor condition.
The remaining buildings, such as Ludwig Mos-
hamer's and Gustav Wolff's "minimalist" town
houses and the individual homes by Theo
Effenberger, Paul Häusler, and Emil Lange, explored different types of structure and means
of grouping them. The buildings of the Werkbund exhibition urgently require the kind of
exemplary restoration recently accorded the
Weissenhof Siedlung.

Selected Sources

Wladimír Šlapeta, "Neues Bauen in Breslau,"
Rassegna 11, no. 40 (December 1989), pp. 14-62;
Theodor Heuss, *Hans Poelzig: Bauten und Entwürfe*
(Berlin, 1959); "Neuer Flughafen in Breslau," *Der
Baumeister* (1933), pp. 119-21; "Wohnung und
Werkraum: Werkbund-Ausstellung Breslau 1929,"
Der Baumeister (1929), pp. 285-303; Georg Munter,
"Wohnung und Werkraum: Ein Versuch, die Werk-
bund-Ausstellung in Breslau 1929 zu würdigen,"
Wasmuths Monatshefte für Baukunst und Städtebau
(1929), pp. 441-53; "Arbeiten von Dipl.-Ing. H. Lau-
terbach, Breslau," *Der Baumeister* (1929), pp. 372-
75; *Heinrich Lauterbach: Bauten 1925-1965* (Berlin,
1971); Peter Pfankuch, *Adolf Rading: Bauten, Entwürfe und Erläuterungen* (Berlin, 1970); "Breslau,"
Die Form (1929), pp. 305-21; "Werkbundausstellung
'Wohnung und Werkraum', Breslau," *Die Form*
(1929), pp. 357-60; Fritz Behrendt, "Das neue Breslau," *Deutsche Bauzeitung* (August 21, 1929),
pp. 577-84.

opposite:
Albrecht Jäger. Apartment building, Ulica Olszewskiego, Breslau (Wrocław), 1929. Photograph 1992.

Heinrich Lauterbach. Apartment building, Ulica Kraszewskiego, Breslau (Wrocław), 1926-27. Photograph 1990.

this page:
Paul Heim and Adolf Kempter. Apartment building, Zimpel (now Sempolno) estate, Breslau (Wrocław), 1928-29. Photograph 1990.

The construction of public housing was as important in Breslau as in other major German cities: between 1919 and 1929, 13,296 apartments were built there, almost as many as were erected by the GEHAG agency in Berlin and more than in Frankfurt am Main. In Breslau, too, they ranged in style from the more or less conservative to the decidedly modernist. The Zimpel (today Sempolno) estate of 1928 by the team of Paul Heim and Adolf Kempter belongs in the former category. One of the finest of all German garden cities of the twenties, its buildings, with pitched roofs and conservative detailing, were erected on an elongated, concentric plan around a central strip of greenery. Breslau's other large estate, the Popelwitzsiedlung (now Osiedle Popowice) by Theo Effenberger, is equally picturesque, with its gently curving streets and buildings, pitched roofs, and brick facades. Unfortunately, part of it was destroyed in World War II. In 1929 Fritz Behrendt designed another estate in Breslau with picturesque features. Located near the Szczytniki park in the eastern area of the city, it was constructed on the single loaded slab principle with circulating galleries attached to its rear elevations. The curved buildings, with steeply pitched roofs containing dormer windows, housed a large variety of excellent modern apartment types.

Among the more distinctly modernist residential structures in Breslau is Heinrich Lauterbach's infill apartment building of 1926-27 on

what is now Ulica Kraszewskiego. Its flat facade, arranged in a strictly symmetrical manner around a central staircase and punctuated by simple horizontal and square windows and small circular ones at attic level, is a fine embodiment of the functionalist aesthetic. Lauterbach, a relatively prominent representative of German modernism, was born in 1893 in Dresden and studied architecture there and in Darmstadt. He practiced in Breslau from 1925 to 1940, when he moved to Stuttgart. Lauterbach taught in Stuttgart between 1947 and 1950, and in Kassel from 1950 to 1958. He died in 1971.

Two housing estates were designed in a functionalist spirit in Breslau at this time. The first, located on Ulica Olszewskiego in the immediate vicinity of the Zimpel estate, was designed by Albrecht Jäger, a pupil of Adolf Radling who had worked for Bruno Taut, and is possibly the most interesting modernist housing project in Breslau after the Werkbund exhibition complex. The other modernist estate, similar in character to that in the Neu-Gohlis district of Leipzig (see p. 218), is located in the Ksiaże Male area and was designed by Hans Thomas.

Selected Sources
Šlapeta, "Neues Bauen in Breslau"; "Breslau," *Die Form* (1929), pp. 305-21; Behrendt, "Das neue Breslau"; "Arbeiten von Dipl.-Ing. H. Lauterbach, Breslau"; *Heinrich Lauterbach: Bauten 1925-1965.*

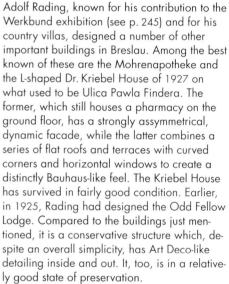

Adolf Rading. Mohrenapotheke, Rynek Solny, Breslau (Wrocław), 1928. Photograph 1990.

Adolf Rading. Odd Fellow Lodge (later, Kino Przodownik), formerly Ulica Przodowników, Breslau (Wrocław), 1925. Photograph 1990.

Adolf Rading, known for his contribution to the Werkbund exhibition (see p. 245) and for his country villas, designed a number of other important buildings in Breslau. Among the best known of these are the Mohrenapotheke and the L-shaped Dr. Kriebel House of 1927 on what used to be Ulica Pawla Findera. The former, which still houses a pharmacy on the ground floor, has a strongly assymmetrical, dynamic facade, while the latter combines a series of flat roofs and terraces with curved corners and horizontal windows to create a distinctly Bauhaus-like feel. The Kriebel House has survived in fairly good condition. Earlier, in 1925, Rading had designed the Odd Fellow Lodge. Compared to the buildings just mentioned, it is a conservative structure which, despite an overall simplicity, has Art Deco-like detailing inside and out. It, too, is in a relatively good state of preservation.

The ten-story Städtische Sparkasse (city savings bank) building, located next to Rading's Mohrenapotheke and still occupied by a bank, was one of two high-rises erected in Breslau at this time (see p. 237) and one of the earliest tall buildings in Germany to have been constructed on a steel skeleton. Its stone cladding and its fenestration were applied in a severe, rationalist manner.

Other non-residential buildings in Breslau were designed by Richard Konwiarz, a local architect whose work is not easy to classify. He was born in Kempten, Bavaria, in 1883 and studied in Dresden, where he became assistant to Lossow and Kühne. He subsequently established a successful practice in Breslau. After World War II, Konwiarz was professor of architecture in Dresden until 1950, when he moved to Hanover. He died in 1960. Konwiarz designed a wide variety of buildings, always concerned to give expression to structural systems. With their vigorous articulation, the two open-air swimming stadia on the Oder (Odra) River are fine examples of this approach. Konwiarz also built the Olympic Stadium, part of a large sports complex in the

Unknown architect. Städtische Sparkasse building, Rynek, Breslau (Wrocław), 1932. Photograph 1990.

Althoff. Volksschule, Osiedle Sepolno, Breslau
(Wrocław), 1928. Photograph 1990.

Zalesie district. The stadium was enlarged
and remodeled just before the 1936 Berlin
Olympics.

The construction of school buildings in
Breslau is represented here by a characteristic
example of hybrid late twenties design: the
Volksschule (elementary school) in the Zimpel
district by City Architect Althoff. Erected in
brick with a certain amount of picturesque
sculptural detail and a steeply pitched roof,
the building's plan and massing are symmetrical.

Selected Sources

Šlapeta, "Neues Bauen in Breslau"; Behrendt, "Das
neue Breslau"; Pfankuch, *Adolf Rading*; Wladimír
Šlapeta, "Luxury Country Houses," *Rassegna* 11,
no. 40 (December 1989), pp. 78-88; "Hochhaus der
Städt. Sparkasse, Breslau," *Deutsche Bauzeitung*
(April 5, 1933), p. 264; "Die neuen Freibadanlagen
in Breslau," *Deutsche Bauzeitung* (July 22, 1931),
pp. 365-69; "Breslau," *Die Form* (1929), pp. 305-21;
"Die neue Volksschule in Breslau-Zimpel," *Deutsche
Bauzeitung* (August 18, 1928), pp. 561-67.

250   The East

Indexes

Index of Architects, Artists, and Designers

Numerals in **bold type** refer to pages with illustrations

Index of Places

Photography Credits

Photographs were provided by the authors, except as noted below.

Introduction
Figs. 1, 3, 4: courtesy Wolfgang Voigt; Fig. 5: Bauhaus-Archiv, Berlin (Otto Hagemann); Figs. 6, 8: Hamburgisches Architekturarchiv, Hamburg (Cäsar Pinnau papers); Figs. 9, 10: courtesy Marion Bembé.

Berlin
Fig. 4: courtesy Bauhaus-Archiv, Berlin; p. 28 (top left): courtesy Bauhaus-Archiv, Berlin (Hedrich-Blessing); p. 36 (top, center left): courtesy Wolfgang Voigt; p. 49 (center): Landesbildstelle, Berlin; p. 52 (top): courtesy The Art Institute of Chicago; p. 55 (top): Almut Eckell.

Frankfurt
p. 65 (bottom): Staatliche Landesbildstelle Hessen, Frankfurt am Main.

The West
pp. 76 (top left, bottom), 98 (bottom), 110 (bottom), 111 (top right, center): Architektur-museum der Technischen Universität, Munich; p. 101: courtesy Bauhaus-Archiv, Berlin.

Hamburg, Hanover
Fig. 4: Hamburgisches Architekturarchiv, Hamburg; p. 116: Kunstbibliothek, Berlin; p. 144 (top): courtesy Hamburgisches Architekturarchiv, Hamburg; p. 154 (bottom): Johann Schmidt.

Stuttgart, Munich
p. 173 (bottom): Franziska Windt; p. 189 (bottom): courtesy The Art Institute of Chicago; p. 193 (top): courtesy Marion Bembé; p. 196 (center left): courtesy Franz Stauder; p. 196 (center right): Werner Buch; p. 198 (bottom): Bilderdienst des Süddeutschen Verlags, Munich; p. 199: Stadtarchiv, Munich.

The East
p. 237 (bottom): Architekturmuseum der Technischen Universität, Munich.